TV-PRO
YO

TV-PROOF YOUR KIDS

A Parent's Guide to Safe and Healthy Viewing

LAURYN AXELROD

With a Foreword by Renée Hobbs, Ph.D.,
Founding Director, Harvard Institute on Media Education

A CITADEL PRESS BOOK
Published by Carol Publishing Group

For my family

A Citadel Press Book
Published by Carol Publishing Group
Citadel Press is a registered trademark of Carol Communications, Inc.

Editorial, sales and distribution, rights and permissions inquiries should be addressed to Carol Publishing Group, 120 Enterprise Avenue, Secaucus, N.J. 07094

In Canada: Canadian Manda Group, One Atlantic Avenue, Suite 105, Toronto, Ontario M6K 3E7

Carol Publishing books may be purchased in bulk at special discounts for sales promotion, fund-raising, or educational purposes. Special editions can be created to specifications. For details, contact Special Sales Department, 120 Enterprise Avenue, Secaucus, N.J. 07094.

Manufactured in the United States of America
10 9 8 7 6 5 4 3 2 1

Library of Congress Cataloging-in-Publication Data
Axelrod, Lauryn.
TV-proof your kids: a parent's guide to safe and healthy viewing / Lauryn Axelrod; with a foreword by Renée Hobbs.
p.   cm.
"A Citadel Press book."
Includes bibliographical references (p.).
ISBN 1-55972-408-0 (pbk.)
1. Television and children—United States.   2. Television and family—United States.   3. Mass media and children.   4. Media literacy.   5. Parenting—United States.   I. Title.
HQ784.T4A94   1997
302.23′45′083—dc21   97-12069
                                                       CIP

Contents

Foreword

by Renée Hobbs, Ph.D.

If you're concerned about TV's effects on your children, but don't know quite what to do about it, you're not alone. You'll find a lot of parents like you in the pages of this book; parents stuck, like most of us, in the middle of a love-hate relationship with contemporary media. They recognize the pleasures that television offers and appreciate its power as a learning tool. But they have also begun to notice the impact of TV on children's behavior and are deeply concerned about the attitudes that television promotes.

But rather than complain, rationalize, or ignore the problem, the parents in this book have begun to reshape the way they use television in the home. They haven't thrown out the TV. They still watch and enjoy TV. They recognize that TV is not the enemy. Passive, mindless, uncritical viewing habits are the real problem. These parents have come to understand the importance of creating opportunities to talk with their children about TV, and of giving them the habits, knowledge, and skills they need to critically analyze its messages.

Lauryn Axelrod knows how powerful it is to talk about TV. She knows how to talk about TV with children and young people of different ages and from different backgrounds. As a talented teacher, filmmaker, and parent, she has written a remarkable book that provides parents a wealth of practical strategies to manage their family's use of television. She shows how parents can find opportunities for the kind of talk that builds children's critical thinking skills.

More and more, we recognize that our children face risks to their future. According to the Carnegie Council on Adolescent Development, 25 percent of seventeen-year-olds have engaged in behaviors that are harmful or dangerous to themselves and others—getting pregnant, using drugs, being aggressive or antisocial, or failing school. According to the

Carnegie report "Great Transitions," nearly half of American adolescents are at high or moderate risk of seriously damaging their life chances. Young people's media consumption has an impact on the kinds of attitudes and behaviors that relate to the important choices young people make as they grow older. Critical thinking about media can improve young people's decision-making, reasoning, and communication skills.

This book is for real parents and real families. It invites you to reflect deeply on your children's relationship with media culture. It offers useful information to help you understand how your children interpret media messages, how to limit media use without starting World War III, and how to build children's media literacy skills in the home. It will probably change your life for the better—because the advice it offers will end the family fights about TV viewing, enhance your family's appreciation of quality programming, and give your family the knowledge and skills to "pull back the curtain" on the role of television in our culture today. *TV-Proof Your Kids* will help your family build skills that will serve you and your children in maintaining an active, engaged life in a media-saturated society.

Renée Hobbs
Communications Department
Babson College

Acknowledgments

This book would not have been possible without the help and support of the following people: Deborah Leveranz of Media Analysis and Practice, for first throwing me into a classroom, showing me the ropes, and always being there to push me on; Renée Hobbs and Kathleen Tyner for their early encouragement and continued good advice and friendship; The Rev. Dr. Warren R. "Jess" Borg, for unfailing support in allowing me to teach TV in his school; Janet Spencer, for finding a way to let me do it; Jay Dover, for convincing me to write my ideas and experience down; Liz Thoman and the Center for Media Literacy for the work they have done and the forum to express myself; Dorcas Hand, for being an astute reader, a great librarian, motivator, and generous friend; Cyndi Hamilton, for sympathy, encouragement, babysitting, and relief; the hundreds of students who have passed through my classrooms for their invaluable contributions and enthusiasm; Sam, Eddie, Sharifa, Lucy, Dynah, Julia, Cherry, Jennifer, Mark, Shawn, Colin, Karla, Lucy II, Maisie, Kelly, Pam, Meredith, and Ellen—you remind me that it's worth it and keep me going—big hugs and immeasurable thanks for your challenges and belief; the many parents who organized and came to workshops and shared their experiences; the inspiring teachers who listened and chose to give media literacy a chance in their classrooms; my incomparable agent, Natasha Kern, and her assistant, Orianna, who believed in this book, found it a home, took care of the dirty work and always had time to talk; my editor, Lisa Kaufman, whose wise, patient advice and sense of humor kept me believing; my parents; and especially, my husband, Chris, an expert at proofing and critiques, and my son, Joshua, both of whom have endured years of listening to me blabber on about TV while they were watching! I owe you all endless gratitude.

Introduction: TV-Proof Kids, A Workable Goal

If you are like most parents, you are worried about the time your children spend watching television and what they might be learning from it. You wonder if TV is healthy and if you should let your children watch it. If so, how much viewing time should be permitted? Which programs are safe?

You aren't alone. In workshops around the country, I have heard the exasperated cries of parents seeking workable solutions to the problem of kids and TV. Having tried a number of unsuccessful approaches to TV management, many parents like you wish there were some easy way to effectively "TV-proof" their kids.

Since television first made its way into most American homes in the 1950s, educators and parents have struggled with how to control its use and its effects on children. Derided as *The Plug-In Drug* by researcher and writer Marie Winn, a "vast wasteland" by former FCC commissioner Newton N. Minow, and "unredeemable" by advertising critic Jerry Mander, TV has been regarded alternately as an addictive box of evil that should be eliminated or as nothing more harmful than a "toaster with pictures."

The truth is that television as a medium is inherently neither evil nor harmful. Nor can it be regarded simply as an appliance. Television is our communal experience: a cultural mythology shared by millions of Americans over generations. It is the thing we talk about on coffee breaks, around the dinner table, on the playground. We fondly recall our special moments with TV, sing well-remembered theme songs, and repeat our favorite jokes. Television is the national "electronic hearth," and through it we commiserate together, laugh together, and are shocked together. More than any other medium in contemporary America, TV has been our most constant source of information and has defined our collective opinions and ideals. For children, it is the modern storyteller and their lifeline to the adult world.

Nonetheless, parents, educators, and legislators justly feel compelled to do something about TV. Noting statistics that state that the average American child will have watched nearly 40,000 hours of TV by his eighteenth birthday and, consequently, will have been exposed to more than 850,000 commercials, 200,000 acts of violence, and incalculable incidents of sexual or otherwise inappropriate material, alarms are sounding. Researchers produce study after study claiming that TV lowers children's test scores, shortens attention spans, encourages poor nutrition and obesity, and promotes antisocial behavior. Some researchers, such as Jane Healy, Ph.D., believe that TV is changing the actual physical structure of children's brains.

While there is little doubt that excessive television viewing can worsen some of these problems, much of the current research has proven inconclusive. There is very little proof that these negative effects are caused solely by television. However, operating under the essential belief that TV is harmful to children's academic and social development, parent groups, educators, and legislators have proposed and employed a number of regulatory measures in an attempt to solve the problem of children and television.

"Turn it off!" scream parents. "Pull the plug!" "Let them watch only educational programming," demand educators. Better yet, say the politicians, regulate the television industry and make the broadcasters responsible for what they purvey. Following these dictums, educators exclude TV from schools; parents attempt to limit the hours and programs their children watch; engineers invent new technological gadgets to monitor and control TV content; and, because the First Amendment prohibits the actual censorship of television, legislators suggest and broadcasters grudgingly agree to ratings and warning labels on some programs that contain graphic sexual or violent content.

But do these actions work? Research and common sense say no. Such gadgets as the V-chip or TV Allowance are overcomplicated to use and easily circumvented; rating systems are flawed; and the networks don't label every program. Moreover, as many adults know, telling children that they can not do a particular thing is guaranteed to make the forbidden act more appealing. If Johnny can't watch TV at home, he'll go to Sally's house. If you tell him that a specific program is off-limits, that's exactly the program he will watch when he gets to Sally's. Despite our best intentions, prohibitive measures rarely work.

Both parents and educators need to recognize that TV is something that children learn from and enjoy. Moreover, we need to accept that regulatory measures do not prevent our children from being better versed in *The Simpsons* than in Shakespeare, and to expect children to watch only educational programming is unrealistic.

The fact is that children watch television. Almost every home in America has at least one television set, which is on for an average of seven hours a day, and much of what children watch on TV is not designed for children. The information superhighway, complete with a choice of 500 channels, is scheduled to come roaring through our living rooms any minute. Since TV isn't going away, nor is it likely to become, as one might hope, free from any objectionable programming, we need to look for other safe and healthy solutions. Should we throw the TV out the window forever, or is there an easy way to effectively TV-proof our kids?

In 1986, I was asked to conduct several residency classes in video production and media for inner-city children in Houston's public schools. Many of my students were in academic or disciplinary trouble, at risk of dropping out or becoming juvenile probationers. The school district authorities thought that my classes in TV would help these kids stay in school and take their education seriously. Surprisingly, they were right. Most of these kids had spent much of their young lives in front of the television set and were eager to know how it all worked. We talked a lot about television, what it meant to them, and how it affected them, and then we made some TV programs of our own.

After a few months, it became clear to me that what I was teaching was invaluable to the students' academic achievement and self-esteem. Their teachers told me how much better they were doing in classes, how much happier they seemed, that they were more involved in other activities, and, oddly, that they seemed to be watching less television. I didn't understand it at first. After all, TV was supposed to be bad for kids. Then I learned that what I was teaching was empowering kids to understand and evaluate the messages of TV. In the academic world, it is called media literacy.

Buoyed by other successful residencies and further studies, I was convinced that all children could benefit from learning about television. In 1990, I developed the Media Arts Department at Episcopal High School in Houston, basing the program entirely on the theories of media literacy. During the last seven years, my students have both inspired and educated me. Together, we have learned how to see through the messages of TV and how to use TV consciously and critically. While many of these kids have gone on to further studies in media or careers in television and film, those who haven't still call me to tell me their thoughts and feelings about the TV shows and movies they see and to express their gratitude for having been taught a better way to watch TV.

In ten years of teaching media literacy and video production, I have received positive feedback from countless students, parents, and educators. Across the board, students report better critical viewing skills, greater enjoyment of the good side of television, and fewer hours in front of the TV. Parents tell me how much their son or daughter has learned, and other teachers ask me to show them how to teach about television in their classes. Responding to these requests for help, I began conducting workshops for parent and teacher organizations, showing how they could apply the same techniques in their homes and schools. Again, the success stories have poured in.

I wrote this book because I have experienced the value of these techniques not only with my students, other teachers, and parents but also with my own son, Joshua. I began using these TV management and media literacy techniques with him when he was just two years old, and the results have been more than I could have hoped for. At six, he rarely asks to watch TV, but when he does, he is very choosy about his programs. However, he is always ready to point out fallacies and errors in what he sees. He does well in school, loves to read and to play outside, and is always finding something with which to experiment. Although his friends all watch far more TV than he does and talk endlessly about the latest movies and shows, Josh is resolute; most of it simply doesn't interest him. Today, I sleep nights knowing that these simple techniques have given my child a strong foundation for safe and healthy lifelong learning *with* television, but without a fight. In other words, because of these techniques, my child is TV-proof!

This personal experience in addition to that of my students, other teachers, and concerned parents around the country provides the basis for this book. By including the observations and insights of the participants as well as my own, I have attempted to go beyond prescribed academic theories about media literacy to illustrate how and why it works, especially in the home. In the first part of this book, you will learn the basic techniques of media literacy and how to begin using them to TV-proof your own children. In Part II you will learn how certain kinds of programs affect your children and ways to combat those negative effects. In Part III we will explore ways to make the use of other kinds of screens—videogames, movies, and computers—a healthy, safe, and positive activity in your home and in the world beyond it. Each chapter suggests simple activities that will help you put these ideas into practice and discussion ideas to share with your children.

TV-proofing your children isn't as difficult as it sounds. In fact, it only requires a little bit of time each week. With practice, your children will learn to apply these techniques on their own, and your job will be finished! There is a viable solution to the problem of kids and TV, and that is to teach them about it.

PART I

A NEW WAY TO WATCH TV

If you are reading this book, you are concerned that TV might harm your children. You worry because, despite your intervention, they spend hours glued to the set watching programs that you feel are inappropriate. You witness them repeating negative attitudes, language, and actions learned from TV shows and you watch them choose TV over schoolwork, creative play, friends, and other previously enjoyed activities. To top it off, you read countless articles and books condemning television and blaming it for children's academic, social, and behavioral problems. You are, like many other parents, justifiably concerned about TV's influence on your children.

In truth there are problems with TV, making it potentially detrimental to children. However, through the time-tested techniques of media literacy, you can change the way your children watch TV so that it is a safe and healthy experience.

I

All TV Is Educational
Why Children Learn From Television

To a child, everything on TV is educational. By that I mean that children learn from everything that they see on television, whether it be a commercial, a cartoon, a sitcom, or a nature program. Without even realizing it, children learn what behaviors and products are desirable and acceptable, what is important to know or think about, what criminals and police are like, how rich people live, and how a happy family supposedly behaves.

Because television is such a constant and successful teacher, some critics refer to TV as an "alternate curriculum," more appealing and more influential than the one we parents, educators, and concerned citizens would like our children to be studying. But just as important as *what* children learn from TV is *how* they learn from TV.

The information in this chapter is intended to help you understand why television has such a strong hold on your children—why they are attracted to it, how it teaches them, and why they learn from it.

Learning to Watch TV: The Drone Zone

Kathy and Mike were having trouble with their eight-year-old son, Zach. Apparently, whenever Zach sat down to watch TV, he became a "zombie," passive and unresponsive, watching anything that came on, for hours each day. Endless arguments and fights erupted as Kathy or Mike tried to pry him away from the TV for dinner, homework, or other activities. But nothing could convince Zach to turn off the TV. They were at their wits'

3

end, sure that their son was "addicted" to TV, when they arrived at a
workshop. "Help us," they cried. "We don't understand why Zach is so
hooked on TV!"

Children aren't born knowing to watch TV. Like reading, writing, or
eating vegetables, TV watching is a learned behavior. And although no
parent has TV watching on their list of things to teach their children, we
are inadvertently responsible for their learning it.

As it stands now, most American children are taught to watch television almost from birth. In a common scenario, infants see and hear the
TV while their parents are watching, and within a few months the child
itself will probably be placed in front of the TV by its parents and told to
watch . . . quietly. By age two, after months of watching *Sesame Street*
and other children's shows, the child will have learned that TV watching
is an acceptable pastime and a pattern of TV viewing will have been
established. By age five, the pattern is firmly set. This pattern is what I
call the "Drone Zone," and it is the most common way in which people
watch television—habitually, passively, and uncritically.

Several years ago I conducted a TV workshop for parents in which a
participant, the mother of two young children, admitted that she put her
kids in front of the TV each morning so that they would "go limp" and
she could easily dress them for school. As astounding as that may seem, it
is more common than we would like to think. Although most of us are
diligent parents and try to monitor and control our children's TV use,
we are often tempted to make convenient use of the TV as a kind of
sedative—a baby-sitter that pacifies our children, keeping them company
and out of our hair while we conduct other business. Admittedly, we lead
busy lives. Many of us work at too many things. When we come home at
the end of the day, we simply want a few minutes to gather our thoughts,
do housework, or attend to other duties. The TV is there, and our
children are easily distracted by it. Without thinking, we say OK. Go
watch. So what's the harm in that?

On the surface, the TV is a welcome respite. It affords us those precious few moments of quiet when the kids are occupied. However, beneath this seemingly harmless diversion lurks a deeper problem. While
we are busy tending to our other responsibilities, our children are learning about the Drone Zone.

The primary root of the Drone Zone begins in early childhood. The
child whose mother places him in front of the TV to make him "go
limp" learns that this is what the TV is for—watching quietly, zoning
out and disconnecting from the world around him. The same is true for

the young child who comes home from school and is told to watch TV quietly so his parents can get some work done. As for the child who is allowed to watch TV before bed to calm down, he learns that TV's purpose is to make him tune out and become passive. Even if what they are watching is "educational," these children will develop a *pattern* of TV use that becomes habitual and encourages inactivity. They will have learned to watch TV at certain times and for certain reasons, regardless of what is on, and the pattern remains as children grow.

TV can only teach if we have learned to watch it. And if we have learned to watch it passively, uncritically, and habitually, we are its willing students. In our rush to condemn television, we often overlook that the way we have learned to *use* television can be as big a problem as what we see on the screen.

TV Use and Children's Health

In 1996, the American Medical Association issued a statement calling for a reduction in children's TV viewing. Citing studies which claimed that excessive and habitual TV watching was partly responsible for childhood obesity, attention deficit disorders, and other health problems, the AMA asked doctors to take a TV history, along with a medical history, of children being treated for these problems. The statement also recommended that children who watch TV habitually and excessively try to reduce their TV viewing as partial treatment for their problems.

Sounds and Images: TV's Teaching Style

Once children have begun to learn to watch TV, they are captive pupils. And since many children spend more time watching TV than they do in school, the television set becomes their primary teacher, and, alas in some ways, TV is a better teacher than we humans could ever be.

Melanie was a happy, bright three-year-old, whose favorite TV program was Sesame Street. *Alice, her mother, was thrilled that Melanie liked the show and encouraged her to watch it. Alice happily noticed that, after a few weeks, Melanie was beginning to recognize numbers and letters and could sing along with songs. Alice also noticed that Melanie could sing the corporate sponsor jingle that came on at the beginning and end of the show, and would often imitate Cookie Monster, roaring "Cookie!"*

throughout the house at the top of her lungs. These lessons and behaviors irritated Alice.

Alice was confused. She didn't understand how Melanie could learn both good and bad things from TV. Why couldn't she just learn the good stuff? After attending a workshop, Alice understood that TV's way of teaching didn't discriminate between good and bad, but made all information learnable.

As a student teacher, I was instructed in a methodology of teaching that was designed to maximize children's learning abilities. Based on children's natural learning styles, I was told that the successful teacher does the following three things:

Presents information in a variety of forms, both visual and aural.
Repeats information.
Makes the information attractive to students.

It sounds simple enough, and for basic instruction it works fine. It works on television too.

Children are visual learners, beginning from the first few days after birth. A newborn baby learns to recognize his mother visually, even though he can only see a few inches in front of his face. As children grow, they learn by observing the world around them. They learn to recognize familiar people, places, and objects by sight and to imitate the behaviors of others by watching what they do. They learn to speak by listening to others talk. Well before children can read or write, they have learned a tremendous amount by simply watching and listening.

Since children are strong visual and aural learners, television, as a visual and aural medium, is a perfectly designed tool for teaching children. A landmark Canadian study substantiated this when researchers proved that children exposed to the same information in a variety of media—print, public speaking, and television—will retain more from television than from any other format. Because television's basic structure is so closely aligned with a child's learning style, it is attractive to them and easy for them to learn from what they see and hear on TV. Since all information is presented on TV in the same way, there is no distinction between "good" and "bad" information.

Children also learn by repetition—the more often something is repeated, the more likely it is to be recognized and learned. Once again, in this regard television proves itself unrivaled. The jingles, characters, and actions of television commercials are repeated daily, sometimes hourly, before a child's eyes and ears, cementing their messages in a child's mind and further strengthening the teaching ability of television. Most children can sing a product jingle or the theme song to their favorite show just as well as they can sing a familiar children's song. Sometimes, better.

Young children are naturally attracted to bright colors, fast movements, humor, songs, and sounds. Older children are equally as attracted and respond well to teachers who use these elements in the classroom. Television producers know this, and so in order to attract children to their programs, they fill the screen with images and sounds designed to appeal to kids. It works. Children watch and learn.

Public television's award-winning *Sesame Street* is often cited as the ideal children's educational show because it matches its structure with the learning style of young children. It is bright and colorful, uses songs and strong graphics to teach concepts, and repeats main ideas throughout the program. In other words, it is specifically designed so that children will learn from it, and countless studies have proved that *Sesame Street*'s formula is successful at teaching children at a basic level. But even noneducational shows use the same techniques to attract audiences, and because these techniques form the language of learning for children, all TV information is absorbed and learned. Even if what children are learning from television is not what we would like them to learn, television, as a teacher, has taken the basic methodology of teaching and learning to its highest degree. We human teachers should have so much success.

Gimmicks on Kids' Shows

Even educational children's shows rely on gimmicks and hooks designed to attract audiences. Not too long ago, the producer of a popular and acclaimed children's educational television show, *The Electric Company,* resigned in protest over how gimmicky and entertainment-oriented his show had become. He complained that the show was moving too quickly for children to absorb its content and therefore had lost its purpose. But what this producer was upset about is the very thing that attracts children to TV programs.

TV as Storyteller: Teaching Through Stories

Austin, eight years old, was having a bad day. He had been sent to the principal for chewing gum in class, skinned his knee during recess, and gotten into a shouting match with another boy on the bus. By the time he arrived home, he was in a foul mood and went directly to his room and slammed the door.

Within minutes, his parents, Mark and Kristin, heard shouting and what sounded like walls being kicked. Mark went upstairs to see what was happening and discovered Austin screaming and throwing books.

Once he had calmed Austin down and heard about the events of the day, Mark asked Austin who he had been screaming at and why he was throwing books. It turned out that Austin was screaming at an imaginary TV character and was throwing books because he had seen a character on TV do the same thing when he was upset.

Mark explained to Austin that what he had seen on TV was only a story and not a model for proper behavior, but Austin said the "lesson" of the story he'd seen on TV was that when one was angry, the right thing to do was to yell and throw books.

For hundreds of years, children learned the basic tenets of their culture through storytelling. Myths, fables, and fairytales were passed down from generation to generation, first orally and then through the written word. In these symbolic stories were contained the culture's ideals of proper behavior, respect for authority, and the expectations of adulthood, which both fed the child's imagination and answered childhood's important questions about identity and future. In *The Book of Virtues*, former secretary of education William Bennett claims that the old stories "anchor our children in their culture, its history and traditions. . . . [they] welcome our children to a common world, a world of shared ideals. . . ." The late Bruno Bettelheim, a renowned child psychologist and an expert on fairytales, believed that storytelling of this nature was not just instructional but also crucial to a child's development into adulthood. Children need stories, said Bettelheim, and without them they grow up insecure about the world they live in and their role in it.

Today children still learn from stories, identifying with their characters and getting involved in their conflicts and resolutions, but the campfire storyteller and fairytale book have been mostly replaced by the television set. Like the old fairytales, these new stories tell us about the world and how we should live in it. But while children learn from these entertaining TV tales, the tales were never intended to carry the same kind of instructional weight—nor the deep meaning—of the classic fairytale.

Helping children find meaning in their lives is one of the primary functions of storytelling, and Bettelheim suggested that real stories do more than simply entertain a child; they stimulate his imagination, help him develop his intellect and emotions, and provide him with solutions to childhood problems. Bettelheim believed that when children are young, literature is the best source of those meaningful stories. However, recent studies have shown that children today read far less and far less well than children even a generation ago. Parents read less frequently to their young children than they did before and rarely take the time to tell a story that isn't in a book. With this absence of written and oral story-telling, the need for instruction and modeling is "satisfied" with the stories of television. For many children, the stories told by television and movies are the only instructional stories that they ever learn.

As William Bennett says, "Nothing in recent years, on television or anywhere else, has improved on a good story that begins 'Once upon a time. . . .' " But nonetheless, TV stories fill the gaping void of instruc-tional tales and make television the primary guide for identities, expecta-tions, imagination, and cultural development of children.

Why Do Children Like TV?

According to researchers, children like to watch TV for three main rea-sons:

- *Friends:* The characters on TV shows become like intimate, reliable friends who are always there when you need them to make you laugh.
- *Time Passer:* TV provides children with an easy way to pass time without requiring them to do anything.
- *Empowerment:* TV provides children with fantasy situations and roles through which they can try out actions and ideas without conse-quences.

Get Involved: Teaching Through Emotions

Erin, four years old, was watching TV in the living room when her mother, Jan, heard crying. Thinking Erin must be hurt, Jan ran to the room, only to discover the TV turned off and Erin huddled on the sofa, sobbing.

"What happened, Erin?" asked Jan.

"The Beast died!" wailed Erin. "The adults killed the Beast!" She broke down in a fit of tears.

"Erin, honey," calmed Jan, "it's only a TV show. And he lives in the end."

Erin could not be consoled. For weeks, she cried about the Beast's death and was convinced that all adults were mean and cruel. She wouldn't watch the show again and it took Jan months to put an end to Erin's emotional outbursts. It wasn't until Jan attended a workshop that she understood what had caused Erin to react so emotionally to TV.

Studies show that children learn best when they are emotionally connected to the material being presented. A good teacher knows that if he or she can get students personally and emotionally involved with the subject, they will be more likely to learn it and remember it. Children themselves will tell you that they learn best when they feel connected to the information.

Television is an emotional medium, telling stories that explore and dramatically expose human emotion. Being emotional creatures, children easily identify with the human characters they see on TV and with the emotions those characters express. They are saddened when their favorite character is hurt or betrayed, angered when someone is wronged, and pleased when someone succeeds or is vindicated.

Through television, children learn the look and feel of various emotions. For better or worse, they learn how to react, emotionally, to certain situations and to categorize their own emotions according to what they see on TV. But most important, they learn because they are emotionally involved in what is happening on the screen.

If you watch children watch TV, you will often see this emotional connection. While watching, children laugh; they yell to TV characters on the screen; they become irate; they jump up and down when the hero wins and cry when he or she is defeated. They are very involved. If you talk to children about their favorite shows, you will notice that they express their delight emotionally, and if you tell them they can't watch that show, they will react with violent emotion. Children are often so caught up in the emotionalism of TV that they seem transfixed by it, or "addicted."

Although younger children, whose emotional life is still immature, are often frightened or confused by extreme emotions, they are also attracted to and easily aroused by them. Older children revel in the thrill and excitement of high emotion, and adults, who are used to emotional stimulation, require ever higher doses. TV producers know this and pack their programs with compelling and dramatic emotions to attract and involve viewers. Situations involving sex, violence, and humor are guaranteed to provoke emotion and get attention. Even commercials are emotionally based, showing characters to be intensely pleased or upset over a product. The whole of TV's twenty-four-hour emotional smorgasbord is both naturally attractive and engaging, adding to television's already powerful teaching ability.

Window on the World:
Teaching Through Experience

Philip, ten years old, was writing a social studies report on Africa for school. When he proudly brought the rough draft to his mother, Pam, for proofreading, she was stunned by what she read.

"Africa is a large continent and all the people are starving, with big stomachs and flies in their eyes. Even though there are many animals in Africa, they are all endangered and the people can't kill them for food.

"There are also wars in Africa and all the people are being killed by evil drug lords. Even though America sends money and food and soldiers to help the Africans, the African people steal the money and the food and kill the soldiers. Soon, Africa will be destroyed."

Pam, utterly shocked, asked Philip where he got his information. "We watched some TV shows on Africa in class," he replied, "and I know what Africa is really like." Although Pam told Philip that the TV shows he saw weren't entirely accurate, he refused to change his mind. "I saw it on TV, so it must be true," he declared.

TV is our window on the world, creating a global village in which everyone is connected and given the opportunity to experience things they could only dream of before. In his book *The Age of Missing Information*, critic and nature writer Bill McKibben says that, "Television is the chief way that most of us partake of the larger world," and because of this, two-thirds of the population of the United States say that they get "most of their information" about the world from TV rather than through actual experience.

If we remember that all TV is educational to children, it is not surprising that TV's vast array of faraway places and different kinds of people and situations would be naturally appealing and instructional. Television, more than any other communications medium, shows children a world such as most of them could never imagine. In vivid moving images and sounds, children witness events and are exposed to people and places that they might never otherwise experience, and because of television's unique teaching power, these experiences are not forgotten.

Joshua Meyrowitz, a media scholar, has credited television with opening up the previously protected world of adult secrets to children. Media

---

What I Learn From TV: Children's Views

One day, I asked my then three-and-a-half-year-old son, Joshua, why he liked to watch TV. I was surprised by the simplicity of his answer and by how well it conformed to research on children and TV. Very plainly, he said, "I like TV because it moves and it has lots of colors and songs. I like songs."

Figuring I was on a roll here, I asked him if he thought he learned from TV. Once again, his answer was amazingly straightforward. "Of course," he said, "I learn how to grow up and how to make friends."

When I asked Joshua if he thought he ever learned anything bad from television, he looked at me slyly, grinned his I-didn't-do-anything-wrong grin, and said, "Sometimes."

Joshua watches very little television, but when he does, he watches videos or select children's shows. Of particular interest was that he was conscious of having learned from TV and that he knew why he was attracted to it. Most children are aware of TV's special teaching powers but don't always have the ability or opportunity to express what they know. Given the chance, however, even high school children will explain why they like TV and what it teaches them.

Says seventeen-year-old Jarrett: "I think I have gained a large percentage of my out-of-school knowledge from TV and movies. This includes everything from trivia to history to women. I learn important lessons from the fictional lives of characters. I also learn about other people's feelings, concerns, and needs."

"I will be watching a movie or a TV show and the next day, I will have picked up a cool line to say!" declares fourteen-year-old Will.

"I learn different ways to act in whatever kinds of moods I am in," reveals fourteen-year-old Kim.

---

critic Neil Postman agrees, blaming television for the disappearance of childhood innocence. In some ways, both men are correct. Television's unrivaled capacity for bringing the world to your living room takes a child's primary experience of different people, places, and situations well beyond the ordinary scope of childhood. Without television, very few children would be exposed to famine, political intrigue, adult violence, or sexual scandal. They might also never experience a safari in Africa, the surface of Mars, or the tragedy of war. Television shows all of it, the good and the bad, in full color and glorious detail, and children soak it all in, unconditionally.

Although experiencing something on television is not the same as experiencing it in real life, many children can't tell the difference. Until the age of six, most children have a very difficult time separating reality from fantasy. Even older children sometimes have trouble discerning what is real and what is make-believe on TV. Television experience looks and feels real, even if it is not, and children are prone to accept television's version of the world, partly because they don't know any better. How can a five-year-old, or even a ten-year-old, with limited experience of the bigger world, know if a situation on television is portrayed accurately? They can't, and because they can't, they accept TV's window as a real and accurate one, and learn from it whether it is truthful or not. Seeing is believing, and for children, TV experience is equal to and, in more cases than not, a replacement for limited real-life experience.

Activity: Do Your Children Learn From TV?

In a calm moment, ask your children why they like TV. Ask them what attracts them to television. Is it the movement? The music? The characters or the stories? Do they find TV exciting?

Next, ask them if they think they learn from television. If so, what kinds of things do they learn? Don't push for specifics; allow them to be expressed naturally.

The purpose of this activity is to encourage children to understand that TV teaches them and to prepare all of you for further discussions about television.

2

Media Literacy
The Key to TV-Proof Kids

Children learn from television; it provides them with most of their information about the world at large. But most children do not think critically about the information they receive from television and other media. They simply absorb it without evaluating it or considering how it might affect them. Consequently, they can be inadvertently harmed by what they are learning.

In the 1960s and 1970s, educators in Great Britain and Australia recognized that their students were learning from the media, especially from television. Concerned that children were being negatively affected by what they learned, they sought to control the media's influence and to immunize their children against it. They developed a way of teaching children about media that included studies in how different media were produced, why they were produced, what messages they carried, and how to analyze those messages. These visionary British and Australian teachers hoped that, through learning about television and other media, children would become more selective and more critical of the information they received, and, therefore, less easily influenced by it. They called their new approach media literacy, and it was so successful that it became a standard in their schools.

In the early 1980s, educators in Ontario, Canada, also adopted media literacy education and mandated it in their schools. Since its inclusion in the national curricula of Canada, Australia, and Great Britain, educators and parents have noticed a substantial improvement in children's critical awareness of television, as well as a significant reduction in the amount of time they spend watching TV. Through media literacy education, children developed a greater appreciation for quality programs and little tolerance for poor ones. Their test scores and attention spans improved, and they appeared to be less easily influenced by what they saw and read and heard in the print and broadcast media. All this without a fight for the remote, tossing out the TV set, or government regulation.

Media literacy education has a large following and media educators are found in almost every country in the world. At last count, at least five countries believed that media literacy was a necessary skill for the twenty-first century and had instituted some form of media literacy in their educational mandates. But here in the United States, perhaps the television capital of the world, we are only beginning to accept media literacy as a solution to the problem of kids and media information.

In 1994, New Mexico became the first state to require media education in its schools. In recent years, other states and national organizations have begun to investigate media literacy's role in curbing youth violence, stemming such health hazards as smoking and alcohol use in teens, and tackling other social and educational problems. The National Council of Teachers of English has adopted a media literacy plank, and a National Media Literacy Conference is held yearly. Through pilot programs around the country, individuals, community groups, the media industry, and educational institutions are realizing that the best way to help children become critical consumers of media messages (those of television in particular) is to teach them about it. However, we've got a long way to go before media literacy education is available in most of our schools.

As parents, however, we do have the opportunity to use the techniques of media literacy in our own homes to help our children understand what they are learning from TV, be more critical of what they see, reduce the amount of television they watch, and most important, arm them against the negative influences of television messages. In this chapter you will learn how to become involved in your children's TV education and how to begin using the basic techniques of media literacy in your home to TV-proof your kids.

Sharing Goals: Parents and Media Literacy

Whenever parents come to a workshop asking for help with their children and TV, I begin by asking two questions: What do they see as the problem, and how would they like it to change? Although the problems range from children who are suffering with academic problems because

What Kids Say About Media Literacy

"In the information age, it is crucial that people learn to watch, listen, and read critically. Just like many things from cars to medicine have necessary warning labels, safety guides, or training courses in how to be used, the media need one too!"

—Sam, 18

"Through media literacy, I came to realize what a huge role the media have played in my life. [The media] give us what we consider to be values and we eat it all up and then go on to boast that we do things the way they 'should' be done!"

—Cherry, 16

"Once I began to learn about the media, everything became clear to me. I started to look at everything differently. It changed my life. Now I think about the clothes I buy, the food I buy, what I do for fun, and the way the country is run. I hope that other kids learn to think about TV this way, too. Maybe people will stop calling us all slackers when they see how well we think."

—Lucy, 15

"Teenagers are especially vulnerable to the media. We are constantly told what music to listen to, what clothes to wear, what to think, and who to be. But teenagers aren't the only ones influenced by the media. Everyone is, from children watching cartoons to adults watching CNN. If we become aware that the media are manipulating us, however, they lose their hold on us and we regain the power over our own minds."

—Shawn, 17

they watch too much TV to children whose behavior is being negatively affected by what they watch, most parents' goals are essentially the same:

To encourage their children to watch less TV.

To encourage their children to watch better shows.

To protect their children from the negative influences of TV.

Media literacy is defined as the "ability to access, analyze, evaluate, and produce media" and its primary goals are as follows:

To help children learn to use TV and other media consciously and selectively.

To help children think critically about the messages they receive from television and other media.

In other words, media literacy educators and parents share the same goals. If our children are conscious, choosy, and critical of what they see on TV, they will watch less and be less easily influenced by its messages. And isn't that what TV-proofing is all about?

A Note About Critical Thinking

Critical thinking is a big buzzword in education these days, and for good reason. If children have the ability to think critically about something it means that they are going beyond the surface, delving deeper, asking questions, and learning on a higher level. A child who is thinking critically can identify, analyze, interpret, and understand information, not just absorb it. Children who think critically are more likely to question the sources and meanings of information and, therefore, be less easily influenced by it. In educational lingo, critical thinking is the highest cognitive skill a student can master, and children who think critically do far better in school and in life than children who don't.

Even very young children are capable of critical thinking. If you ask a preschool child to tell you what she thinks about a book that was read to her, she would be able to. Although her language may be simple, she might tell you what parts she liked and why. She might explain her interpretation of what happened in the book and even offer an analysis of why it happened! Older children are even more capable of critical thinking. Their increased vocabulary and reasoning skills allow them to go beyond the obvious and ask questions, interpret and analyze information.

It is important to note that critical thinking is a learned skill; something that must be taught. As you work with your children to develop their critical thinking skills about TV messages, remember that *critical thinking doesn't necessarily mean criticizing; it means analyzing.* Encourage your children to ask questions, delve deeper, interpret, and draw conclusions about what they see. It is only through the skills of critical thinking that children will become less easily influenced or harmed by the messages they receive from TV.

TV Teaching: Using the Techniques of Media Literacy in Your Home

To help our children become selective, critical TV viewers, we need to do a little TV Teaching. Many parents cringe at the idea of teaching their children about TV, believing that because they aren't certified teachers or media experts, they don't have the necessary skills, time, or knowledge. But neither media literacy nor television is as complicated as it appears. You don't need any special skills or equipment, and the basic goals don't take long to accomplish. To guide your children toward conscious, selective, critical TV consumption, you only have to be able to do three things: watch, listen, and talk.

Watching

Throughout this book, it is recommended that you watch television with and for your children. The purpose of this activity is to familiarize you with what your children are watching, enable you to help them make decisions about a particular program's appropriateness, and give you the opportunity to discuss the messages of the programs with them.

Before you panic, think about some of the other things we do with and for our children. Don't we go to their schools and meet with their teachers to get a feel for what is going on in the classroom? Don't we attend athletic games, dance recitals, and plays to encourage and support our children's efforts? Don't we buy toys based on what we think might be appropriate for our children, read with them and guide them in their book choices? Watching TV with your children is the same as any of these other activities: it takes a little time but we do it for our children's benefit.

It is not necessary to watch everything that your children watch, nor is it necessary to watch with them every day. However, plan to watch TV with your children at least once a week, if not more often at first. You may also want to watch the shows your children watch without them present if you are making decisions about a particular program.

You may find that, despite the loss of "baby-sitting" time, you and your children enjoy watching TV together. Young children, especially, enjoy a parent's company while they watch and love to point things out to you. Older children also appreciate your interest and are likely to invite you to watch with them. After several years of watching TV with us, my son, Joshua, hates to watch TV alone. When he does, he often comes running into the kitchen or study to tell us all about what's happening on the screen and urges us to come watch! Even if I am in the middle of something, I always try to accept his invitation, knowing that he is giving me a great opportunity to do some TV Teaching.

Listening

In their best-selling book, *How to Talk So Kids Will Listen, and Listen So Kids Will Talk*, Adele Faber and Elaine Mazlish encourage parents to listen to their children and accept and respect their feelings, even if they don't agree with them. Faber and Mazlish say that children have a deep need to be heard and an empathetic, listening ear does wonders for eliciting cooperation and trust.

Using our listening skills is an important part of TV Teaching. Often, our children's feelings and thoughts about TV will be quite different from our own, but no less valid. If we want to understand how our children are being affected by TV and guide them toward a more critical awareness, we have to be very careful to respect their opinions and not to impose our own. If our children believe that we are truly interested in what they say, they will be more likely to talk to us about TV. Moreover, if we listen without judging, we will learn a great deal from our children.

Media literacy is not about dictating what our children should think about TV, but guiding them toward thinking about it critically. Each chapter in this book recommends activities to do *with* your children and questions to ask as you watch TV with them. The activities and questions are designed to allow your children to respond according to their feelings and impressions. As you listen to your children talk about TV, accept that they have their own thoughts and opinions and try to work with them. Be careful in your responses and try not to deny or belittle their feelings and ideas. Although this may take some practice, how well we listen to our children will determine how successful we are at guiding them toward conscious, selective, critical TV viewing.

Talking

One of the most successful methods of TV Teaching is talking about TV, or TV Talk, as I call it. The purpose of talking about television is to help your children learn to think critically about what they see by verbally analyzing it and discussing it with you. Talking about TV also enables you to counterbalance negative messages or point out things that you feel your children should be aware of. However, most children and adults aren't used to talking about TV in a critical way, so it takes some practice.

Throughout this book you will be encouraged to talk to your children about what they see on television. Each chapter will provide you with suggestions for discussion topics and will help you make talking about TV a fun, learning experience for both you and your kids.

Again, before you moan about having no time to talk about TV, remember that it's not necessary to talk about TV all the time. Once or twice a week, while watching TV together, will be sufficient at first. Obviously, as you and your children become more interested in and adept at talking about TV, it will happen spontaneously. Often, my son, Joshua, will bring up a TV topic in the car on the way to school! Sometimes he wants to discuss a show he watched last night, but frequently the topic is related to something he saw months ago. I am always surprised by his interest because it indicates that he has been thinking about something he saw on TV and really wants to talk about it. Sometimes, those car conversations are the best ones and provide the most constructive TV-Teaching time.

It is important that you approach talking about TV just as you will any other topic of conversation with your children: lightly and enthusiastically. Try not to think of TV Talk as a lecture or a lesson, but rather as a dialogue and a discussion. Sometimes it's helpful to think of a conversation about TV as though you were asking your child about his day at school. However, be prepared to listen to and learn from your child.

In time, you and your children will not view talking about TV as a chore, but as an enjoyable, quality family experience. And, of course, the real benefit is that your children will have learned to think critically about what they watch and, therefore, will be fast on their way to being TV-proof.

Activity: Preparing Your Family for Media Literacy

Before you begin to tackle the activities and discussions in this book, you need to do a little mental preparation. For a moment, imagine yourself a school teacher, going into a class for the first time, excited, nervous, filled with anticipation of and expectations about all the wonderful things you and your students will learn together. For any teacher, the first few days are the hardest; getting to know your material and your students, determining what they need to know and how best to teach them. Most teachers, therefore, have a few tricks to help them get past the initial obstacles and be successful.

To begin, make a list of your goals. What do you want your children to learn? What is your desired end result? It is sometimes helpful for parents to ask themselves the following questions:

From a Parent

After months of frustration trying to make my children watch less TV, I attended your workshop at the advice of a friend. To be honest, I was skeptical. How could talking to my kids about TV make them watch less and be less influenced by what they saw? Wouldn't it just be easier to buy a TV locking device or, better yet, get rid of the TV altogether?

Your techniques convinced me that this was the only way to accomplish my goals. I left the workshop excited and hopeful, ready to watch TV, talk about it, and help my children learn to be more critical of what they saw. I began the very next day with the TV Use Chart and Family TV Menu.

I can't begin to tell you what a difference this has made. TV watching is no longer a battleground in my home. My children watch less, think about what they see, and much to my surprise, like to talk to me about it! I won't lie to you, though. It took some time. But I'm glad I stuck with it. Thanks to these techniques, both my children and I have learned so much. Now we are *all* TV-proof!

—*Janice, mother of Ellen, 6, and Daniel, 9*

- Do I want my children to watch less TV? How much less?
- Do I want my children to watch only quality programs?
- Do I want my children to learn how TV affects them?
- Do I want my children to be less influenced by the messages of TV?
- Do I want my children to understand how TV is made?

Once you have made a list of your goals, examine them. Are they realistic? Make another list of your expectations. How do you think your children will respond? What obstacles do you foresee? The following checklist has proved helpful:

- Do I expect my children to change overnight?
- Do I expect my children to lose all interest in TV?
- Do I expect changing TV habits to be difficult?
- Do I expect my children to rebel?
- Do I expect my spouse or partner to help?
- Do I anticipate having the time to do this?
- How much time am I willing to devote?

Using these two lists, make some plans for yourself. Acknowledge that TV-proofing your children might take some time and that you may run into a few obstacles. Do some advance trouble shooting. If you know that your schedule is very busy, plan for a specific time during the week to begin each activity. If you know that your teenage children are likely to run away from any attempt you make to talk, think about a strategy to involve them. If you anticipate that your spouse may not be cooperative, plan to explain your goals and ask for help. Arrange to talk to your family about what you are trying to accomplish and why. The following chapters will give you some advice along these lines, but do what works best for you and your family.

Above all else, be flexible and forgiving with yourself. You are trying to change old habits and teach your children a whole new way of looking at TV. Take it slow, one step at a time. Remind yourself that, like any other parenting activity, teaching your children to use TV constructively and critically takes a little time, but it is time well spent. Within only a few weeks, your children will begin looking at TV differently, watching less and being less easily influenced by its messages. That's what TV-proof means.

3

TV or Not TV?
Making TV a Choice, Not a Habit

One of the goals of media literacy is to help children learn to use TV consciously and selectively—to teach them that TV viewing is a *choice*, not a habit. Conscious, selective viewing encourages children to watch less TV, make better choices about what they watch, and be less easily influenced by what they see. Making TV viewing a *choice* frees children from TV's powerful and potentially harmful grip.

Helping your children kick the Drone Zone habit is the first step toward TV-proof kids. The information and activities in this chapter will help you guide your children away from habitual, passive, dangerous TV use and teach them how to make TV viewing an active, safe, and healthy choice.

It's Not About Time

Greta and Eric were concerned that their daughters, Danielle, 11, and Sophie, 7, were watching too much TV. On the average, the girls watched between three to four hours each day, and on weekends they watched at least four hours each day and a video movie each night. Eric feared that the girls' excessive TV watching was affecting their schoolwork, and Greta was worried that they weren't getting enough exercise or stimulation. Both parents were also concerned about what the girls were learning from all that TV.

They encouraged their girls to try other activities instead of watching TV. They enrolled them in extracurricular classes, took them on field

trips, and even attempted to bribe them with rewards for not watching
TV, but nothing seemed to work. After reading parenting articles about
TV management, Greta and Mike decided to set a TV time limit of two
hours each day. Danielle and Sophie protested loudly and pleaded for more
time. They threw fits and refused to talk to their parents for an entire
week, but Greta and Eric remained firm. Soon they noticed that although
the girls seemed to be watching less TV at home, they were sneaking off to
watch TV at friends' houses, and their cumulative TV time was exceeding
the two-hour limit. Greta and Eric realized that setting a TV time limit
wasn't the answer.

Statistics tell us that the average American child watches four to five
hours of TV each day! The American Medical Association, the American
Academy of Pediatrics, the PTA, and the National Education Association
all recommend that children watch no more that two hours of TV each
day to allow time for other activities, including reading, schoolwork,
playtime, and family time. Many experts recommend that young children
watch less than one hour each day. Most of us would probably agree that
limiting our children's TV watching can only be beneficial.

Many of us have tried setting time limits for our children. Some of us
have even purchased TV devices that monitor and control how long the
TV is on. Most of us believe that if we can limit the amount of time our
children spend watching TV, we can limit their exposure to negative
influences. But this is only true to a degree. Of course, less time spent
watching TV does decrease the amount of exposure to harmful influences, but it doesn't necessarily reduce the possibility of negative effects
from what the children *do* see.

If you tell a child how much TV he *can* watch, that's how much he *will*
watch, regardless of what is on, and limiting your children to one or two
hours a day spent watching terrible TV shows won't solve the problem of
negative influence. They are still watching terrible shows and may still be
watching habitually and passively. Counting minutes doesn't make children selective about what they watch or think critically about it; it only
makes them aware of time.

If we want to encourage our children to use TV selectively and consciously, we need to stop thinking in terms of the amount of time spent
watching TV and instead focus our energy on *how* the time watching TV
is spent. We want to help our children become aware of how they use
TV and teach them that TV watching is a choice, not a habit or something to do when bored. Children need to learn that we watch TV *pro-*

grams, not TV, and turn the TV off when the program is over. And what is more important, when we watch TV programs, we think about them.

So for the time being, forget about counting the minutes your children spend in front of the TV set and concentrate instead on *what* they are watching, *why* they are watching it, and *how* they are watching it.

Where Is Your TV?

Most homes today have at least one TV. Many have several. Some of my students have revealed that their homes have seven or eight TV sets—one in each room of the house! Experts agree that one of the best ways to eliminate unplanned, unconscious, and excessive TV viewing is to eliminate extra TVs and centralize all TV viewing in one room—the way it used to be when we were kids!

Take stock of where the TVs are in your home. Do your kids each have their own TV? Is there one in the kitchen? Are these TVs used frequently? If they aren't, try to negotiate with your family about moving them. Put them in a closet and pull them out only under special circumstances, such as when a child is sick. If removing the extra sets is too traumatic, make children ask before watching, keep a log of what they watch, and turn the TV off when the show is finished. In that way, they will at least become more aware of when they turn it on.

How Does Your Family Watch TV?:
The Family TV Use Chart

To aid you in assessing your family's TV-watching patterns, the first activity I recommend is the Family TV Use Chart. This tool enables parents to discover the ways in which they and their children use TV and to work toward making TV a conscious, selective choice.

To begin, have each member of your family fill out the Family TV Use Chart (provided in appendix A). Since most family's TV weeks are pretty consistent, filling out the chart for one day should give you a good idea of what the whole week is like and help you determine where the problem areas are. Make sure to include everyone in the household on the chart—parents, children, caregivers. Note every time that the TV is on, whether it is actually being watched or not. Write down what is being watched by whom and pay careful attention to *why* the TV is on. This is probably the hardest part, since most of us don't really know why we are watching TV. Ask your children and do your best to answer, but if you or your kids are not sure why you are watching, put a question mark. If you or your kids aren't sure of what is being watched, put a question mark in that column too.

After you have filled out the chart, determine when TV is being used to fill time, baby-sit, or calm children or if it is on for a specific purpose or program. Flag those times when the TV is not a *conscious* choice. By conscious choice, I mean that the TV is on in order to watch a chosen, specific program for a known, productive purpose that is not to fill time, calm down, relax, or be kept company. For example, if your children are watching something specific because they like the show, that is a conscious choice and is acceptable. If you or another adult watch the news to get information, that is a conscious purpose. If you or your children watch a special program because you are interested in its topic, that is also a conscious purpose. However, if the TV is on and no one knows what is on or why it is on, that's a red flag.

You may be surprised to learn that your family's TV use is overwhelmingly habitual. To begin making TV watching a conscious choice in your home, you and your family will have to address this problem. Remember, the goal is to make TV watching a conscious, planned activity for your whole family, not a habit or something to do when bored. Discuss the results with your children. Help them become aware of how they are using TV. Explain that from now on, TV watching will be a planned activity, not a default action, and that, as a family, you will try to cut down on unplanned TV watching, one day at a time. Expect some dispute, particularly from older children, but be firm. It won't take long for children to learn, and even very young children can be taught to make a choice about watching television and not to use it unconsciously.

Sample Family TV Use Chart

David and Allison were frustrated by the amount of TV and the types of shows their three children watched. As responsible parents, they tried setting time limits for their kids and even tried to eliminate TV altogether for a week at a time. Nothing worked. They arrived at a workshop desperate for a solution. They began by filling out the Family TV Use Chart for themselves and their children, Darryl, fourteen, Jeff, eight, and Susan, six. Darryl has a TV in his room. There is a TV in the kitchen, one in the den, and one in the younger children's playroom. What follows is their chart for a typical Monday.

Time of Day	Shows Watched	By Whom	Why?
6:00 A.M.			
7:00 A.M.	*Good Morning America*	Allison	Get going*
	Goof Troop	Susan and Jeff	Eating breakfast*
8:00 A.M.			
9:00 A.M.	*Regis & Kathy*	Allison	Getting dressed*
10:00 A.M.	*Oprah*	Allison	On while working*
11:00 A.M.	*Fit-TV*	Allison	Exercise
12:00 P.M.			
1:00 P.M.			
2:00 P.M.			
3:00 P.M.	*Darkwing Duck, Batman*	Jeff	After school*
	Barney, Sesame Street	Susan	After school*
4:00 P.M.	*Power Rangers*	Jeff	He likes it. Favorite show.
	Wishbone	Susan	We think it's a good show.
5:00 P.M.	*MTV* (all night usually?)	Darryl	Background music, relax*
6:00 P.M.	*News*	David and Allison	Information (habit?)
	Family Matters	Jeff and Susan	While eating dinner*
7:00 P.M.	*Seinfeld*	David	He likes it.
	Doug	Jeff and Susan	Calm down before bed*
8:00 P.M.	*Melrose Place*	Darryl	He thinks Taylor is pretty.
9:00 P.M.	*Savannah*	Allison	I'm tired*
	Monday Night Football	David	He likes football.
10:00 P.M.	Channel surfs (?)	David	? Relaxes him*
11:00 P.M.			
12:00 A.M.			

* Indicates habitual, passive, or unconscious TV use.

David and Allison's chart is pretty typical, and after filling it in they realized that most of their family's TV viewing was habitual and not for a productive purpose. In fact, if they were to eliminate all viewing except that which was planned and chosen, Darryl, Jeff, and Susan would all be watching less than two hours of TV each day! Even David and Allison would watch less TV.

David and Allison discussed this chart with their children during the workshop and decided that they would all work together to make TV viewing a conscious choice in their home, beginning with changing their attitude about TV.

The Invited Guest: Changing Your Family's Attitude About TV

In most American homes, the TV is viewed as a fixture of daily life; always there, always on, ready, willing, and able to do whatever we ask of it, from baby-sitting to curing the blues. And that's how most of us use it. A thirteen-year study by researchers Robert Kubey and Mihaly Cziksentmihaly reported that most people viewed TV as a kind of therapist that helped them feel less lonely, depressed, or tired and that more than 70 percent of TV viewers watch TV for escape. Children also learn to view TV as a kind of pacifier or pick-me-up and treat the TV as though that were its purpose.

Before we can teach our children to use TV differently, we need to change our family's attitude toward the TV itself. Think for a moment about how you and your family view TV. Is the TV on all the time, regarded as a permanent resident, baby-sitter, relaxant, or time filler? Or is the TV like any other appliance: useful for a specific purpose?

Let's start thinking of the television as an invited guest in our homes, not as a permanent resident. This simple change in attitude allows us to invite the TV in when we want it to be there and ask it to leave by turning it off when the visit is over. It allows us to determine if we want and enjoy its company or if we can do without it. If every time we turn on the TV, we ask, "Do we want to invite the TV guest?" we will be more likely to examine our reasons for watching and less likely to turn the TV on.

If your children want to watch TV, ask them what they want to watch and why they want to watch it. If they can't answer with a specific, conscious choice, deny the request and suggest an alternative. If they answer with a specific show and a conscious purpose, you may let them watch, but remind them that the *TV goes off when the show is over*. If you do this in conjunction with your Family TV Use Chart, you will notice an immediate decrease in the amount of time your children spend watching TV and be well on your way toward making TV use a conscious choice for your children instead of a habitual one.

TV's Off Button

Every TV comes equipped with a very simple device to help you make TV viewing a conscious, selective choice in your home. It is called the off button. The off button can be used anytime you or your children don't wish to invite the TV guest into your home.

Even though twenty-four-hour programming makes it seem as though the TV was designed to be on all the time, it really isn't. In fact, in most homes, the TV is *off* seventeen hours each day! But in many homes, the TV is left on almost all day, no matter what's on or who's watching it.

Most people are pretty easily swayed into leaving the TV on, even after the show they wanted to watch is over. That's why TV producers tease us with commercials about the next show before the previous show is even finished. They want us to watch TV! Next thing we know, a planned, half-hour program becomes a three-hour TV night, and all our goals for conscious TV use are out the window.

If you want your children to become more conscious and selective about their TV use, show them where the off button is and teach them to *turn the TV off when the show they choose to watch is over*. With practice, turning the TV off will become as automatic as turning the TV on.

When Can We Watch?: Building Family Viewing Guidelines

When you allow your children to choose to watch TV is up to you, but most experts believe that it is important to establish guidelines for choosing appropriate times. Guidelines, however, are not designed to limit the amount of time spent watching TV; they are intended to specify times when TV viewing is an option that can be chosen.

Although there are no hard and fast rules for when children should or should not watch TV, there are a number of recommendations from experts around the country. National teacher groups suggest that children not watch TV before school or while doing homework because it affects their academic performance. The American Academy of Pediatrics believes that watching TV during meals leads to obesity and poor nutrition and recommends that parents not allow children to eat in front of the TV. Parenting experts suggest that children watch TV only when their homework and chores have been completed.

Your family's guidelines don't have to fill up a rule book, but it is important that you have some and that they are consistent. In my family, we have only a few guidelines for when TV viewing is *not* an option: before school, during meals, after 7:00 P.M. on school nights, when friends come over to play, and when the weather is nice. Occasionally, my son wants to watch TV during dinner or on a cool, sunny afternoon, and I have to remind him that, as a family, we decided not to choose TV at those times. He usually remembers and then scampers off to find something else to do.

As you build TV-viewing guidelines for your family, it is important to discuss them with your children. Explain that TV watching is one of several possible activities at any given time, but, like any other activity, there are times when it is more or less appropriate. For example, going swimming is not usually an appropriate choice at midnight, but sleeping is!

Encourage your children to help you select appropriate times for television watching by asking questions.

- Are mealtimes important family times? Should they be interrupted by TV?
- Are weekends good times for other activities and family outings?
- Is it appropriate to watch TV before school? On weekday afternoons?
- Should all homework and chores be finished before watching TV?
- What other activities deserve equal time with TV?

Ask your children to explain when they think TV viewing shouldn't be an option and why. You might be surprised to hear them establish their own guidelines. I know several children who voluntarily chose not to watch TV while doing their homework because they wanted to make good grades and they knew they couldn't concentrate while the TV was on!

Although it is important to stick to your family guidelines, a little flexibility won't hurt. For example, we generally don't allow our son to choose to watch television after 7:00 P.M. on school nights. However, occasionally, there is a special program on at that time that he would like to see or that we think he might enjoy. On those rare occasions, we bend our rules a little, but we remind him that this is a special event, not a permanent change in the guidelines.

You may want to post your family's guidelines near the TV as a reminder to your children. But if you are consistent in following your guidelines, it won't take long for them to realize that those are the rules, and you will have made great strides toward helping your children make TV a choice, not a habit.

Possible Family TV Viewing Guidelines

No TV before school.
No TV before or during homework and chores.
No TV during meals.
No TV after a certain time on school nights.
No TV when friends visit.
No TV during quiet times or before napping.
TV is turned off when shows are over.

Guidelines for Younger Children

Statistically, preschool-aged children watch more TV than older children simply because they are home more often. If you wish to apply viewing guidelines to your preschool-aged child's TV habits, it is best to choose those guidelines which can carry over as your child grows and enters school. For example, even if your preschool child does not yet have "school nights," try treating weeknights as school nights and do not allow your child to watch TV at that time. It is also a good idea to start choosing *not* to eat in front of the TV when children are young, as it is a difficult habit to break when children get older.

If your young child is old enough to discuss the guidelines with you, do so, and remember that children are always more likely to abide by rules if they have a say in what the rules are. Don't forget to watch TV with your young child and, if she is old enough, begin discussing what she sees on TV with her. The sooner children learn to watch TV selectively and critically, the better, and if your family TV viewing guidelines are in place early in a child's life, you will have less trouble maintaining them as children grow.

Interage Differences

Remember that these TV viewing guidelines should be *family* guidelines suitable for all members of the family. Therefore, as you select guidelines with your children, it is important to choose *consistent* TV viewing guidelines which apply to all of your children, even if they are of different ages. If everyone knows what the rules are and understands that they are the same for every member of the family, your family will change their TV viewing habits together and there will be less confusion, bargaining, and rebellion.

Sharing TV Time

If your family has chosen to have only one TV in the home, there will be some discussion about who gets to watch it at any given time. This is completely normal and can teach children valuable lessons about sharing and compromise. However, to make TV sharing discussions a little less volatile, you may want to adopt some of the following suggestions.

- The TV should operate as a first come, first served privilege. Therefore, children who complete their chores and homework before others may choose a program to watch.
- To insure that no one child can monopolize the TV during a viewing period, children may select only one program per viewing time and must relinquish the TV when that program is over.
- Since TV time must be shared over the week, have children make a chart of their daily TV program choices and work with them to develop a schedule that allows each child to watch his or her favorite program at least once a week.
- If at all possible, have children work together to select programs that can be watched together.
- If one child wants to watch a program that is on at the same time as another child's choice, use your VCR to record it (many VCRs can record one program while another is on) and let the child watch it later.

Making TV Watching an "Active-ity"

Once we have begun to change our family's attitude about TV and use it consciously, we can begin teaching our children to watch TV selectively and critically. In other words, we can help our children become *active*, not passive, TV watchers. Kathryn Montgomery, president of the Center for Media Education in Washington, D.C., says that "active TV watching is a skill that we have to teach our children." But fortunately, this isn't as tricky as it sounds.

One of the primary goals of media literacy has been to help children learn to evaluate and selectively choose TV programs from the hundreds of possible options. The active process of selectively choosing programs helps children learn to think critically about what they are watching and why they are watching it, before the TV is ever turned on!

The Case Against Channel Surfing

Channel surfing is an American pastime and a real problem when it comes to helping children learn to use TV consciously and selectively. People channel surf because they don't know what they want to watch; they simply turn on the TV, pick up the remote, and start flipping away until they find something that looks interesting. TV programmers know this and go out of their way to make shows look enticing, even if seen for only a split second. It's called the "Least-Objectionable-Program Theory" by TV executives and works because, provided with a number of choices, most people will watch whatever bothers them least or catches their attention first.

Channel surfing doesn't encourage children to plan their screen time or to watch a specific TV *program* and turn it off when through. Instead, channel surfing teaches children to use TV as a habitual time filler, as they mindlessly change channels, watching anything that comes on, until they get bored with it or are called away to do something else.

As you work with your children to help them learn to watch TV actively, consciously, and selectively, say no to channel surfing. It will make TV-proofing much easier!

Choosing TV Programs With Your Kids:
The Family TV Menu

The one question I am most frequently asked is "What shows should my children watch?" Unfortunately, I can't answer that question with specifics because every family is different and TV shows change each season. The chapters in Part II of this book will give you more information about different types of shows that your children may want to watch and how they may be affected by them. The guidelines below will help you and your children choose programs that are less potentially harmful.

Most parenting experts agree that if children are involved in family decision making, they are more likely to abide by the decisions that are made. This is especially true with television. Consequently, the goal here is to provide your children with safe options—a menu—from which to choose and to *actively involve them in the process of making the decision.*

To start with, buy a *TV Guide* each week or check your local newspaper for the TV listing. I recommend *TV Guide* because it tends to be more comprehensive and provides cable listings and ratings, as well as descriptions of programs. Sit down with your children each week and go through *TV Guide* or listing together. Obviously, no one has time to read *TV Guide* cover to cover, but you don't have to. Many of the shows children want to watch are only on in the mornings, after school, or early evenings, and a large number of those are series shows that are on at the same time each week. The *TV Guide* will also give you information about special programs that might be appropriate and interesting choices. Use your TV Guide in conjunction with the following guidelines to help your children select shows that might be possible viewing options for them.

Age Appropriateness

Not all TV shows are appropriate for all ages. A thriller or cop show, for example, is not age appropriate for a five-year-old. She wouldn't understand what was happening and might be confused or frightened by what she saw. By the same token, *Sesame Street* is not age appropriate for a twelve-year-old. Naturally, he would think it childish and not enjoy it. Most children prefer to "view up," or watch shows that are designed for an older age group because they appeal to children's natural curiosity about what life is like as an eight-year-old, a teenager, or a twentysomething adult. Although rated for younger children, many of these shows, unfortunately, are not age appropriate and might contain messages that are detrimental.

The following checklist will help you determine if a show is age appropriate for your children.

- Note your children's ages. Are they preschool? Elementary age? Preteen or teenagers?
- How old are the show's main characters? Are they close in age to your child or much older?
- Are the situations in the show similar to what your child might experience in real life?
- Is the language or humor something that your child would understand?
- Is the theme of the show something that would be meaningful to your child?

- Is the show free of material that might frighten, confuse, or upset your child?

If the answer to any of the above questions is no, then the program is not age appropriate and would not make a good choice for your child's viewing. The new TV rating system will also help you determine if a program is age appropriate. However, bear in mind that ratings are only a guide, not a definitive "child-safe" seal of approval. Use your best judgment.

Time of Day

TV programs are on twenty-four hours a day, seven days a week. However, most programming that is appropriate for children is only offered at certain times, such as early morning, mid-afternoon, and early evening prime time. Occasionally, there will be a special child-appropriate TV program that is offered only in the evening.

When choosing shows, it is important to select only those which are on at appropriate times for your children. To a certain extent, your family's TV viewing guidelines will dictate when and what your children watch. For example, if your guidelines say that TV viewing isn't a choice after 9:00 P.M., certain sitcoms, dramas, and other adult-oriented shows won't be options. If your guidelines prohibit watching TV before school, then programs that are on between 6:00 and 8:00 A.M. won't be choices for your children.

As you and your children select programs, make sure that they choose from those programs that fit within the times specified in your family's guidelines.

Content

Decisions regarding content are the trickiest ones because it is sometimes hard to know what the content of a particular program is. The *TV Guide* can give you a basic idea about a particular show, and the following chapters will better inform you about the content and messages of certain types of programs, but generally the rule here is that if you don't know what the show is about, watch it before making a decision as to its appropriateness.

It is important to listen to your children's opinions about the shows they want to watch, while encouraging them to evaluate their choices. If you are unsure about the content of a show that they are already watching, ask them to tell you about it, and, together, decide if it is an appropriate show. For example, my son, Joshua, had watched a cartoon that I was unfamiliar with at friend's house. He wanted to include that program on his menu. I asked him to tell me about the show and led him with specific questions about the content. Was there any fighting or hitting in the show? Who were the characters? What sorts of things did they do? Was it funny? Why did he like it? What did he learn from it? Although it was not an ideal program, together we determined that the show was acceptable and could remain on the menu. I watched an episode with him the following day and was convinced that although the show wasn't great, he liked it and it could stay, but that we would watch it together and talk about it.

Once you and your children have made decisions about which shows are appropriate choices, write the list down and post it near the TV so your children always know what their choices are. Each child should have his or her own menu from which to choose.

If the menus need to be amended periodically, you may add or subtract shows. In my family, we change our son's TV menu several times a year. Each season, we check for new shows that might be appropriate, watch an episode of each, then consider which shows should be included on the menu. If Joshua has decided he might like to watch a new or different show, we check for appropriateness and amend the list. We also change the menu on his birthday, adding or subtracting shows based on his developmental stage and interests.

Obviously, your children may want to watch TV programs that are not what you would ideally choose for them. However, even if your children are watching less-than-appropriate programs, the critical thinking and discussion techniques you will learn in the next chapter will mitigate any possible negative effects.

Activity: What Are Your Children's Favorite Shows?

Most of us have a favorite program or two that we would be hard-pressed to give up, even in the best interests of our family. Children are especially attached to their favorite shows, and any attempt to "take them away" will be seen as tyranny on your part. Therefore, it is important that we recognize their favorite shows and work with our children to ensure that they are watching them consciously and selectively.

The purpose of this activity is to help you and your children avoid conflict and reach an agreement about favorite shows when building family TV guidelines and menus. To begin, ask your children to make a list of their favorite shows, when they are on, and why they like them. Remember to be careful about passing judgment on these shows. We

---

Joshua's TV Menu

As I mentioned before, my six-year-old son, Joshua, has certain TV viewing guidelines: No TV before school, during meals, when friends are over, after 7:00 P.M., or when the weather is nice. Below is a TV menu that he and I constructed, based on those viewing guidelines, program appropriateness, and the shows he likes to watch. This menu lists his options, but he rarely, if ever, watches this much TV. He usually only chooses to watch one show in each time frame, if that. Some days, he doesn't choose to watch at all!

Monday–Friday afternoon (2:30–6:00): *Looney Tunes, Cartoon Express, Tom and Jerry, Barney and Friends, Where Is Carmen Sandiego?, Ghostwriter, Reading Rainbow, Bill Nye, the Science Guy, Charlie Brown and Snoopy, Arthur, Kratt's Kreatures, Wishbone, Fraggle Rock, The Flintstones*

Monday–Friday evening (6:30–7:00): *Doug* (occasionally), *Looney Tunes*

Saturday morning: *Goosebumps, Bugaloos, Biography for Kids, Doug, Rugrats, Reading Rainbow*

Sunday morning: *Mr. Rogers' Neighborhood, Ghostwriter, Where Is Carmen Sandiego?, The Magic School Bus, Rugrats, Captain Planet, Looney Tunes, Scooby Doo*

---

don't want to make TV watching any more of a battleground than it already is!

Next check to see if any of the shows conflict with your family TV guidelines or menu appropriateness. If they do, work out a compromise that allows your child to see the show under certain conditions. For example, my son's favorite show is *Doug*, a cartoon that airs at 7:00 P.M., weeknights. Joshua likes it because it is funny and the main character gets away with things that he wouldn't be able to get away with. Although the show doesn't fit within our family TV guidelines and contains some less than appropriate humor for a six-year-old, for the purposes of family sanity we decided it could stay. However, we put some limits on it. My husband and I decided that Josh could watch *Doug* two nights a week, if he wanted to, and at least one night each week we would watch with him and talk about it. Everybody seemed to accept that plan, and our guidelines and menu remained pretty much intact.

In another example, my neighbor's little girl, Darcie, who is ten, wanted to watch *Saved by the Bell*, her favorite show. Unfortunately, the show is on at 5:30 P.M., and the family had agreed that there would be no TV on school nights until after dinner at 6:30. This was a potential conflict. However, disaster was avoided when Darcie and her parents agreed that she could watch *Saved by the Bell*, if and only if her homework was completed and checked by her parents. They also suggested taping the show for her to watch after dinner if homework wasn't completed. These solutions worked out well. Darcie usually only finished her homework before the show once or twice a week. And on the nights that Darcie didn't finish her homework on time, the family taped the show for her to watch after dinner, if she wanted to. They also used the taped show for TV-Talk discussions.

You might also consider using your child's favorite TV show to begin TV Talk. The next chapter will teach you how!

4

TV Talk
The Road to Critical Thinking

Studies show that children are better able to think critically about television if they are watching with an adult and talking about what they see. A 1978 study concluded that "adult interaction with television—not just adult presence while children watch—was necessary for significant learning." Another landmark study suggested that children's attitudes and behaviors related most closely to "the presence and behavior of parents when the TV was on." Still another important study, conducted by the United States Office of Education, concluded that adult mediation of television was central to effective media education.

In order for children to become aware of TV messages and how they are affected by them, we need to guide them toward that awareness and analysis through discussion and dialogue. What this means is that, as parents, the most significant and effective portion of our TV Teaching will be done through discussion with our children before, during, and after they watch television. I call it TV Talk.

Three Things You and Your Kids Need to Know About TV

Before you panic about talking about TV, rest assured that it's not hard, and you don't have to be some kind of expert to do it. In fact, there are only three basic concepts that you need to know about TV before you begin talking about it with your children, and if you have watched any television yourself, you probably already know them. These three concepts are

1. TV is not reality, but a version of reality.
2. TV shapes our beliefs, opinions, ideals, attitudes, and behavior.
3. TV is commercially driven.

These three basic themes are central to any discussion about TV and will guide you and your children toward a more critical understanding of TV messages.

TV Is Only a Version of Reality

Most children and many adults believe that TV presents "reality." After all, TV works hard to appear as an omniscient, all-seeing power with access to everything and everybody and we tend to think of it as our "window on the world," telling us what the world is really like. However, what most children don't understand is that TV's world is not an accurate reflection of the real world. A TV show or movie is a carefully created *version* of reality.

"Version" is the key word here. Someone—a writer, a producer, a director, a camera operator—has taken reality and *interpreted* it for the audience through techniques of film and video production. All TV shows are interpretations: scripts are written, actors are cast and rehearsed, costumes and sets are chosen, makeup is applied, lights are set, camera angles and composition of shots are selected, sound and special effects are added, and the final product is edited to give the audience the illusion of real life. Even the most "real" TV show, documentary, or news story is prepared for the audience through techniques such as choice of camera angle, editing, interview questions, locations, and sound.

The way that something appears on the screen affects what it means, and so TV producers are very careful about the way that things appear, using certain codes and conventions to carry meaning. For example, if we see a man dressed in dark clothing walking along the street at night and hear scary music, producers know that we will most likely interpret that to mean that this is a bad guy on his way to do something dastardly. If, in contrast, he were wearing bright colors, it was a sunny day, and we heard birds chirping, the producers know that we might assume that he was a good guy who was happy and in no danger.

Other codes and conventions include the way in which an image is shot with the camera. If something is shot from below, it appears bigger than in real life and will seem scary. If the same object is shot from high above, it will appear small, insignificant, or frightened. Lighting is also an important code. If the light in the shot is shadowy and dark, we might think something suspenseful is going on. If it is clear and bright, we will feel happy.

How a show is edited or put together also affects its meaning. If a show has a large number of very fast shots, it will excite us and make us anticipate what comes next. If the pace is slow, it might seem less urgent. If music or sound effects have been added, they carry certain meanings too.

Interestingly, these codes and conventions are not natural to us but, like TV watching itself, are learned through experience. Young children who haven't been exposed to much television ask a lot of questions while watching. What's happening? Who is that guy? What is he doing? Where is that sound coming from? They are trying to figure out what is going on and what it means, and because they don't yet understand the codes and conventions of television, it doesn't make sense to them. However, it doesn't take long for children to learn.

All television audiences are actively processing the information that appears before them on the screen. For children, that means that they are learning the codes and conventions of television, as well as trying to understand them in context. As you begin to employ the techniques of media literacy to arm your kids against TV's influence, it is important to help them recognize that TV is only a version of reality and to understand and question how TV's codes and conventions affect the meaning of what they see (see Appendix B, "Glossary of Production Terms"). Once they understand this concept, it becomes easy for them to distance themselves from TV's "reality" and to think critically about its messages and their effects.

TV Shapes Beliefs, Opinions, Attitudes, Behaviors, and Ideals

The way in which people, places, objects, and events are portrayed on television has a strong impact on what we think about them. Because TV appears real, we readily accept as truth what TV shows us and tells us and therefore embrace TV's attitudes, beliefs, opinions, and ideals as our own.

If, for example, we constantly see women on TV behaving stupidly or dressing suggestively, we may come to believe that women are dumb and sex crazed. If we see a show on Africa and only see poor, starving villagers in a fly-infested barren field, we may believe that Africa is a desolate land filled only with famine-stricken, disease-wracked people. If most of the criminals we see on TV are young men of color, we may assume that most criminals are young men of color and that most young minority men are criminals. If we are constantly told by TV advertisers that we are inadequate, unattractive, or unsuccessful without certain products, we are likely to believe it, feel terrible about ourselves, and rush out to buy their products.

Consider your own beliefs about yourself and the world as a whole. How many of them do you think are influenced by TV? George Gerbner, a TV researcher and dean emeritus of the Annenberg School for Communication at the University of Pennsylvania, constructed a test to determine how much people's beliefs and opinions were influenced by television. The test comprised multiple-choice questions about the U.S. population, crime statistics, employment, race, and women, which reflected current TV and popular opinion and belief. After giving the test to a large number of adults, Professor Gerbner discovered that the more television people watched, the more answers they got wrong, proving that heavy TV watchers were very likely to accept TV's often inaccurate portrayal of the world as true.

But even if you don't watch a lot of television, what little you do see will still influence what you think and feel about certain topics. If you watch the news, what you think and believe about the country and the world are directly affected by what is shown and said about them each night. If you watch an educational program on underwater life, you will most likely accept the opinions and attitudes presented by the makers of the show.

Children are especially prone to TV's influence on their developing attitudes and beliefs. Because they have so little real life experience to compare to TV's version of the world, they have no way to determine if what they see and hear is accurate or not. Therefore, it is important that children realize that everything they see and hear on TV influences them and to question how and why they are being influenced.

Money Makes TV Go Round

Television producers would like us to think that TV exists for the sole benevolent purpose of providing viewers with twenty-four-hour news and entertainment, and many of us believe it, especially children. But television does not exist to entertain or inform us; television exists to make money. That is its real purpose. If we are entertained or informed in the process, it is because by doing so, television makes money. How does TV make money? By selling audiences to advertisers.

Dr. Gerbner's TV Influence Test

Below are a few questions from Dr. George Gerbner's test, which measures how much TV influences our beliefs and opinions. Try the test and see how you score.

1. What percent of the world's population lives in the U.S.?
   (a) 1%   (b) 5%   (c) 10%   (d) 15%   (e) 20%
2. What percentage of American workers are in law-enforcement jobs?
   (a) .25%   (b) .5%   (c) 1%   (d) 2%   (e) 5
3. What percent of the victims of crime are black?
   (a) 70%   (b) 55%   (c) 40%   (d) 25%   (e) 10%
4. What percent of married women work at jobs outside the home?
   (a) 60%   (b) 50%   (c) 30%   (d) 20%   (e) 10%
5. What percent of workers have jobs in professional athletics or entertainment?
   (a) .25%   (b) .5%   (c) 1%   (d) 2%   (e) 3%

Answers: the correct answer to each question is (b).

When TV was first invented, its makers claimed that it would revolutionize the world by making access to information and programming available to everyone. TV pioneers envisioned television as a great democratic tool, and their lofty ideals included TV as a public service, a bringer of information to the disadvantaged, and a means by which to unify the country and the world. In many ways, their dreams have come true, but not exactly the way they had planned.

In order to make these dreams a reality, someone had to finance the venture. TV was expensive, and someone had to pay for the programming to be produced and aired. Along came advertisers. Companies and the makers of products realized that television was an ideal way to reach lots of potential consumers of their goods. So what was it to them if, for a few hundred or thousand dollars, they could get their name and product to appear on TV? Millions of people would see it and the money would be recouped in sales. So television and the makers of products joined forces. TV promised large audiences for advertisers' messages, and, in turn, advertisers footed the bill for the programs that would bring them audiences. The larger the audience, the more money the advertiser had to pay to reach it.

Consequently, TV producers created programs that they hoped would

attract large audiences and, therefore, advertisers. More and more companies recognized TV's power to reach and sell to potential consumers
and TV recognized that there was a killing to be made. A symbiotic
relationship was born.

Today, advertising revenues account for most of television's profits. A
successful show can command hundreds of thousands of dollars for a
thirty-second commercial slot. Highly watched shows such as the Super
Bowl can demand close to half a million dollars for each commercial! If a
program fails to attract an audience, it is canceled: No audience, no
advertisers; no advertisers, no profit; no profit, no show.

In his book *The Sponsor*, media historian Erik Barnouw says that
"Sponsorship is basic to American television. Even noncommercial television looks to it for survival . . . [and a] vast industry has grown up
around the needs and wishes of sponsors [advertisers]. Its program formulas, business practices, ratings, and demographic surveys have all
evolved in ways to satisfy sponsor requirements."

Millions of dollars are spent each year on what is called "audience
research," in which producers try to determine what kinds of shows
people will watch. Ratings, or measurements of audience, are tallied
daily, and advertising rates are based on the ratings. If one kind of show
is successful and draws large ratings, others just like it will follow. If a
certain style or topic is hot, there will be programs about it. If a show
reaches a small audience, but one that is important or attractive to advertisers, it will remain. Anything that will attract audiences that can then be
sold to advertisers will be on the air, no matter how dumb, offensive, or
risqué. High-paying advertisers can even control the content of a TV
show by demanding that producers follow guidelines for the show's story
line, characters, and the like.

"TV is advertising. Advertising is TV," says a prominent advertising
executive. But TV is a money-making enterprise beyond selling advertising. It is also a billion-dollar export industry, selling reruns and syndi-
cated shows around the globe. Videotape sales and rentals account for a
large share of profits, and sales of products associated with TV shows
rake in even more money. Everywhere we look, TV is selling to us and
being sold to us.

While it is important to know that TV's bottom line is the bottom
line, it is even more important to encourage kids to look for what they
are being sold and to question why and how the selling is being done. In
his book *Selling Out America's Children*, psychologist David Walsh says
that children need to know that they are being sold to and how advertising works, so that they will not be as easily influenced by its messages.

Otherwise, says Dr. Walsh, they are easy prey for the harmful negative values of consumerism.

The Cost of Commercials

It costs a lot of money to make and air a commercial. In 1996, the cost of producing a thirty-second ad was between $500,000 and $800,000. To purchase time on a popular sitcom, the CPM (cost per thousand viewers—what networks charge to air an ad) was $9.42, and the CPM for national news was $5.00. In 1995, the CPM for *The Simpsons* was $15.51, and *20/20* cost $7.73!

On the average, it will cost an advertiser $800,000 to $1,000,000 to produce and broadcast one thirty-second commercial during prime time! And if a half-hour TV show costs only $800,000 to produce, after selling sixteen or so commercials at $150,000 to $250,000 each, that's quite a profit!

In 1994, advertisers spent almost $63 billion on television advertising, and according to *USA Today*, approximately 50 percent of an advertised product's profit went back into advertising!

Join Your Children

Now that you know the basic themes of TV Talk, you can begin to use them to introduce your children to thinking critically about TV. But in order to do that, you are going to have to watch some TV with them. Don't panic. As we noted before, you don't have to watch TV with your children all the time; just a few times to start with, and then occasionally afterward.

Kerri and Ray both grew up in households that had only one TV and fondly remember family TV nights spent watching Wild Kingdom *or* The Smothers Brothers Comedy Hour. *But when they learned in a workshop that they needed to watch TV with their children, they were apprehensive. They had good family TV memories, but how would the kids react? TV was so different now; would they even enjoy the programs their kids watched?*

After one family TV night, Kerri and Ray's fears subsided. Not only did the children enjoy their parents' company, but the show they watched, a family sitcom, actually had some funny moments. Kerri and Ray were even more delighted to discover that talking about TV was easier if they

*watched with their children, and their conversation was enlightening and
fun. In fact, everyone was so pleased with the family TV night that it
became a regular weekly event, and has been so for years!*

Watching TV together can be a fun, quality, family experience. Many
of my students tell me that TV watching is more fun with other people
and that they enjoy the opportunity to share their thoughts and ideas
with each other. Parents note that they enjoy watching TV with their
children—plus it enables them to see firsthand what their children are
watching and observe their children's behavior and responses. They also
report that their children are more willing to talk to them about what
they see if they are sharing the viewing experience together.

To begin, choose one show from your children's TV menu to watch
together. It doesn't matter which show you choose. You might offer to
watch your children's favorite show, ask your child which show he would
like to share with you, or suggest a show that might interest you both. If,
however, your children are watching a show that bothers you, you might
consider starting with that one.

Plan to watch at least one show a week for the first month. Organizing
a family TV night is a good way to make watching TV with your kids a
regular habit. In my family, Friday night is our family TV night. Often
we rent a movie to watch together or we check the *TV Guide* for a special
program that we all might enjoy. These Fridays are sacred time to us,
and we try not to interrupt them. In fact, my son enjoys them so much
that he often plans all week for the movie or TV show he wants to share
with us! Most important, my husband and I know that at least once a
week, talking to Josh about TV is a priority. And with our busy sched-
ules, having a set family TV night helps insure that TV Teaching doesn't
get away from us.

Watch First, Talk Later, TV-Talk Guidelines

Parents often arrive at workshops saying, "I know I'm supposed to talk to
my kids about what they see on TV, but I don't know how. What am I
supposed to talk about?" or "I've tried talking about TV, but my kids
won't cooperate. How can I get them to discuss it with me?" Although
each of the following chapters provides specific suggestions for discussion topics, you will find that talking to your kids about TV is easier if
you follow these TV-Talk guidelines.

*Respect the fact that your children want to watch the show and might enjoy
it.* We adults have to be very careful about imposing our tastes on our

children: We might unwittingly make a bad show irresistible simply by expressing our disdain for it. In fact, I have heard children claim that they love a certain show, just because their parents hate it! But even if they haven't heard us pan a program, they may sense how much we dislike it and be unwilling to discuss it with us.

Although we might not like a show that our children want to watch, we must respect their feelings and reserve our negative comments. Don't begin discussions with "I really think this show is awful!" You won't get much cooperation with such an introduction. If something bothers you about the show, save it for discussion and point it out in a constructive way.

Observe the show quietly for points of interest and discussion. While watching with your children, take mental notes about things that interest you or would be good topics for conversation. If it's easier for you, keep a notepad by the TV to jot down ideas. Remember that you have a lot of discussion possibilities, ranging from production techniques to what your children are learning from the commercials! But don't feel compelled to discuss everything at one time. Start with one or two topics and slowly add more. We don't want to overwhelm our children or ourselves, especially in the beginning.

At first, it's best not to interrupt the program with comments. Children get very resentful of such intrusion. Remember, they want to watch the show! However, if something requires immediate attention, you can discuss it during the commercial break or save it for after the program.

As you and your children get more experienced at talking about TV, you can begin to discuss things as they are happening. This is great for helping children learn to think while they are watching, not just after it's all over. You can also begin your TV viewing time by asking your children to look for certain things and point them out to you as they see them. This is a very good game for younger children and develops their critical observation skills. Bear in mind, even after you've finished talking about the show, someone can bring up a subject. Anytime can be a good TV-Talk time.

Question your children gently about their thoughts and feelings. Kids are very perceptive and easily sense when we are trying to teach them something. We don't want our children to feel threatened or lectured to by talking about television. We want our children to *want* to talk to us about TV. So, in discussions, try to be as gentle and as relaxed as possible.

When you begin your TV Talk, start with an easy question, such as "Did you like the show?" Ask your children why they liked it, what they liked about it, or what they didn't like. Think of it as though you were asking them about their school day. But try not to pressure your children into talking about big issues as soon as the show is over. It may take them a while to formulate their thoughts and opinions. Try again later.

If the first conversations only last a minute or two, don't be alarmed. Remember, it may take your children some time to adjust. With time and practice, they will be more willing and able to discuss TV with you. Soon, they will start talking without being questioned!

Listen carefully and respectfully to what your children say about the show. It is important to practice our listening skills while talking to our children about TV. We want our children to feel that discussing television with us is a safe, fun activity, but if we interrupt them, deny their feelings, or belittle their opinions, they won't want to talk.

As you question your children about what they see, remember that they may see things differently from the way that we see them. Try to work *with* how they feel about a show, not against it. If they say that they love a show that you dislike, be careful of how you respond. The safest bet is to ask them why they liked it, then offer to share your feelings, without denying or belittling theirs.

Reinforce positive comments and positive aspects of the show. When children do respond to your questions, encourage them by telling them how interesting you find their answers. When your children offer a viewpoint that shows their critical understanding, don't be afraid to tell them how pleased you are with their thoughts. Urge your children to think critically by being supportive and enthusiastic of their attempts.

It is also important to reinforce anything that is positive in the show. It's very easy to get wrapped up in the negative aspects of television, once you become aware of them, but we don't want our kids to think that whenever we talk about TV, it's just to point out the negative things. That isn't fun and makes the discussions very tedious. Besides, even a really crummy show might have something good in it! It might only be the costumes or the acting, but it's still good. Talk about the good parts, as well as the bad ones. Remember that we don't want our children to hate TV, we just want them to be critical of what they see. But thinking critically about something doesn't mean criticizing it, it means analyzing it—both the negatives *and* the positives.

TV Talk With Children of Different Ages and Abilities

Not all children are able to carry on an in-depth conversation about TV. A preschool child, for example, would have a difficult time talking specif-

TV Talk Topics

Although the following chapters will provide you with more detailed suggestions for discussion, here are a few general topics and questions which can be covered in any TV-Talk discussion. Don't forget to talk about the commercials too!

- Did you like the show? Why or why not?
- Did anything in the show upset you, frighten you, or make you feel bad?
- How were the characters portrayed?
- What is the situation or conflict?
- Do you think that the characters behaved appropriately or realistically?
- How was the conflict or problem solved? Was that a good way to solve it?
- Could this happen in real life? Why or why not? How would it be different?
- How did the production elements affect what you thought about the program?
- If you were writing this show, how would it be different?
- What did you learn from this show?

ically about his feelings or analyzing the moral implications of a character's actions. Nonetheless, if you keep it simple, you can talk to your young children about what they see on TV and start developing their critical thinking skills.

Since children under the age of six or seven need practice separating reality from fantasy on TV, talking about production elements is accessible to them and works well. Young children are fascinated by the workings of TV, and demystifying it by pointing out techniques of animation, actors, costumes, and music helps them understand that TV isn't reality but rather a constructed version of reality.

Engaging younger children in conversation about characters and their actions also works well. Asking your children if they agree or disagree with a character's behavior or how they might feel if the same thing were done to them in real life is a good way to start children thinking about the meaning of a program. Don't forget to ask them what they learned from the show.

Older children between the ages of eight and twelve are better able to tackle tougher topics, but again, the trick is to begin simple and light and with a good sense of humor. Production elements are good discussion starters, as are questions about characters, conflict, and problem solving. Children in this age group also like the game of making up their own version of the show and are likely to get very involved in discussion this way. Older children also enjoy talking about commercials and are excited to learn how they are made. Point out production techniques here too! And, as always, ask your older child what he has learned from the show.

Teenagers are probably the most difficult to engage in TV Talk. Most teens are extra sensitive to anything that seems like a lesson or a lecture, and their growing sense of identity and independence feels threatened by any perceived attempt at control or manipulation. When trying to watch TV with your teen, consider asking her if she *minds* if you watch a show with her. That way, she may not feel that you've intruded on her space and may be more likely to share her ideas with you.

In discussions, it's often best to approach your teen casually, informally, and after you have watched the show. Again, start simple and light, as though you were asking about the events of her day. Don't worry if she doesn't want to talk immediately or if the conversation feels like a failure. Give her plenty of time to think about your questions and be extra careful not to deny her feelings or opinions. If it doesn't work, try it again later.

Teenagers need to trust that you aren't ridiculing their show or, indirectly, their emerging identity. Remember to respect their ideas and their interest in the show and use your listening skills. With time and patience, your teen will realize that you aren't trying to control or manipulate her; you are only trying to hear what she has to say. Soon, you will be engaged in some very fascinating discussions on a number of different levels.

If you have children of vastly different ages, it is important that you talk to each of them at their level and at different times. This may mean that you are watching TV and talking about it twice or three times a week, but remember, it's only for a short time. Soon, your kids will be on their own, with only an occasional reminder.

Sample TV Talk

The following conversation between a father and his twelve-year-old child might help you begin TV-Talk discussions with your children.

Andrew and his Dad, Allen, had just finished watching Andrew's favorite action-adventure show together, and Allen was concerned that Andrew

---

What Kids and Parents Say About TV Talk

"I never knew how commercials were made or how they convinced me to buy things until Mom talked to me about the Nike ad. I feel really stupid for having let Nike make me believe that they were the best shoes. I'm glad my Mom pointed it out and I'll never fall for their tricks again!"

—*Alex, age 11*

"I always thought that my family was different or wrong because it wasn't like the ones I saw on TV, but after talking with my Mom about how TV isn't like real life, I don't feel so bad."

—*Cassie, age 13*

"I was hesitant to begin talking about TV with my kids, thinking I couldn't teach them anything because I didn't know anything about TV. But I discovered that I actually knew more than I thought, and more important, I learned a lot just from watching and talking. I really enjoy TV Talk now, and my husband and I even do it together without the kids!"

—*Amy, mother of 3*

"My son, Jeremy [age six], has been a fan of *Power Rangers* since it first aired. I never could figure out why he liked it so much and I was curious to know what he was learning from it, so one afternoon we talked about it. I learned that he liked the show because it made him feel strong, but that he knew it was pretend and people didn't act that way in real life. He also told me that the one thing he had learned from it was that being bad doesn't get you anywhere. I'm very relieved, and I'm glad to know that he is thinking about what he's watching. I'm going to keep talking to him about what he sees."

—*John, father of Jeremy*

---

might be learning negative values from it, so he initiated a TV-Talk discussion.

ALLEN: That was pretty good, huh?

ANDREW: Yeah. I liked the part where the bad guy got hit by the train. That was cool!

ALLEN: What was so cool about it?

ANDREW: It was neat the way the train slowed down and you could see everything that was happening real slowly.

ALLEN: I wonder why the director chose to use the slow-motion effect there?

ANDREW: Maybe so that you could see all the details like the way the guy's head came off. How'd they do that, anyway?

ALLEN: The special-effects department probably created a dummy whose head could come off and then switched the dummy for the actor when they shot that scene. It wasn't a real person.

ANDREW: I know.

ALLEN: They sure used a lot of fake blood, though. I wouldn't want to be on the clean-up crew.

ANDREW: Me, either.

ALLEN: Do you think that the bad guy deserved to be hit by the train?

ANDREW: Yeah. Of course. He was a bad guy.

ALLEN: How do you know?

ANDREW: 'Cuz he did bad things, duh.

ALLEN: Like what?

ANDREW: (groaning) Dad . . .

ALLEN: No, really, Andrew. I'm curious. What bad things did he do?

ANDREW: Well, he robbed that store and then he stole that car and then he hurt all those people.

ALLEN: You're right. I guess he did do some pretty bad things.

ANDREW: So he deserved to be hit by the train, didn't he?

ALLEN: It's hard for me say that anyone deserves to have such a terrible thing happen to them, even if they do some bad things.

ANDREW: I guess so. Okay. He didn't deserve to be hit by the train, but it did make him stop.

ALLEN: Do you think it's like that in real life?

ANDREW: What?

ALLEN: Do bad guys get hit by trains and then the problem is solved?

ANDREW: No. In real life, bad guys get away or maybe they get caught and go to jail.

ALLEN: So, if you were going to rewrite this show to be more like real life, what would be different?

ANDREW: The bad guy would get caught and put in jail.

ALLEN: That sure is a different story.

ANDREW: It would be boring.

ALLEN: No slow-motion bloody train scene to make it exciting, huh?

ANDREW: Yeah.

ALLEN: Do you think they put that scene in there for a reason?

ANDREW: To make the show interesting to watch!

ALLEN: I agree. So, what do you think you learned from this show?

ANDREW: Uh . . . I guess not to do bad things? Oh, and you told me
about the dummy.
ALLEN: That's good. I'm impressed! How about next time, we look for
more dummies, okay?
ANDREW: Deal.

This conversation took only a few minutes, but it covered almost all of
the main TV Talk topics. As a result of this conversation, Allen felt better
about what Andrew was learning from the show, and Andrew learned
some valuable things about TV production and how messages are conveyed.

Activity: What Should I Talk About?

The following simple activity is designed to help you define target
areas for TV Talk with your kids. To begin, make a list of the things
about TV that concern or upset you. Is it the violence? Is it the stereotyping? Is it the messages about values? Advertising? Lack of positive
role models?

Next, ask your children if there is anything that bothers them about
what they see on TV. Listen carefully, without judging, and make a list
of those things.

Finally, make a list of things that you think are important for your
children to know about TV. Is it important that your children know how
to "see through" commercials? Do you want them to know how TV
shows are created? Do you think they ought to know about how news
decisions are made?

Keep these lists near the TV set for easy reference during TV Talk.
They will help guide your discussions and even help you determine
which shows need to be talked about. The chapters in Part II will give
you helpful hints for discussing the things that are important to your
family.

PART II

SEEING THROUGH TV

You have already learned simple techniques to help your children watch TV consciously and selectively. In the following chapters, you will discover what your children might be learning from the television shows they watch and how to help them see through TV's tricks and messages to watch more critically and be less easily influenced.

"Buy Me That!"

Exposing the Tricks in Advertising

Have you ever made what you thought would be a quick trip to the grocery store, only to end up angry and exhausted after a big fight with your kids in the cereal aisle? Do you dread trips to the toy store to buy a birthday present for a child's classmate, knowing that you won't get out of there without buying the latest cartoon character toy for your own child? Does a simple shopping excursion with your teenager turn into a brand-name nightmare? Is "Buy me that!" a frequently heard and hated phrase in your home?

The lesson of consumerism is the earliest and most powerful lesson children learn from television. The average child will see more than 700,000 television commercials by the age of eighteen, and each year millions of dollars are invested to develop products and ads that will appeal to kids. In 1992, $6.8 billion was spent advertising to kids between the ages of four and twelve. Another $5 to 7 billion was spent on kids ages twelve to seventeen. Over $100 million is spent annually for advertising on Saturday morning TV. Whole cable networks and TV programs are created simply to take advantage of the potential advertising dollars earned from reaching millions of kids.

And, for business, it pays off: Each year, American children spend over $50 billion on advertised goods, including snack foods, toys, clothing, and entertainment. Millions of children demand that their parents purchase Nike or Reebok sneakers because of TV ads, and millions more whine for the latest TV-inspired toy peddled on Saturday morning cartoons. Advertising to kids is a highly profitable, but dangerous business. How does it work and how can we prevent our kids from falling prey to TV-sponsored consumerism?

There is no way to keep your children from ever being exposed to advertising. You can, however, help them become less influenced by advertising messages by using the TV-Talk techniques of media literacy to teach them about commercials—their purpose, how they are made, and the tricks they use to get viewers to buy their products. Once kids know how ads work, they will be less inclined to demand, "Buy me that!"

The Child Consumer

According to James McNeal, a marketing professor at Texas A&M University, children constitute the most lucrative market for many businesses because they are actually three markets in one: A *current* market that spends over $50 billion a year, an *influential* market that causes parents and grandparents to spend more than $160 billion more annually, and a *future* market whose needs and wants for products and services will be conditioned while they are children. As the number of American children increases and they begin to influence purchasing decisions for other household items, from soap to cars, the total purchasing power of children is now calculated at over $340 billion a year!

What Is a Commercial?

The first step in helping children become aware of the influence and impact of advertising is to explain what a commercial is and its purpose. Since many children don't know what those entertaining thirty-second blurbs are that interrupt their shows every seven to ten minutes, it is important to go back to the basics: A commercial is a persuasive combination of sounds and/or images designed to entice the viewer to buy something.

A standard broadcast commercial is thirty seconds long and features the name and logo of the product for easy recognition. Some commercials are shorter and some are longer. A sponsor tag—"brought to you by . . ."—is usually only five seconds long, while an infomercial can be sixty minutes in length or longer.

Commercials are also hidden inside programs. News stories and talk shows contain "promotions" for products, and other types of shows use an advertising technique called "product placement," in which a product is placed in a prominent position during a scene. Sometimes a whole show can be one long commercial, as are many children's cartoons.

It is important that children learn to recognize ads and to find both the "hidden" ones and the obvious ones. Once they can do that, they can begin to examine what the commercials are selling and how they are being affected by commercial messages.

Why Are There So Many Commercials?

In 1996, the Federal Trade Commission (FTC), which governs TV commercial times and practices, allowed network television to sell eight minutes of commercial time for each half hour of programming. That meant that during every thirty-minute program, your children saw sixteen commercials. In each hour, they saw thirty-two commercials. Over the course of a year, the average child would have seen almost 40,000 commercials. At that rate, the average child will have seen almost 700,000 commercials by the time he turns eighteen!

However, networks sometimes disregard the FTC limits, and the amount of TV time allotted to commercials has been creeping up. Not long ago, a broadcast network was cited for airing almost 9½ minutes of commercials during a half-hour program!

This alarming statistic doesn't include the number of "hidden" commercials in shows that use tie-ins or feature products as part of the show. In 1996, every children's show on network television licensed a toy or other product that could be purchased. The hit program *Friends,* which has a large teenage audience, even built an entire episode around a can of Diet Coke. It was one of the most highly rated shows of that season!

The bottom line in television is the bottom line, and since commercials are there to make a profit for the network, is it any wonder that there are so many?

Activity: Counting Commercials

Most children are aware that TV programs are annoyingly interrupted by commercials, but they don't necessarily know why they are there or why there are so many of them. Younger children often have difficulty differentiating a commercial from a program or separating one commercial from another. A simple and fun way to introduce children of all ages to thinking critically about the influence and impact of commercial messages is to have them count the number of commercials that appear during a TV show and to discuss the findings.

During a family TV viewing time, ask your children to keep count of the number of commercials they see, including hidden commercials. Young children may need your help to determine if something is a commercial and to separate commercials from each other. After the show, tally your score and discuss the results using the following TV-Talk questions:

- How can you tell that something is a commercial?
- Were there any hidden commercials? Where?
- Were you surprised by the number of commercials you saw?
- Why do you think there are so many commercials?
- Why do you think commercials are there? What do you think is their purpose?
- How do you think people are affected by commercials?
- How are you affected by commercials?

Your children will probably be shocked to realize how many commercials there are during a regular TV show and will be curious to know why there are so many and why they are there. This is the perfect TV-Teaching opportunity to explain the relationship between TV and advertising and to introduce your children to thinking about the effects of commercial messages.

How Does Advertising Work?

Although most of us would be inclined to deny it, advertising clearly works. But how does it work? What makes us want to buy whatever we see in commercials?

All advertising is based on the theory of creating demand for a product. If people have choices between products or don't really need a particular item, the producer must somehow convince the buyer that the product is either desirable or necessary or both. In other words, it is up to the advertiser to make the consumer *want* the product or create an artificial need for it. To create demand, advertisers play on our emotions, take advantage of our insecurities and fears, and manipulate our values.

Helping children to learn to recognize how advertisers create demand is an important part of TV teaching, and the following explanations will help you guide your children toward a better understanding of commercial messages.

Selling a Feeling

Have you ever seen a commercial and thought to yourself, "Boy, that looks like fun!" or "Gosh, that sure looks like it feels good!" If you have, it is because the advertiser has tried to make you feel that way in hopes that you will buy the product that will provide that feeling. It's an advertising technique called "selling a feeling."

Making a consumer feel good about purchasing a product is one of the primary goals of an advertiser. After all, why would you buy something that makes you feel bad? Joy, happiness, pride, comfort, and fun are all feelings that advertisers try to provoke in consumers, knowing that if they can convince a viewer that the product will bring them that feeling, they will buy it. So they create commercials that show people having fun with the product and enjoying themselves or feeling good about themselves because of the product. In some cases, advertisers will evoke an emotion like fear or sadness, show people overcoming that emotion with the help of a product, and then being happy or relieved. For example, an ad for an insurance company might show people saddened over a fire in their home, frightened by how much it will cost to repair, and then happy and comforted to know that such-and-such insurance company will take care of them.

Advertisers will go to great lengths to make products look fun, exciting, or rewarding for kids. They will show children squealing with delight over a toy or feeling good about themselves because of an acne cream. Since children learn through emotions and are especially susceptible to portrayals of emotion on television, is it any wonder that they would identify with the emotions portrayed in the commercials and believe the advertisers' claims?

Children need to learn that advertisers will always try to make a consumer feel good about a product in order to sell it, but that it is a technique that advertisers use, not an accurate representation of how they will feel when they get the product home. In fact, many kids are disappointed when they finally get a toy or game home and discover that it's not nearly as exciting or as much fun as they were led to believe it was going to be. My friend's seven-year-old daughter, Anna, said it best. After playing with a new toy that she demanded her mother buy, she brought the toy to her mother and asked, "Can we take it back?" When her mother asked if the toy was broken, Anna replied, "No. But it wasn't as much fun as it was on TV!"

Selling an Image

Another powerful way that advertisers create demand for a product is to endow the product and its users with a certain desirable image. Attractiveness, sophistication, elegance, sportiness, popularity, power, wealth, and healthiness are all images that advertisers promote, knowing that consumers will buy a product that promises that image to the user.

To endow a product with a particular image, an advertiser will design a commercial that presents the product being used or endorsed by people who convey that image or surround the product with props to make it look more beautiful, powerful, elegant, and so forth. For example, if an advertiser wanted to make a particular brand of shoes look as if they would make the user a great athlete, he might have a famous athlete endorse the shoes or show them being worn by people who run fast or jump high. If an advertiser wanted to convince a consumer that a beauty product would make her irresistible to the opposite sex, he might have a beautiful woman using the product in a romantic setting surrounded by a number of handsome men.

Once advertisers have endowed a product with an image, they then try to convince us that without the product, we will never attain the image we desire. They tell us that without that product, we are inferior or unworthy or there is something wrong with us, and that the something can only be cured by having this product. For example, if elegance or beauty is an image that we want, advertisers might tell us that without a certain beauty aid, we will not be beautiful or elegant.

Teens and preteens are particularly vulnerable to the claims of image advertising. Concerned as they are about their own emerging identities, they are easy prey for any advertiser who can convince them that his product will make them appear attractive or cool or athletic. Even younger children can be hooked by the techniques of image advertising, believing that a certain food or toy will make them happy or popular.

It is important that children learn to recognize the techniques of image advertising and to be aware of how they are being manipulated to believe that a product can make them cool or popular or a star basketball player. A former student of mine had the right idea when he said, "The right brand of shoes won't make me popular; they'll only make me broke!"

Selling Values

Perhaps the most insidious of all of advertising's tricks is the creation of demand through the creation or support of certain values, the most influential of which is the value of consumption itself.

In the world of advertising, to have things is considered good and not to have them is bad. We are taught to buy things not only because we are told we need them or even want them, but because it is the thing to do. We are supposed to consume. Constant repetition of the advertising message "buy this" teaches children that buying things is a value in and of itself.

Other values promoted by the advertising industry include the value of fun, the value of attractiveness, the values of wealth, power, efficiency, security, and success. Commercials frequently imply that those values are necessary for "the good life," and without certain products, such a life and lifestyle cannot be achieved. For example, an ad for a security system might state that protecting your family should be important to you, and you need their product to do it right. Another ad might tell you that since getting women is important to you, you need to buy this car, which will attract women to you.

In many ways, advertising defines our value systems. Although advertising frequently plays on existing values, it overemphasizes certain ones—like attractiveness, wealth, excitement and fun—and under-represents or ignores others—education, honesty, family, and traditions—affecting our value systems and weighting them toward those things that advertising promotes. For children, whose value systems are just forming, this can be extremely detrimental.

Selling values is perhaps the most difficult sales pitch to detect, but it is important that children learn to recognize that much of what they might consider to have value has been dictated to them through advertising. Learning to see the difference between real values and those propagated by advertising is a crucial step in helping children become immune to the harmful messages of TV.

Activity: What Is Being Sold?

Since all commercials are selling something besides the product, helping children determine what feeling, image, or value an ad is selling is a good exercise in critical thinking and encourages them to understand how advertising creates artificial needs. To do this, simply watch a commercial together and discuss it using the following TV-Talk questions.

Selling Addiction to Kids

Children see over 100,000 alcohol ads before they reach drinking age, and many parent, health, and consumer groups are justly concerned about alcohol and tobacco commercials that are targeted to kids. In recent years, Joe Camel and the Budweiser frogs have been attacked as being highly influential on children's desires to smoke and drink.

In 1995, a study by the National Cancer Institute and the American Heart Association revealed that of all the influences that can draw children into a lifelong habit of smoking, cigarette advertising is the most persuasive. "Tobacco marketing is much stronger than peer pressure in getting a youngster to take the first step toward smoking," says Dr. John P. Pierce, coauthor of the study.

Out of the 3,536 California adolescents interviewed by Dr. Pierce, 76.2 percent said cigarette ads depict the habit as enjoyable; 73 percent viewed it as relaxing; 67 percent thought ads sold cigarettes as a way of reducing stress; and 41 percent said that cigarettes were promoted as a way of staying thin! Although cigarette ads do not appear on TV, it is important to note that they use the same advertising techniques—selling feelings, images, and values—and have the same effects.

In another study, it was found that beer ads were overwhelmingly popular among both boys and girls aged eight to twelve. A 1996 marketing survey found that the Budweiser frogs were more recognized among youngsters twelve to seventeen than any other television character and more than half of children aged six to eleven knew the bullfrogs well.

Many teenage boys cite beer advertising as a major influence on their decision to drink. "Beer ads make drinking look like so much fun," said one fourteen-year-old. And now that the liquor industry has reversed its voluntary ban on TV advertising, one public interest advocate has claimed that "the liquor industry has declared open season on kids."

You may have to do a little modeling for your kids by explaining how TV commercials sell feelings, images, and values.

- What product is being sold in this ad?
- Does the commercial make you want the product? Why?
- Does the ad convince you that you need the product? How?
- What feeling do you get from this ad? How did the ad make you feel that way?

- Does this ad seem to promise you something? What? How does it promise it?
- Do you think that the product can really do what it promises?
- What does the ad tell you is important? Is that important to you? To others?
- Why do you think ads use these other feelings, images, and values to sell a product?

While discussing ads, make sure to talk to your kids about the consumption ethic. This might be a good time to suggest limits on spending or allowances. It might also be a good opportunity to think about your own consumption patterns and the degree to which they are influenced by advertising.

Advertising Tricks Aimed at Kids

The techniques described in the previous section are as effective for kids as they are for adults. However, advertisers use some very specific production techniques targeted especially to kids. Helping your children learn to recognize these "tricks" is a fun and effective way to encourage their critical thinking.

Perfect Kids

The kids in commercials are always a little older and a little more perfect than the target audience for the ad. This trick is a good example of image advertising as the children in the ad are intended to be role models for what the advertiser thinks kids want to be like. For instance, a commercial targeting five-year-olds will feature seven- or eight-year-old actors. This technique is also used in TV shows targeted to kids.

Animated Characters

Since children love anthropomorphized characters, a favorite advertising trick is to use animated characters as representatives for the product. Do you remember Tony the Tiger, the spokestiger for Sugar Frosted Flakes? Now, Ninja Turtles sell snack foods, and Disney characters sell bath products. Part of the appeal to cigarette and beer advertisers of animated characters like Joe Cool and the Bud Frogs is that they help build product loyalty among children, even before these "customers" can buy the products!

Amazing Toys

Many toy commercials show their product doing things it can't possibly do, like flying in the air without strings, talking, or moving in a lifelike fashion. Recently, a Barbie commercial was singled out as deceptive because the dolls were shown moving in ways that seemed real, though everyone except kids who are unacquainted with the product knows that Barbies can only move stiffly. Commercials for athletic toys often show the product zooming high in the air or depict their users doing amazing stunts. These tricks are accomplished through camera effects and selective editing, in which missed catches, flopped jumps, or other mistakes are taken out. Toy commercials also show the product surrounded by additional amazing props, which make the featured item seem more appealing. However, those extra accessories aren't included in the box and "must be purchased separately."

Sounds and Music

Loud or realistic sound effects and upbeat music are tricks advertisers use to grab kids' interest and make products seem more exciting or lifelike. A toy airplane, for instance, might be shown flying through the air with the sound of a real airplane edited in, or a snack food might be featured with a loud hip-hop soundtrack performed by some well-known rock star. Memorable musical jingles are also a trick used by advertisers to target children who are susceptible to sing-along songs. And since many people don't actually watch commercials unless they are intrigued, any music or catchy sound effect is a great way to get kids' attention.

Visual Hype

As we already learned, children are attracted to bright colors and fast movements on the screen, and so of course advertisers use these techniques to appeal to kids. Neon colored, highly patterned backgrounds surround objects that fly across the screen in all different directions. Camera angles are tilted to generate excitement, and everything seems filled with energy and fun. This technique works as well for young children as it does for teens, and most ads from toys to sodas to clothes use it.

Celebrity Endorsements

A surefire trick used not only by advertisers of children's products but also for teens and adults is the celebrity endorsement. A supermodel hawking makeup, a well-known musician selling snack foods, or a star athlete selling shoes all help make a product seem more appealing to consumers. However, most children are unaware that the celebrity on the screen probably doesn't use the product but is paid millions of dollars to tell them how great the product is. This is another example of image advertising.

Faked Food

Do you ever wonder why those fast-food hamburgers look so juicy and tasty on TV, but when you buy them they're dry and tasteless? Faked food is a basic trick of TV advertising, and everything from fruit to ice cream is doctored to look fresher and more appealing for the camera. For example, milk in cereal is really Elmer's Glue. Fruits are dipped in oil to make them shine, and ice cream is made from Crisco and food coloring! Snack foods are presented in colorful, exciting packages that make them look more like a toy than something to eat, and this subtle deception is designed to make kids go nuts in the grocery store, demanding "Buy me this!"

Humor

We have already seen that children are attracted to humor and easily learn from it, so making things funny is a great ploy to trick both younger and older kids into watching, liking, and remembering commercials. Cartoon characters that beat each other up over snack foods or funny-looking spokespeople are sure hits. Anything that smacks of the unusual or humorous will get attention and most likely be remembered for its funniness.

Boy-Girl Strife

A favorite trick for targeting teens is to show some dating- or romance-related problem miraculously solved by a product. Imagine, a teenage girl is getting ready for her big date with the class hunk, but oh no, she has a pimple on her chin! Life is over! Compassionately, her friend recommends the facial product and guarantees that the blemish will be gone overnight. Shazam! The next day, she looks beautiful, and her date is a smashing success! This is a typical scenario for teens, and acne creams, sodas, and even clothing are sold by targeting teen insecurities. This technique is a perfect example of selling a feeling.

Bandwagon

The bandwagon approach is another favorite trick targeting teens, wherein the advertiser implies or states that *everyone* is using the product and that you will be left out, disgraced, and exiled if you don't. Again, teenage insecurities and fears about popularity make them easy prey to this technique, and any ad that promises instant peer acceptance is a sure hit. Paradoxically, commercials that promise the product's user individuality or attention are equally effective on teens. Since teens are working on their independence and personality, they want to stand out in the crowd, and products that they think will help them do this are instant successes.

Did You Know That . . .

- According to *Advertising Age* magazine, Michael Jordan is probably the highest paid commercial spokesman in the country, earning more than $30 million a year for his endorsements for McDonald's, Nike, Quaker, and Hanes. Would advertisers spend the money if Michael Jordan's face and name didn't attract consumers?
- Of the topmost appealing advertising tricks, a 1993 survey stated that 52 percent of kids were more easily persuaded by commercials containing humor than any other kind.
- In 1993, the top ten companies in advertising spending included Kellogg's breakfast cereals, McDonald's, and Disney.

Activity: Find the Advertising Trick

Finding the trick is an easy and fun activity for children of all ages and helps them learn to recognize how advertisers manipulate consumers through production techniques. While watching TV with your kids, make it a game to see who can pick out the tricks in the commercials. Point out the tricks you see, and use the following TV-Talk questions as discussion starters.

- Why do you think the children in this ad are older than you?
- Why did the advertiser use an animated character in this ad? Does it make the product more appealing?
- Do you think that the product can really do what it is doing in the commercial?

- How do you think the advertiser made the product appear to do amazing things?
- How do you think the advertiser makes the food look so good? Does it look like that in real life?
- How do the sound effects or music affect what you think about the product?
- Does the advertiser make this product look exciting? How?
- Do you think that the celebrity spokesperson really uses the product?
- Do you think that this product will really make you popular or attractive or cool, or whatever?
- Why do you think the advertisers use these tricks?

As you and your children discuss these advertising tricks, you can also ask your children if they have ever bought anything because of an ad and then been disappointed by the product when they got it home. Chances are, they will have had that experience and be willing to talk about it. This is a perfect TV-Teaching opportunity to discuss how commercials can be deceptive. A good follow-up activity to this discussion might be to compare real products in stores with their ads. You can do this anytime you go shopping with your kids!

How Children Are Affected by Advertising

Children are naturally attracted to commercials and can easily be deceived by advertising that influences them to buy products that they don't really need. Advertising also affects the way children view themselves, others, and the world around them. These effects can be quite subtle but, ultimately, extremely harmful.

Self-Esteem

Over the past few months, Diana had noticed a change in her thirteen-year-old daughter, April. She had taken to spending hours in the bathroom each night and was constantly looking in mirrors. April's clothing had changed too. She was wearing clothes that were either too tight or very revealing. After school, she would run upstairs to her room and not talk to anyone.

Diana had been leaving April alone, figuring that she was going through some kind of normal preadolescent phase, but one night she heard April crying in her room and went to help.

"I'm ugly and fat!" cried April, huddled with her pillow and stuffed animals on the bed. "No one will ever ask me out on a date!"

"Oh, April." Diana was understanding. "You're not ugly or fat. You're a very pretty girl! And besides, you don't have to worry about dating yet!"

April wailed. "Yes, I do! And besides, look at me! I have stringy hair, two pimples, and cellulite! No matter what I do, I'll never be beautiful." She collapsed in a fit of tears.

A few hours later, after Diana was able to calm April down and put her to bed, she noticed a bag lying beside the trash can in the bathroom. When she opened it, she discovered a treasure trove of half-empty beauty products that April had been buying and using to make herself "beautiful" but had discarded in frustration earlier that night.

One of the most harmful techniques employed by advertising is the creation of a problem that can only be solved through the purchase of a product. Bad breath, yellowed teeth, pimples, stringy hair, cellulite, baldness, dandruff, and body odor are all problems created by advertisers who play on our insecurities and fears. According to advertisers, we are all imperfect, flawed, and unacceptable in some way; our appearance isn't right, we don't have the appropriate clothing or car, or our business isn't functioning as efficiently as it could. Consequently, we cannot and should not feel good about ourselves until we have corrected these problems by purchasing a product.

Advertisers bombard us with idealized images of perfection and urge us to strive for them. Beautiful models tell us that we will never be beautiful without the right shampoos, makeup, and clothes. Athletic superstars declare that we will never be good athletes unless we have the right clothes, sneakers, or deodorant. Actors who appear wealthy and powerful tell us that we will never have wealth or power without the right computer or car, and everyone tells us that we have bad breath, perspiration odor, embarrassing stains, and other minor flaws that will prevent us from ever being perfect.

The truth of the matter is that these ideals are unattainable for most of us. The average fashion model weighs 23 percent less than the average woman and spends between three to five hours each day working on her appearance. Less than 0.5 percent of the national population are professional athletes, and more than 38 percent of the population wears eyeglasses (compared to 14 percent on TV)! But, unfortunately, children don't realize that the perfect people they see on TV are just that—highly crafted, finely detailed ideals.

Children's self-esteem can be seriously damaged by advertising's promotion of idealized perfection. It is well known that young girls are easily affected by the constant images of idealized beauty seen in advertising. Girls as young as seven and eight go on diets to achieve the "waif" look popular in clothing ads, and 80 percent of fourth-grade girls claim to be dieting! Eating disorders among adolescent and preadolescent girls are at an all-time high, and suicide rates and depression have skyrocketed among girls who are dissatisfied with their less-than-perfect bodies. In her book, *Reviving Ophelia*, Mary Pipher, Ph.D., says that advertising traumatizes young girls into feeling ashamed and upset over their bodies. "The omnipresent media consistently portrays desirable women as thin . . . [and] . . . girls compare their own bodies to our cultural ideals and find them wanting."

Even very young girls' self-esteem can be affected by advertising images. Ads for "girl toys," such as dolls and playhouses, show young girls engaged in stereotypical play, which emphasizes the accepted feminine role as mother or housewife. Consequently, most young girls accept those images and behaviors as appropriate, acceptable, and desirable. Young girls who don't wish to play with dolls feel ashamed because they are "different." And because girls rarely see diverse advertising images of women as, say, engineers or pilots, they view real women who are not sexy or domestic as though they are unworthy of the kind of exaltation given the beautiful, feminine, or domestic woman.

Boys also have self-esteem problems that may arise from advertising's influences. A boy who is not good at sports may feel ashamed or depressed about his lack of ability because athletic prowess is such an important value in advertising. The heavy emphasis on health and slimness in male advertising has also led to an unprecedented increase in dieting and eating disorders in boys.

Since commercials often feature men surrounded by a bevy of women, young boys feel they should be entitled to the same treatment and feel bad about themselves if they aren't as attractive to the opposite sex as advertising says they should be. Many boys (a) don't realize that those images are largely fantasy images and (b) internalize the value that advertising places on attractiveness. The increase in early sexual activity in young boys has a lot to do with the emphasis advertising places on sexual activity as proof of manliness and worth.

The self-esteem of very young boys can also be affected by advertising. "Boy toys" are defined in advertising as things that shoot, snort, scream, and shout, and commercials for these items feature rough-and-tumble boys shooting, killing, and destroying everything in their path.

My son, Joshua, once explained the problem this way. When I asked him why he didn't want any of the action figure toys he saw advertised on TV, he said, "Because boys play rough and I don't like to get hurt." I explained that that was OK, he didn't have to play like the boys on TV, to which he responded, "But then I'm not a real boy!"

Since advertising also portrays the world and its inhabitants as perpetually happy, children learn that happy is what everyone is supposed to be. This message can compound the other problems of advertising's idealized world because children who aren't "happy" feel that there must be something terribly wrong with them, in addition to all the other things advertisers say are wrong. It's a deadly combination that spirals into depression and leads, in extreme cases, to suicide.

Along with all the other possible effects on children's self-esteem, the most pervasive one is the simplest. If children don't have the things that other children do, they feel bad about themselves. Advertising's bandwagon technique always makes it seem that everyone else has something and children are afraid that they are missing out or won't be accepted if they don't have it to.

Acceptance of Others

Since according to advertisers having the right things is a prerequisite to acceptance, those who don't have the right things are not accepted by others. Children are deeply affected by this notion.

> *Fourteen-year-old Ben was telling his cousin Aaron about his new classmates at boarding school.*
>
> *"Well, Charlie, he's great. He's cool. His Dad drives this awesome Maserati, and Charlie's got this incredible mountain bike with Rock Shox and everything. And Dave's okay too. He's got the coolest clothes and he's real laid back. He's got a kicking stereo too—I think it's a Sony—and the best CD collection I've ever seen!"*
>
> *"We've got a few losers, though. They don't have anything cool and nobody likes them at all!"*

In school yards around the country, divisions based on who has what things are commonplace. Group identities are forged around clothing or shoes or cars, and those who have the "right" things are accepted, whereas those who don't are condemned.

Children take peer acceptance very seriously. Teenagers have been known to do all kinds of things to acquire the goods necessary for acceptance into the group, including lying, stealing, and even killing for that certain pair of sneakers guaranteed to make them popular with the "in" crowd. On the other hand, children whose families can't afford the "right" things are often made to feel like outcasts—taunted and shunned. In recent years, there have even been reports of attempted youth suicides over peer acceptance based on such materialism!

Not long ago, some public school systems around the country instituted school uniforms in an attempt to eliminate the problems associated with having the "right" clothes. Having witnessed a barrage of incidents, from name calling to assaults, school administrators decided that uniforms would level the playing field, making the haves indistinguishable from the have-nots and discouraging the social importance of material goods. While the effort should be applauded, it doesn't change the fundamental principle of peer acceptance and the way in which advertising plays on children's insecurities about fitting in outside of the school yard.

On a more personal level, advertising's exaggerated vision of the way people are supposed to look and act affects the way children view others. Boys internalize advertising's idealized images of female beauty and behavior, thus altering their ability to see women and girls realistically. Girls are equally affected by advertising's portrayal of the tanned, athletic "hunk" and often judge boys by that standard. Even relationships are frequently viewed through advertising's funhouse mirror, affecting the way kids relate to each other, their parents, and their teachers and setting up unrealistic expectations of how things should be between people. After all, if ads continually show beautiful people in beautiful settings having a wonderful time together, why shouldn't children expect life to be like that.

Advertising and Children's Worldview

At lunch, Jesse and two classmates, Alexis and Seth, were discussing a news film they had seen in social studies on the economy of Southeast Asia.

"I'm sure glad I don't live there," declared Jesse.

"Me too," chimed Alexis. "The streets are all crowded and dirty and the people probably stink!"

"Yeah," added Seth, "and they probably don't have any decent restaurants, either!"

"I wouldn't want to go anywhere that didn't have a McDonald's," agreed Alexis, "or anything to buy!"

"All I know is that anyplace that doesn't have a mall or a McDonald's can't be worth much," pronounced Jesse. "Someone ought to buy it and fix

it up right, if they want people like us to go there and improve their economy."

Constant exposure to advertising teaches children that the world is a buyable place, where everything is for sale and everything can be bought. In the world of advertising, acquisition of things becomes a symbol of status—wealth, success, and power—and "he who dies with the most toys, wins."

Consequently, children's worldview is affected. People and nations are judged according to their material wealth, and children often divide the greater world into haves and have-nots, in which the have-nots are somehow less worthy than the haves. Many children who have been exposed to large amounts of television advertising express little sympathy or understanding for the disadvantaged or developing nations and believe that there must be something wrong with them for not having the things that wealthier people and nations have.

This skewed sense of perspective affects not only children's view of other people and nations but also their vision of the natural world. If everything is consumable, then natural resources are also there for the taking. Despite recent emphasis on recycling and preservation, statistics have shown that many children continue to feel that nature itself is a commodity that can be bought, sold, and treated according to desires.

TV advertising's portrayals of the "perfect" world also influence the way children view the real world; if the real world appears grimier, less perfect, or less happy than the world created by advertising, children can be easily disillusioned and become depressed about their world and the future.

Perhaps the most problematic of all of TV advertising's effects on children is the way in which advertising promotes the value of immediate gratification. In the world of advertising, "get it now!" is a familiar refrain. Commercials that urge viewers to "rush to the stores!" and purchase something "while supplies last" teach children that there is little to be gained from waiting or saving. This idea spills over into children's worldview and is most commonly seen in their inability to accept setbacks or cope with misfortunes. They seek easy answers and solutions, just like those promised by ads. In the greater world, children who have been exposed to large amounts of TV advertising tend to support policies and politics that promise them immediate gratification while eschewing consequences and responsibility.

Activity: How Are Your Children Affected by Advertising?

All children are affected by advertising in some way, whether it is simply a case of the "Buy Mes" or a more complicated issue like peer acceptance, self-image, or excessive consumption. Although, it is often hard to pinpoint exactly how advertising is affecting your children, it is important that you and your children begin to recognize advertising's effects and find strategies for coping with them.

This is an activity that you can do alone or with your children to help you identify how your kids are being affected by advertising messages and how to minimize those effects.

To begin, simply take stock of your children's buying patterns.

- What do they spend their money on?
- What do they ask you to buy for them?
- Does your teenage daughter spend her money on makeup and clothing? Is your son buying athletic apparel or alcohol?
- Do your young children insist that you buy the latest TV- or movie-inspired toy?

Next, examine why your children are buying these things. You may need to consult them for answers.

- Ask them why they buy certain products.
- What do they hope to gain from buying them?
- Do they buy them for acceptance, to feel better about themselves, or just to buy things?

Finally, observe your children.

- Does your daughter appear to be overly concerned with her appearance?
- Is your son overly obsessed with sports or girls?
- Is shopping a favorite pastime?
- Do your young children get bored with toys quickly and demand new ones?

If you notice a relationship between what your children buy, why they buy it, and their behavior, you may have located a problem in the way they are affected by advertising. It is now important for you to talk to your kids about advertising's influence and to help them understand how they are being affected.

Discussing advertising's effects will take some practice and a little patience. Remember that children aren't used to thinking about advertising or how it influences them and may need a little prompting from you. Be gentle, though, as advertising's influence is often closely related to how kids feel about themselves, and they can be very sensitive about it.

What Kids Say About Advertising's Effects

"I never realized how much I had been affected by advertising until I found myself in the hospital weighing 97 pounds at 5'6"! For years, I had starved myself to look like Kate Moss. It worked, but what a price I paid!"

—*Ellen, age 17*

"Those beer ads are something else. All those bikini-clad babes swarming around the guys with the beer. I wish I had known that real life wasn't like that. Girls like that would never want to hang with guys that drank that much beer!"

—*Ed, age 16*

"I was always ashamed to go to school in my K-Mart clothes because I knew that the other kids were wearing Calvin Klein or Guess? I used to beg my mother to buy me those clothes because I didn't want to be left out. I wish that I had listened to her instead of the TV."

—*Michelle, age 14*

"Advertising has taught me so many things that I can't begin to list them. Sometimes I lie in bed at night and try to figure out if what I believe has been influenced by advertising. I'm sure it has. Just look at the posters of ads all over my walls!"

—*Nona, age 15*

TV Talk About Advertising

As we have seen, television advertising is a rich subject and contains the seeds of all other TV-Talk topics. When we talk about advertising to our kids, we can talk about the business of advertising, why it is there, how it affects what we see on TV, how advertising works, and how we are affected by it. We can also point out production techniques and value messages that apply to all TV shows. However, the most helpful thing we can do is talk to our kids about the difference between advertising's version of the world and the real world.

Demystifying the illusions created by advertising helps children understand that advertising not only creates false needs and wants but also defines the way we view ourselves, others, and the world around us. Pointing out discrepancies between advertising's pseudo-reality and the real world reinforces one of media literacy's primary themes, namely, that all TV is a construction—a fabricated version of reality—and helps children distance themselves from advertising's influence. As one of my students said, "Once you know how commercials work, you'll never be fooled by them again!"

The activities suggested in this chapter will help you talk to your children about advertising while you watch TV with them, but talking to your children about advertising is something you can do anywhere and at any time. Since advertising is everywhere and influences all parts of our lives, driving to school or to after-school activities, grocery shopping, cleaning the house, or even taking a walk all provide us with ideal TV-Teaching opportunities. I know of a family whose favorite time for TV Talk about advertising is when they are stuck in traffic, surrounded by billboards and radio ads!

However, as pervasive and harmful as advertising can be, it also has some redeeming features. Many ads are tours de force of production values and cleverness and are great for talking about camera techniques, special effects, and editing. In fact, most of us have an ad that we really like because of its unique or clever production styles, and are curious to know how it was made. What a great opportunity to talk about production techniques!

When you talk to your kids about advertising, acknowledge and accept that children like advertising and probably have a favorite commercial or two that they would be happy to talk about. Use their fascination and curiosity to your advantage, and together you can learn some interesting things about how TV ads are made and how they affect people.

Starting discussions with children's favorite commercials is a good way to ease into TV Talk, but whenever you decide to discuss advertising, be sure to remember the basic rules for TV Talk with kids:

- *Respect* their right to like what they see.
- *Observe* quietly before talking.
- *Question* gently.
- *Listen* carefully.
- *Reinforce* positive values and responses.

Remember that talking to your kids about TV advertising reinforces the idea of TV as an active-ity, rather than as a passive time waster, and stimulates their critical thinking skills, making them less vulnerable to advertising's messages. More than anything else, it's a fun activity that both you and your children can share and learn from.

Discussion Starters for Kids

The following questions are useful discussion starters for TV Talk with children of all ages. Remember, however, that younger children might be less able to discuss more complex ideas than older children. However, each of the following questions can be modified for your children's ages and abilities. Of course, for a special activity, you might suggest that your children try making a commercial of their own! Chapter 12, "Kid TV," will give you hints to get them started.

1. What is advertising? Why do you think there are commercials on TV? Why are there so many commercials? Do you think there should be commercials? Would TV be different if there weren't commercials? Can you think of any TV that doesn't have commercials? How is it different?

2. How do you feel when you see commercials? Do you like to watch them? Do they bother you?

3. What is your favorite commercial? Why do you like it? How do you think the commercial was made?

4. Have you ever bought something because of a commercial? What convinced you to buy the product? Were you satisfied with the product when you got it home? Why or why not? In your opinion, do you think the commercial was untruthful?

5. Do you think that TV commercials can be deceptive? Can you think of any that are? How are they deceptive? Why do you think advertisers say that products can do things that they can't really do? Is that fair to consumers?

6. If you were going to make a commercial for your favorite toy/food/product, what would it be like? What would you show? What would you say? How would you convince the viewer to buy that product? Would it be deceptive or honest? Would your advertising scheme work for you and your friends?

7. If you could make some rules about how commercials should be made, what would they be? Would you allow false claims? Would you allow certain kinds of images? Why or why not?

8. Are there any kinds of "good" commercials? Can good commercials be deceptive too? How?

9. How do you think commercials differ from real life?

10. Do you think commercials affect the way that people feel about themselves, each other, or the world around them? Do they affect you? How?

Sample TV Talk About Commercials

Thirteen-year-old Lori and her mother, Liz, had been watching TV together when Liz decided that it might be a good time to talk about advertising.

LIZ: I really like that commercial.

LORI: Me too. Those polar bears are funny.

LIZ: What's so funny about them?

LORI: Polar bears don't drink Coke, Mom!

LIZ: You're right. They don't. They eat fish. But those aren't real polar bears, are they?

LORI: I don't think so. They look like robots—like the ones we saw in Disney World.

LIZ: They do look like robots, don't they?

LORI: I wonder how they make them look so real?

LIZ: I think it's done with computers, but we'll have to do some research. But why do you think they used polar bears drinking Coke to sell us Coke?

LORI: Because it's funny.

LIZ: Why do they want their ad to be funny?

LORI: So we'll watch it and then go buy Cokes.

LIZ: Ah, so they tricked us!

LORI: Yeah. I guess it is a trick. But it works.

LIZ: Can you think of any other commercials that trick us?

LORI: What about that Maybelline ad? The one that makes it look like you'll be a supermodel, if you buy their makeup?

LIZ: How does it make you think that?

LORI: Well, it shows those models putting on the makeup and says that they use the makeup. And since they're beautiful, it looks like the makeup makes them look that way.

LIZ: So, it seems like they are beautiful because they use the products?

LORI: Yeah.

LIZ: Do you think that's true?

LORI: No, not really. I mean it's a trick too. The models are beautiful to start with.

LIZ: Why do you think advertisers use tricks like that?

LORI: So you'll buy makeup and Cokes and stuff?

LIZ: Probably. How does it make you feel when advertisers try to trick you?

LORI: It makes me angry. They shouldn't do that. It's not fair.

LIZ: I agree. If you were making the ad, would you do it differently?

LORI: I would tell the truth.

LIZ: What would the truth be?

LORI: Maybe that the makeup won't make you look like Naomi Campbell? That it's just like any other makeup?

liz: That would be honest. Lori, does that ad make you feel bad about yourself?

LORI: Well, kind of. I mean, no one can ever look like those models, really. I mean, even if you do use all that makeup. Why can't people just be who they are?

LIZ: That's a really good question. Do you think commercials make people unhappy?

LORI: Some do.

LIZ: Well, what should we do about it?

LORI: Maybe write them a letter or just not believe the ads.

LIZ: Both of those things sound like good ideas. Why don't we work on them, okay?

LORI: Okay.

Liz was very good at listening to Lori and asking questions that helped her think critically about what she had seen. She was also able to guide Lori toward thinking about advertising's effect on her own views.

While not all children will be able to articulate their feelings about advertising as well as Lori could, it is important that they begin to discuss them at any level that is appropriate. With time and practice, they will be dissecting commercials like frogs in biology class, but enjoying it a lot more and becoming TV-proof in the process!

6

"Why Is My Family Different From the Ones on TV?"
Combating Stereotypes and Negative Values

Several years ago, I was teaching at an "at-risk" middle school in Houston, Texas. My students and I were discussing their favorite sitcoms and I asked them to describe the "typical American family," according to TV. A few children offered their versions—white; rich; important jobs; big houses; kids and a Mom and Dad—all of which reflected a very different world from that in which these inner-city kids lived.

A few moments later, one little boy, Roy, began to cry. I went over to him and asked him what the matter was and he sobbed, "My family's wrong, isn't it?" Some of the other children in the class immediately echoed his sentiment, each one feeling as though there must be something wrong with his or her family because it wasn't at all like the ones they saw on TV each night. Some children also explained that when they did see families like theirs represented on TV, the feeling of "wrongness" was further reinforced by the negative way in which they were portrayed.

Stereotypes and negative values carry some of the most harmful messages on TV, and yet they are everywhere from commercials to news programs. For children, who have little real-life experience to measure against TV stereotypes and values, they can be extremely damaging. Helping children learn to see through TV stereotypes and negative values is an important part of TV-proofing, and the information and activities in this chapter will show you how.

TV's Funhouse Mirror

According to a *USA Today* report on TV stereotypes, more than 60 percent of TV's fictional employees are professionals and executives, compared to 26 percent of real-life workers. Only 21 percent of TV's workers are employed in labor or service, compared to 72 percent of those in the real world, and 19 percent of TV's working population are in law enforcement, compared to only 2 percent of real workers!

In addition, TV characters eat in restaurants 30 percent of the time, whereas real Americans only eat in restaurants 16 percent. On TV, there are more blond-haired women than there are in real life, and only 10 percent of TV's population is overweight, compared to 68 percent of the real U.S. population. Over 80 percent of all the characters on TV are between the ages of eighteen and fifty-nine, leaving young children, teens, and senior citizens grossly underrepresented.

These statistics offer a fascinating picture of how TV distorts reality through stereotypes and provide a glimpse of how that funhouse mirror image can affect how we view ourselves, others, and our world.

The Primary TV Stereotypes

There are many different stereotypes on TV, but there are just four primary categories of stereotypical TV images that affect kids. Helping children recognize and think critically about these TV stereotypes will diffuse the images' influence.

"And They All Lived Happily Ever After": The Typical American TV Family

Since the early days of TV, television programs have told the stories of families. Ozzie and Harriet Nelson and the boys, the Cleavers, the Brady Bunch, and the Cosbys are all famous TV families with whom generations of Americans identified and against whom they measured themselves. Over the years, we have looked to the TV family as an example of how we were supposed to be, of what was "normal." We asked ourselves: Were our fathers as supportive as Ozzie Nelson? Our mothers as caring as June Cleaver? Were our kids as honest and sweet as "the Beav?" Even today, when people talk about family values, they often have the values, behavior, and lifestyle of the American TV family in mind.

The TV family, however, is not a real family; it is a stereotypical ideal, just like the idealized people in advertising. A "typical TV family" consists of a father who works, a mother who always seems to be at home, even if she supposedly has a job, two or three kids, a nice house, relative wealth, and some minor problems to deal with, which are usually solved within thirty minutes and without serious conflict. After the final commercial break, everyone comes to a peaceful resolution and lives happily ever after. Even when TV families go through hard times—divorces, kid troubles, financial woes—they come out on top. But real families don't always have happy endings and real families don't always look like the ones on TV.

The stereotypical ideal of the American family, as represented by television, has a deep effect on us. How many children wish their father was as laid back as the dad on *Full House*? How many husbands wish their wives were as understanding as Tim's wife on *Home Improvement*? How many parents wish their kids were as good as the ones on *The Cosby Show*, and how many families wish they lived as well and solved their problems as easily as the families on TV? Although most of us recognize that TV families are not real families, we continue to compare ourselves to them, and, sadly, to feel that we can never live up to their ideal.

TV's perpetuation of the stereotype of the ideal family allows others to condemn our families if they do not measure up. Think about the controversies over single parents, gay households, or racially mixed families that regularly make the news. Deviations from the norm spark heated debate and strong public responses. Remember Vice President Dan Quayle's 1992 attack on the TV show *Murphy Brown*? Mr. Quayle publicly condemned the episode in which Murphy decides to bear a child out of wedlock as "mocking the importance of fathers in a family" and turned a TV program into a national debate about single parents and working mothers.

For our children, the stereotype of the typical American family can have serious repercussions. Children will always compare themselves and their families to what they see on TV, and because stereotypes on TV make the ideal appear normal, the disparity between the real family and the ideal TV one can lead to intense criticism, feelings of failure and shame, depression, and self-destructive behavior.

One of my students, Anya, a very bright, articulate but depressed fifteen-year-old, explained another frustrating conflict by revealing that everyone in her family seemed to be trying to act like a TV family, and in the manner of a TV family, they did not discuss or deal with any real issues. Instead, everyone just cracked jokes! More critical, her parents had expected her to act like a TV kid instead of a real teenager with serious problems, and they were angry with her for not living up to the ideal kid role.

Girls Shop and Boys Fight: Gender Stereotypes on TV

A few years ago, I saw an episode of *Full House* that was filled with some of the most blatant gender stereotypes I had ever seen on TV. The plotline involved the dad, who is a TV news reporter, and his conflict between parenting and work. Apparently, a big football game needed to be covered. The assigned reporter was ill and the boss called Dad to cover for him. Dad accepted the assignment, even though it meant that he would miss his daughter's ballet recital and have to back out of a promise to take the girls shopping at the mall.

In the first scene, the youngest daughter is seen dancing around in her tutu while the oldest daughter is talking about the sale at the mall. When Dad accepts the emergency assignment, the girls are disappointed and Dad feels terrible, but everyone is comforted when Joey, one of the roommates, offers to take them shopping, anyway.

Meanwhile, the other "cool" housemate, Jesse, has picked up a mini-skirt-wearing girlfriend and is shown making out with her on his motorcycle parked in the basement. Joey interrupts this romantic scene and complains that he never gets girls like that and wishes that he were more like Jesse. So to fix Joey's image and make him more attractive to women, Jesse takes him shopping for some new cool clothes too.

When Dad comes home from the football game, everyone comes out to model their new clothes. The girls are greeted with catcalls and whistles from the boys, and they beam with pride and satisfaction. Even the baby is congratulated on her new look and is told, "Ooh, you're going to be such a fox when you grow up!"

Joey shows off his new image, complete with leather jacket and boots, which is also met with approval. Jesse's sex-kitten girlfriend gives him a kiss, and everyone swoons. Dad realizes he missed an important day, but, even though the job seems to come first, he tells everyone that he loves them and promises to take them shopping again next week.

Gender stereotypes are everywhere on television—in advertising and in programming—and are so common that we often don't recognize them. This episode of *Full House*, on the other hand, is a prime example of how women and men, boy and girls, are stereotyped on TV.

Young girls on TV are shown in one of two ways—as docile, sweet, nurturing, and innocent or as boy-crazy fashion plates with little more than pink fluff for brains and an unquenchable urge to shop. Older TV girls are usually seen as the latter, preoccupied with boys and their own appearance, but occasionally a preteen or teenage girl is portrayed as being smart, but homely—a terrible fate for a TV girl.

Young boys are often seen as heroic, mischievous troublemakers, in the Dennis the Menace mold, and are usually one step ahead of getting into big trouble for what they do, even if it's the right thing. As TV boys age, however, they become more interested in girls and are portrayed as love struck, desperately trying to get the attention of the opposite sex, or as hopelessly mired in "loserdom," unable to tie their own shoes, let alone get a date. Coolness and peer acceptance also become factors for older boys and, therefore, the cool boys are seen as athletic and attractive, surrounded by girls and always taking things lightly, but they are never shown as being too smart—smartness brands teen boys as pocket-protector nerds.

If we look at how grown men and women are seen on TV, the images become more disturbing. The stereotype of the boy-crazy girl becomes the sex-starved, vacuous bimbo, and the nurturing, sweet ten-year-old girl becomes a passive but neurotic housewife or innocent crime victim. Women are generally seen as half-clothed set decoration, pawns in a male game. Intelligence is never a factor for these kinds of beautiful women, but if it is, they are stereotyped as controlling, vindictive, and cunning or as power hungry and greedy. In occupations, women either have a "typical" woman's job (nurse, decorator, teacher, or the like), or a powerful career, which they are almost always willing to give up for love.

Men are seen more often on TV than women, almost twice as much, and are most often portrayed as aggressors, fighting violence with violence, or as playboys, gathering women around them like flies. *Real* TV men are frequently shown as powerful, courageous, and steadfast and often have important jobs as executives, police officers, lawyers, TV personalities, and doctors. In the TV world, men are clearly in control. Recently, however, the TV stereotype of fathers has gone from being the respected, all-knowing, and compassionate dad like Ozzie Nelson to a bungling fool like Al Bundy, unable to do much of anything right, let alone parent.

After a five-year study, the American Psychological Association determined that television gender stereotypes have a distinctive and damaging effect on children. Since TV stereotypes are often seen as definitions of "normal," we can begin to understand how deeply gender stereotypes might affect children's emerging identities, opinions of others, and expectations for their futures.

If TV stereotypes make it seem normal for young women to be submissive sex toys, then it is not surprising that young girls and teens might aspire to that. In her book *Reviving Ophelia* Dr. Mary Pipher explains that "girls are coming of age in a more dangerous, sexualized, and media saturated culture" and gives examples of young girls who dress provocatively and engage in early sexual relations because the images they see in the media make it seem like they are supposed to act that way. My own students have explained that they feel like something must be wrong with them if they don't "dress sexy" and "try to please guys."

When I talk to my female students about how TV gender stereotypes of women's occupations affect their goals for the future, they respond that it seems like there is only so far they can go in any given field and that much of a woman's success depends on her appearance. They also reveal that they are afraid to appear smart or aggressive because of the way strong women are stereotyped and dismissed. In her book *Where the Girls Are* Susan J. Douglas comments that this historical portrayal of women as submissive nonachievers had a tremendous impact on the women's movement and has influenced the feminist backlash among young women today.

Many young girls today are also deeply afraid of violence toward women. Noting that television frequently portrays women as victims of assault, rape, domestic abuse, and murder, many young women feel that their chances of being victimized are disproportionately high. Most of my female students say that they are afraid to go out at night, afraid to date, and rarely go anywhere alone for fear of what might happen to them.

Many of my young male students are equally as affected by TV gender stereotypes. Most say that they feel compelled to be good at sports, be tough, drink heavily, and sleep around because stereotypical TV images portray those behaviors as normal and acceptable for boys. They also reveal that their attitudes toward girls and women are formed through TV gender stereotypes. Many teenage boys believe that women are supposed to want sex and they have no qualms about forcing it on them or being angry if it is not given.

Today, young boys are behaving more violently than ever and our newspapers and news shows are filled with stories about juvenile violent crime. Many child psychologists believe that much of this violent behavior stems from TV gender stereotypes that portray violent, aggressive men as heroes. Children, they argue, see those stereotypes and believe that violent behavior is normal for boys and men.

As boys grow, their expectations of adulthood are formed by images on TV. Stereotypes of powerful, rich men on TV formulate ideals for manhood, which include notions of sexuality, power, harassment, and violence. The bungling father stereotype does little to provide young boys with a model for responsible parenting, and there is intense fear and speculation about how this stereotype will affect families of the future, if it hasn't already.

Helping children learn to recognize and think critically about gender stereotypes provides an antidote to these powerful and destructive images. My students have often told me that they didn't realize how fully they had accepted TV's stereotypes until we discussed them in class. One fourteen-year-old boy in particular remarked that he was ashamed of how badly he had thought of girls because of what he had seen on TV and wished that someone had said something to him earlier!

Age and Disability on TV

Older Americans are portrayed stereotypically on TV and appear in less than 8 percent of programming. When we do see people of either gender over the age of sixty, they are most often seen as drooling, helpless invalids, overly concerned with the effectiveness of their denture cream or stomach remedy and are frequently the victims of crime. In fact, most victims of crime on TV are female or elderly or both. Consequently, children view them the way TV views them: useless, helpless, expendable, out of sight, and out of mind.

Even stereotypical portrayals of the disabled affect children. Physically disabled people are rarely represented positively on TV, if at all. When the handicapped are seen on TV, they are usually seen as the victims of crime or as depressed, helpless invalids. Rarely do we see a happy, self-reliant disabled person on television. Is it any wonder our children think poorly of the physically or mentally handicapped?

Who's Missing From This Picture? Racial and Ethnic Stereotypes on TV

Do you ever notice that Italians on TV always seem to be mob-related gangsters? Or that Arabs are almost always portrayed as terrorists? Or that the Irish are most frequently seen as drunken revolutionaries? Racial and ethnic stereotypes are rampant on television, and these stereotypical and often negative representations are extremely damaging to children's understanding of other races, other cultures, and themselves.

Studies of TV's racial and ethnic stereotypes began in the 1960's, when there were few TV representations of people of races and cultures other than white Anglo-Saxon Protestants. Recent content studies show that while there have been improvements in both the numbers and portrayals of ethnic and racial groups on TV, non-white, non-Anglo groups are still grossly underrepresented. More disturbing, when minorities or non-Anglo ethnic groups are represented, they are often portrayed with less status than whites and in stereotypically negative ways.

In 1996, Julio, a Hispanic student of mine in Houston, did a class project in which he examined twenty-four hours of TV on the four major networks—ABC, NBC, CBS and Fox—to explore the way in which minorities were represented. His findings, similar to those of other university-level studies, were shocking to him, to his classmates, and to me. In the ninety-six cumulative hours of network TV, he discovered only twelve representations of Hispanics: two were newscasters, two were daytime talk-show guests, one was a minor soap opera character, one was featured in a headache remedy commercial, two were law-breakers featured on the news, two were fictional law-enforcement officers and two were fugitive felons on *Cops*. That's it. There were no Hispanic characters in any other TV shows or commercials. Moreover, in the representations Julio saw, Hispanics were most often portrayed in poverty or negatively.

Julio also looked at representations of other minority groups and discovered that they were treated similarly. On the day he examined, there were only three representations of Asians appearing on network TV: one was an Indian convenience store clerk who was the victim of a robbery and shooting, one was a newscaster, and in a story about human rights in China, Asians were featured as victims and perpetrators of brutality. He also looked for representations of Native Americans and found only one program that showed them at all, complete with feathers, war paint, and bows and arrows!

In his study of how African Americans were portrayed, Julio found that although there were more representations, they were equally as stereotypical. The only black people reading the news were sportscasters, while more than three quarters of the criminals in the news and crime-based TV programs were black. Although African Americans appeared more frequently in advertising than either Hispanics or Asians, they were mostly sports stars endorsing athletic products or women selling cleaning products and health remedies. There was only one black talk-show host, and, on that day, none of the guests on the evening network news-talks was black. With the exception of sports programs, which overwhelmingly featured African Americans, there were only three black characters on soap operas, all in minor roles, and only three sitcoms which featured black families.

Julio's study corroborates many larger studies which indicate that minorities are seriously underrepresented on American television. According to national minority population figures, Hispanics make up over 10 percent of the U.S. population, African Americans 17 percent, Asians 4 percent, and Native Americans 1 percent. Yet, *USA Today* reports that the face of American television is overwhelmingly white. In a weeklong study of the major networks, the paper found that more than 84 percent of the characters on TV are white. Only 12 percent of the TV population is African-American, 2 percent is Hispanic, 1 percent is Asian and 0.04 percent are Native American.

Leaving aside the issue of whether equal representation on TV of all ethnic groups and races is a worthy aim, these studies do make clear that the frequency of TV's representations of nonwhite races is inappropriately imbalanced. Moreover, many studies reveal that when minorities do appear on TV, they are frequently portrayed in stereotypical and often negative ways.

A 1994 report released by La Raza, a Latino civil rights organization, declared that the way in which Hispanics are represented on U.S. entertainment television amounts to "clear, unadulterated racism." The report cites that the representation of Hispanics on TV has fallen to a level far below that of the 1950s and that when Hispanics are shown on TV, one in six is a criminal. On reality-based shows like *Cops* and *America's Most Wanted*, Hispanics make up 8 percent of the characters, over half of whom are criminals. When Hispanics do appear, they are more likely to be shown as lawbreakers than any other ethnic group.

Television industry treatment of African Americans fares little better. According to numerous academic content studies, blacks are most often portrayed as criminals, victims of crime, athletes, musicians, or comedians. They are far less frequently seen as professionals, doctors, lawyers, or business people, despite the growing population of middle-class professional African Americans. Although blacks are more frequently portrayed in advertising, there are few African Americans featured in ads for upscale products such as luxury cars.

The long history of racial stereotyping on TV began with early TV shows such as *Amos and Andy* in 1951, in which minorities were seen as stupid buffoons, entertainers, or servants. These degrading TV stereotypes continue today but are compounded by more dangerous images of minorities as social pariahs: impoverished criminals who abuse social services and harm the rest of the population. Even in children's cartoons, the stereotype of the minority bad guy is perpetuated by villains who have dark skin or foreign accents.

To be fair, there are TV programs that portray minorities in nonstereotypical ways, and all groups of people, like all individuals, do have their negative aspects. But although cable and satellite television offer greater representation of minorities, the majority of our entertainment and news programs persists in depicting minorities in a stereotypical way. "The view of us perpetuated by Hollywood is that of a dysfunctional, angry, frustrated populace prone to violence and self-destruction," says African-American TV veteran and filmmaker Tim Reid. While this treatment of minorities in media is often blamed on racism, director Emily Mann says that "A lot of racist images are made unconsciously, and whites just aren't aware that they are doing it." Actor Morgan Freeman agrees, saying that "whoever's writing is writing what they know about, and I would like to think that the bulk of the writers, like the bulk of the population, is not black."

Even if TV's racial and ethnic stereotypes derive from unconscious cultural stereotypes, the fact that they are perpetuated on TV is harmful. Few people believe that everytime we see a minority or a white person on TV, they should be shown in a positive light. But TV is a mirror in which we Americans see ourselves, and if we see ourselves as a nation in which minorities are excluded or are overwhelmingly represented in negative ways, we are denied the real experience of understanding our fellow citizens and ourselves as complex, individual beings. Without this understanding, we are prone to accept TV's skewed version of the world and to assimilate its inaccurate opinions as our own.

Jerome and Dorothy Singer, founders of the Family Television Research Center at Yale University, have done several studies which indicate that TV's ethnic and racial stereotypes are highly influential on children's beliefs and prejudicial attitudes. They found, for example, that the more programs featuring blacks in criminal roles that a child watched, the more likely the child was to view African Americans negatively. Conversely, if a child watched programs that portrayed minorities nonstereotypically, he was more likely to have positive attitudes.

In an informal survey I took with my mostly white high school students, more than three-fourths of them believed, inaccurately, that most American blacks were on welfare or were single teenage moms, and that most young black males were involved in gangs, drugs, and criminal behavior. More than half of this group also wrongly believed that the majority of Hispanics were illegal immigrants who couldn't speak English, and were lazy, alcoholic criminals. Asians, they claimed, were either really smart or worked in convenience stores. Arabs were all terrorists, and they knew nothing at all about modern-day Native Americans! When I asked them where they got these ideas, they all unanimously responded, "TV."

My minority students are often keenly aware of the way in which TV misrepresents them. In the same informal survey, black students revealed that, as upstanding, hard-working African Americans, they felt ashamed of television's negative and innaccurate representations of their race and culture. The Hispanic students, many of whom come from families who have been in America for generations and may not even speak Spanish, reviled mainstream TV's negative portrayals of Latinos and Latinas and desired to see a real Hispanic middle-class American family shown on something other than a Hispanic station. My Asian students felt completely ignored by TV, and my one Arab student, whose family had left Lebanon during the war there, was so hurt by TV's constant portrayal of Arabs only as terrorists, not as victims, that he refused to watch any American TV shows or movies that had an Arab character.

Unfortunately, minority children are also prone to believe what television stereotypes tell them about themselves and their own culture. I have often heard African American boys claim that since the only black role models that TV provides are sports stars or musicians, they feel their futures are often limited to careers in music or sports. African American girls reveal that, since black women, with the exception of Oprah, are given little positive representation on TV, they view themselves as having little or no importance in the greater world. Hispanic students often try to hide their ethnicity because they claim they have to work twice as hard as white students to overcome TV's stereotype of laziness and stupidity, while Asian kids of average intelligence reveal that they are frequently forced into classroom submission to avoid being harassed about being "too smart."

But perhaps the most telling example of how TV stereotypes affect children is the story of an African American student, Kenny, a soft-spoken, violin-playing, high school football player who told my class how he felt when people judged him according to the racist stereotypes perpetuated by TV. "It hurts my feelings," he explained. "When I am walking down the street, women clutch their purses or cross the street to avoid me, like I'm some kind of criminal! I like people and I'm a nice kid. I'm not like the black gangstas that they see on TV all the time. But they don't know that and are afraid to even find out. It makes me so angry sometimes that I want to yell at them, so I go home and punch a wall or something. And, when I feel that way, I wonder if they are really right about me after all, and I just don't know it."

Racism in Hollywood

In 1996, the U.S. film industry was bashed for its continued exclusion of African Americans. According to *People* magazine, only one of the 166 Academy Award nominees for that year was black—a live action short film director. Roughly 2 percent of Hollywood's directors and writers are African American and there are precious few blacks at the level of studio executive. Although 25 percent of the moviegoing audience is black, Hollywood usually puts out only one or two black-themed movies each year, usually featuring a black singer, comedian, or sports figure. The top black actors also earn less than white actors of similar fame and are most often given roles that portray them as cops, criminals, or buffoons.

Everybody's Rich and Lives in L.A.: Economic Stereotypes on TV

Television's world is filled with economic stereotypes. Fantasy images of wealth and prosperity dominate the screen. These stereotypes can have an enormous effect on children's views about themselves, their lives, and their expectations for their futures, and it isn't by accident.

If we remember that TV's purpose is to sell audiences to advertisers, then we might also recall that the advertisers' goal is to sell products to audiences. Since the target audience for most advertising falls into the middle- to upper-middle-class economic range, the programs that surround the ads are also targeted to that group. If we look at TV programs as "environments" for advertising, then a good environment would be one in which the characters in the show are happy and living well, just like the people in the ads. In other words, the emphasis on wealth and prosperity is designed to appeal to both target audiences, while at the same time providing them with an ideal image of what life can be like. After all, if we see people in TV shows living "the good life," and then we see ads that promise us that kind of life through the purchase of a product, wouldn't we be more likely to want it?

Consequently, the characters in the shows will look and behave like idealized target audience members in ideal middle- to upper-middle-class environments. For example, a show targeted to adult middle-class men might include stereotypical images of upper-middle-class men, with good jobs, power, beautiful women, and a nice house, with nice cars, good tools, and other things that middle-class men might want. The shows will present the ideal of how successful middle-class men should live. However, there is such a thing as being too rich on TV. Since megamillionaires are often portrayed as greedy, selfish, and manipulative, the ideal remains that of the wealthy, but moral, upper-middle class.

When we do see the economically disadvantaged on TV, they are most often portrayed negatively as lazy, alcoholic, drug addicted or criminal. Again, there is a reason for this stereotyping. Poor is bad. Rich is good. Poverty must be viewed negatively to keep consumers wanting to buy things to achieve "goodness." Those people who cannot afford to buy things must be portrayed as wanting them, and so they are shown trying to get them in criminal ways. Since we have seen that most criminals on TV are minorities, the equation is minority = poverty = criminal, or vice versa.

These economic stereotypes are devastating to kids who come to believe that rich is the only way to be and that poor people are lazy, unworthy criminals. Children will always compare themselves and their environments to the ones they see on TV and will often find them wanting. Many children have complained to their parents that they aren't rich enough or don't have a nice car, nice clothes, or a big house because they have seen and accepted the stereotypical images of wealth on TV. I know of one eleven-year-old boy who told his very caring and responsible parents that he wanted to divorce them because they couldn't provide a life like the one he saw on TV. He wanted rich parents, instead!

Children who do live comfortably often view others based on the economic stereotypes they see. Many advantaged children see the poor with little compassion or understanding and have been known to repeat the refrain, "Why don't they work like everyone else?" Because the poor are infrequently seen on TV working and struggling, it's not surprising that wealthier children view them as lazy and irresponsible.

Many economically disadvantaged children view TV's stereotypes of the poor as a condemnation of themselves and a portrait of their inevitable future. An eight-year-old girl who lived in a housing project once told me she thought TV showed all poor people as criminals and was sad because she feared she too would grow up to be one. Another little girl was ashamed to reveal that she lived in a mobile home and that her parents got food stamps because she didn't want people to think she was "trailer trash, like on TV."

Like family, gender, and racial stereotypes, economic stereotypes on TV prevent children from seeing themselves and others clearly and foster an environment devoid of compassion, security, tolerance, and acceptance of others. If we hope to give our children a future as secure, caring, and responsible adults, we need to teach them how these TV stereotypes affect their opinions and behavior and guide them toward a more balanced and positive view of themselves and others.

What Children Say About TV Stereotypes

"When I discovered how women are shown on TV, it changed my life. I got really angry that I had been tricked by these images into buying certain clothes, cutting my hair a certain way, and even acting like a sex goddess. I want to change this: Women aren't objects, but TV treats us that way. Until TV starts showing us as human beings, we won't respect ourselves and neither will anyone else!"

—Gina, age 16

"My dad's a lawyer and it bothers me that everyone thinks we must be rich and live in some mansion, since all lawyers are rich on TV. I wish they understood that my dad works for the ACLU and makes less money than their parents do!"

—Danny, age 14

"I really resent the way they always show foreigners as bad guys on TV. My family emigrated from Ecuador twenty years ago and we are all American citizens. My parents are both doctors, and my oldest sister is graduating from law school this year. But people think that my family is a bunch of lazy, drunk, tortilla-eating welfare thieves. A policeman once asked me if anyone in my family spoke English and people actually tell me we should go back to where we came from and quit ruining America!"

—Carlos, age 15

"Now that I know that TV affects the way I look at myself, I'm much less self-conscious about my appearance. So what if TV shows everyone as healthy and thin and tan. I'm me and I don't have to be like TV."

—Corey, age 14

Activity: Finding TV Stereotypes

Helping children recognize stereotypes on TV is an important part of immunizing them against the negative effects that stereotypes often produce. The following activity is a fun way to introduce children of all ages to TV stereotypes and to help them begin to think critically about their influence.

1. Make a list of common occupations (doctor, lawyer, nurse, police officer, businessperson, teacher, reporter, and so on) and then ask your children to tell you what they think people in those positions are like.

   • Are they male or female?
   • What race?
   • What age?
   • Are they rich or poor?
   • What other qualities are attributed to them?

2. While watching TV together, find representations of these professions on TV shows.

   • Are they similar or different to the way in which your children described them?

3. Ask your children if they know any people who are in those professions.

   • Are they like the people on TV? Why or why not?

4. Ask your children how these stereotypes affect the way they view certain professions?

   • Are some professions more desirable than others?
   • Are some only for men?
   • For women?
   • Are there any occupations that aren't ever seen on TV? What would those be? And what is the effect?

5. Finally, have children revise the list to reflect reality and discuss the ways in which TV might try to be less stereotypical.

This exercise can be repeated with any list—women; men; people of different ages, races, or economic level—at any time. In fact, once children get the hang of recognizing stereotypes, they will be able to point them out to you without any prompting at all.

Whose Values Are These, Anyway?

Without a doubt, the most common complaint I hear about television is the way that it promotes negative or harmful values. Why, people want to know, can't TV promote good values like family, honesty, tradition, compassion, nonviolence, and abstinence? The answer is simple: Good values don't sell.

Sex sells, violence sells, action sells, and humor sells. Countless market studies have proved that people are drawn to these themes, but they don't want to watch anything that smacks of a sermon or a message. Moreover, when TV does try to teach positive values, critics and viewers alike often pan those attempts, saying that they were too mushy.

Consequently, TV producers aren't necessarily concerned with promoting positive values. TV producers also claim, however, that they aren't in the business of promoting bad values, either. They say TV isn't interested in promoting anything other than itself and the commercial products that buy advertising time. Nonetheless, all TV promotes values—good or bad—and even if producers aren't trying to teach moral lessons, children learn them.

Many psychologists and educators have concluded that TV is perhaps a child's most powerful moral teacher. More consistent than parents, more persistent than clergy, and more convincing than a classroom teacher, television has the undeniable capacity to transmit moral values, whether intentionally or not. When children see people on television behaving in certain ways or attributing a positive value to certain behaviors and attitudes, they are prone to think of those behaviors and values as acceptable. And since values are like stereotypes in that their repetition signals normalcy and acceptability, children are even more likely to strive to imitate those values that they see on TV.

Helping children learn to identify and analyze the values that are taught by TV is a crucial step in TV proofing. Faced with the challenges of today's TV, it is also a healthy way of preventing very negative and destructive messages from sending our kids off in the wrong directions.

The Six Most Common TV Values

TV teaches many values, but there are six values in particular commonly promoted by TV that you especially need to help your children recognize and think critically about:

Material goods and wealth buy happiness. The most pervasive and influential value message of TV is the value of consumption and wealth. Children learn through commercials and programs that the key to happiness and success lies on the material plane. And because having things is so important, other values, such as honesty, integrity, hard work, and

---

TV Values and Children's Behavior

In the 1990s, children's behavior has appeared to mimic the values of television. The rise in juvenile crime is attributed to the values of violence promoted by TV. Children are drinking at age eight, having sex at ten and killing over sneakers at thirteen! In fact, the relationship between television values and children's behavior is so close that programs have had to curtail their content to satisfy the outraged cries of parents and psychologists over copycat crimes.

For example, in 1994 the mother of a five-year-old who started a fire that killed his younger sister blamed the MTV cartoon *Beavis and Butthead* for influencing her son's behavior. As a result, pyromania is no longer one of the characters' staple fun activities. Furthermore, each episode now begins with a warning to viewers that Beavis and Butthead are fictional characters and should not be imitated. Despite the efforts of *Beavis and Butthead*'s producers, many public schools have banned *Beavis and Butthead* paraphernalia and have punished children for the use of the epithet "Butthead," noting that the changes in the show have done little to stop children from absorbing the antisocial values exemplified therein.

Studies have shown that children who watch lots of music videos, cartoons, and soap operas are at higher risk for developing patterns of self-destructive behaviors because of the values espoused on these shows. However, other studies conclude that those risks can be decreased through active and critical viewing.

---

perseverance get pushed aside. One of the most dangerous messages of TV is that wealth and material possessions are so important that anything that one needs to do to attain them is acceptable.

Sex is for everyone. A recent study showed that children are exposed to more than 20,000 TV messages about sex each year. The majority of these messages say that sex is good and fun and should be had at every possible opportunity. According to *USA Today*, more than 85 percent of all prime-time shows have at least one reference to sex, and sitcoms refer to sex every four minutes. Most sexual encounters on TV take place between unmarried people, and most of those instances can be categorized as one-night stands. Many ads use sex to sell products and suggest that love and sex are synonymous.

With the exception of a few public service announcements promoting safe sex and contraception, the results of unprotected sex are rarely mentioned on TV. Thus, children learn that sex has no consequences and no responsibilities. Considering the way sex is portrayed on TV, is it any wonder that pregnancy and AIDS are serious problems in the younger population?

Party, party, party! One of the main goals of everyone on TV is to have a good time. TV characters relax over a drink, meet at bars, or get so drunk that they can't remember what they did the night before. Beer commercials show men surrounded by bikini-clad babes while party music plays, and the value of casual drug use is implicitly extolled in music videos. Just like TV messages that promote sexual activity, messages about drinking and drug use show these activities as fun and funny, and rarely show the real consequences of those actions.

Despite concerted efforts by parent, teacher, and law enforcement groups, youth alcohol and drug use is on the rise; children as young as nine and ten are drinking and smoking. This accepting attitude toward drugs and alcohol has a great deal to do with the value they are given on TV. After all, how can we expect children to listen to the message "Just Say No" when TV tells them more vividly and more entertainingly, "Just Do It."

Got a problem? Get a gun. The value of violence as the ultimate problem solver is taught everywhere on TV, from cartoons to the news. Wherever children look, violence is used to solve conflicts and is exalted when used in the name of good.

Our TV heroes use violence. Our TV police use violence. Our TV soldiers use violence. Even our TV "Everyman" uses violence in the name of vengeance or self-defense. Violence is always the solution to a problem and the real consequences of violence are rarely shown. What is to keep children from believing that violence is OK? And even more disturbing, what's to prevent children from becoming numb to the suffering of others?

Get it now! Instant gratification is another common value message of television. The whole of television teaches that you can have what you want and have it quickly. On TV shows, problems are solved quickly and easily, usually within thirty to sixty minutes. Ads promise that you can have what you want by simply going to the store and buying it. Even the news packages international crises in easy-to-swallow, rapidly concluded sound bites on the hour, every hour.

Children are born believing in instant gratification; they cry, they get fed, held, or changed. It is only as they grow that they learn to delay gratification; saving money for a special purchase or studying for a test instead of playing because good grades will help them later in life. TV, however, makes those lessons much harder to learn and certainly less appealing. After all, why delay when the world of TV promises that you can "get it now!" Which one would you rather believe?

It's OK, as long as you're the good guy. In recent years, much has been made of the decline of moral responsibility and culpability in our culture and TV is partly to blame for this tragic development. Although it appears that TV teaches the lesson that crime doesn't pay, the "good guys" are often the worst law breakers and, unlike the "bad guys," suffer no consequences and take no responsibility for their actions. On TV, people lie, steal, cheat, and even murder, but as long as it is in the name of good, it's OK.

Concurrent with this problem of culpability is a decline in the respect for authority. For the most part, on TV, no one is an authority worthy of respect; police, politicians, and businesspeople are corrupt; parents are inept and neurotic; and teachers are idiots. Whom are children supposed to look up to and respect? Who is supposed to model and enforce culpability?

Activity: Detecting TV Values

The following activity will help you initiate discussions with children of all ages about TV values. My students have always found it fascinating, and parents tell me that they learn a tremendous amount from their kids through the discussion that follows. I have also found it successful with my own son.

While watching a TV show together, ask your children to look for what each character considers important and to make a list of those things. After the show is over, ask the following TV-Talk questions:

- What does each character consider to be important to him or her? Is it money? Success? Fun? Girls? Beauty? Power?
- What does each character do to achieve his or her goal? Does she dress a certain way? Act a certain way? Say things?
- Do the characters achieve their goals? What do they get in return? If a character fails, why does he fail? Which characters are considered better? Which goals are considered better?
- What do other characters say about each character? Do they like him or her? Do they respect her? Are they afraid of him? Do they make fun of the characters or put them down? Which characters do you like? Which ones do you dislike? Why?

What Kids Say About TV Values

"When people come to school and talk to us about not smoking or drinking or doing drugs, it kind of doesn't make sense. I mean, everyone on TV does those things, and they're famous! Why should we be any different?"

—*Bethany, age 13*

"I know that the only way not to get pregnant or not to get AIDS is safe sex, but how come no one on TV ever gets AIDS and they don't ever have safe sex?"

—*Erin, age 14*

"My friend Mike got caught buying beer and they called his parents to come get him at the jail. I felt sorry for him. He just broke a little law and everyone does it. He's a good kid and they should have just let him go, like on TV!"

—*Caleb, age 15*

"I asked my parents if they would get me a gun for my birthday and they asked me what I needed it for. I told them that I needed it to defend myself from other kids, but they said I couldn't have one. That kids shouldn't use guns. I don't know why. I mean, according to what I see on TV, guns are necessary!"

—*Marshall, age 13*

- Based on the characters and their goals, what things does the show tell you are good or important? What things are bad? Do you agree? Why or why not?
- What things or kinds of behavior do you think are good? What do you think is bad? Where did you get these values? Do you think that TV has played any part in your value system? How?

Positive Stereotypes and Values on TV

Although it seems that there are only negative and derogatory stereotypes and values on television, there are actually some programs that succeed admirably in presenting positive images and values without being sentimental or overbearing. Shows that portray people in non-stereotypical ways, documentaries, and even some news shows are all valuable resources for counterbalancing the negative stereotypes and values that are so prevalent. Many children's programs on PBS do a terrific job of presenting non-stereotypical characters and positive values. Even some specials on cable are great!

Programs that deal with such controversial topics as drugs, prejudice, or divorce and other family conflicts can actually be good catalysts for family discussions, helping children confront these issues and sort them out. In his book *Raising Good Children*, Dr. Thomas Lickona says that value-filled, but hard-hitting TV programs such as *Roots* or *Holocaust* can actually help children develop a "deeper awareness of society and its moral problems." Even seemingly non-value-laden specials like *The Grinch Who Stole Christmas* can be wonderful for raising children's moral awareness and sensitivity.

Finding these kinds of shows and exposing your children to them is a very good way to teach children about stereotypes and values while encouraging them to recognize and prefer quality programs. Moreover, positive or non-stereotypical portrayals of diverse populations teach children tolerance and acceptance—two attributes that all children everywhere would do well to learn. When you do find these shows, watch them together and be sure to talk to your children about how differently people are portrayed in the show as compared to other programs and what the value messages are.

TV Talk About Stereotypes and Values

Children of all ages can learn to recognize and think critically about the way TV portrays people and their behavior. All it takes is TV Talk. My six year old is an expert at pointing out negative stereotypes of children and doesn't hesitate to condemn the way TV tells him to use violence to solve problems! Older children take great pride in being able to recognize and evaluate TV's stereotypes. I once overheard a group of eleven- and twelve-year-old kids engaged in a very serious and heated debate about the way teachers are represented on TV. Teenagers often attach a moral value to TV's distorted lens and respond by getting angry and offended by what they see. One student of mine feels that the way that TV misrepresents people and their values is a "gross injustice to humanity!"

Whatever your children's ages, TV Talk about stereotypes and values reinforces the idea of TV as an active-ity and helps children learn to think critically about the way they are influenced by TV's messages. It is

---

Finding Shows With Positive Stereotypes and Values

The following suggestions might help you determine if a particular show
has positive stereotypes and values in it.

- *Check your TV guide.* Read the mini-reviews for programs and look for
  shows that feature women and minorities doing something besides
  being criminals and victims. Even certain sitcoms or series might have
  an episode or two that present positive values and stereotypes. Read
  about the weekly special programs and look for varied plots, themes,
  and characters or shows that deal with history or current age-appropriate issues.
- *Look at the TV ads for programs.* Do you see any negative stereotypes
  or values or do you see diverse people in non-stereotypical roles? If
  the commercial for a show depicts people behaving in ways that you
  find unacceptable, don't watch the show.
- *Look for shows that are adaptations of books or short stories.* Try out a
  documentary on cable or PBS. These programs are less likely to
  contain negative stereotypes and values and have the added advantage of teaching something else at the same time!

---

an important part of TV proofing and a crucial step in guiding children
toward safer, healthier, more positive viewing.

Discussion Starters for Kids

As you watch TV with your kids, the following TV-Talk questions
should help you guide them toward a greater understanding of TV's
stereotypes and value messages and can be adapted for children of any
age. As you talk, however, it is important to remember the guidelines
mentioned earlier: mutual respect, careful listening, and positive reinforcement.

1. What is a stereotype? Why does TV use stereotypes? Do you think
   TV should use stereotypes? Can you think of any programs that
   don't use them? Do you ever use stereotypes? How and why?

2. How are women/men/children/minorities/ethnic groups shown in
   this program? What are their main attributes and characteristics?
   How do they talk and what do they talk about? How do they look?
   What is important to them?

3. Are these attributes and qualities accurate? In what ways? How are they inaccurate? Do you know any people that are like the ones on TV? Do you know anyone that is different? What does that tell you about the way in which people are represented on TV? How do you feel when you see certain people or groups portrayed in this way? Does it affect the way you think of them in real life?

4. How do you feel when you see stereotypical representations of yourself on TV? Do you think that others judge you by these images? Do you compare yourself to them?

5. Is there anybody that you see in real life that you don't see on TV? Why do you think that is so? How does it affect the way you think of those people in real life?

6. If you were going to rewrite a show so that it didn't include stereotypes or was a better representation of certain kinds of people, how would it be different? How would you portray each person?

7. What is a value? What do you value? What things are important to you? Where do you get your values? Do you ever see your values represented on TV?

8. What does TV value? Why does it value those things? Do you think that TV's values are right or wrong?

9. What things does this TV show say are good or important? What things does it say are bad? How does it tell you these things? Do you agree with the values that this show is promoting? Do your friends? Why or why not?

10. If you could make a show that promoted good values and non-stereotypical portrayals of people, what would it be like? What would be important to the characters? How would they solve problems? Do you think people would like your show? Why or why not?

Sample TV Talk

Eleven-year-old Dennis and his mother, Carolyn, just finished watching an episode of The Simpsons, *when Carolyn decided that it might be a good time to discuss stereotypes and values.*

CAROLYN: This show is pretty funny, Dennis, I can see why you like it.
DENNIS: I like Bart the best. He's always doing stuff that he should get into trouble for, but he doesn't. I wanna be like Bart.

CAROLYN: I wonder why he doesn't get into trouble for things he does?

DENNIS: Because he never gets caught, Mom! Homer is such a loser and his teachers are stupid. He's much smarter than they are.

CAROLYN: Dennis, do you think it's okay to do the kinds of things that Bart does? Playing tricks on people and being rude?

DENNIS: Yeah, if you don't get caught. I usually get caught, though.

CAROLYN: Why do you think that happens?

DENNIS: 'Cuz I'm not as smart as Bart.

CAROLYN: Dennis, Bart is just a TV-cartoon character, he's not a real person.

DENNIS: I know, but I still wish I were him.

CAROLYN: Do you think your parents and teachers are as dumb as the ones you see on TV?

DENNIS: Sometimes.

CAROLYN: What do you mean?

DENNIS: Sometimes, I don't get caught passing notes in class at school 'cuz my teachers don't see it and sometimes, you and Dad don't punish me for picking on Cindy 'cuz you're not home when I do it.

CAROLYN: Yes, but what about the times you do get caught and punished?

DENNIS: Well, I guess those times you guys are smart and I'm dumb.

CAROLYN: Well, that's not necessarily the case, but why do you think that the makers of the show let Bart get away with things?

DENNIS: I dunno. Maybe because then we will like him.

CAROLYN: Why?

DENNIS: 'Cuz he gets away with stuff and we don't, so we like him.

CAROLYN: And they make the parents and teachers seem dumb so that we won't listen to them or respect them?

DENNIS: Yeah.

CAROLYN: Do you think many children get away with what Bart does?

DENNIS: No, probably not. Parents and teachers are smarter than that.

CAROLYN: So, is Bart a stereotype of a mischievous little boy?

DENNIS: Yeah, I guess he is. And Homer and Marge are stereotypes of dumb parents, right, Mom?

CAROLYN: You're exactly right. It's an exaggeration. So, people aren't really like the Simpsons, are they?

DENNIS: Not really, no. But it's funny 'cuz it's not real life.

CAROLYN: Do you think it's O.K. to do bad things just because a character on TV does them?

DENNIS: No, I guess not, 'cuz they're not like real people.

CAROLYN: If you were going to rewrite *The Simpsons* to be more realistic, how would Bart be different?

DENNIS: I guess he wouldn't do things that he shouldn't do, or if he did them, he'd get in trouble.

CAROLYN: The show might not be as funny then, huh?

DENNIS: Nope. I wouldn't like it as much.

CAROLYN: Can you think of other shows that you like that would be different if they were more realistic?

DENNIS: Yeah, all of them.

CAROLYN: What do you say we watch another one next week and talk about it, okay?

DENNIS: Can we watch *Beavis and Butthead?* They get away with worse stuff than Bart.

CAROLYN: Sure. *Beavis and Butthead* it is.

Carolyn and Dennis had briefly discussed stereotypes the week before, and Dennis was able to recognize Bart and his parents as stereotypes when she mentioned it. And although Carolyn never actually mentioned the word *value*, she was able to discuss the program's values with Dennis in a way that enabled him to understand and think about what the show was teaching. Her questions were gentle, but to the point—and she was a good listener. It would be interesting to hear what they discussed the following week!

7

"Who Will Protect Me When the Bad Guys Come?"
Violence Beyond the V-Chip

More than any other topic on television, it seems, parents are most concerned about violence. It's not hard to understand why. Statistics show that the average American child begins watching violence on TV by age two and, by age eighteen, will have witnessed over 200,000 acts of televised violence.

In 1996, the National Cable Television Association commissioned a three-year, $3.3 million TV violence study, the most comprehensive examination of TV violence ever conducted. This landmark study concluded that "psychologically harmful" violence is pervasive on broadcast and cable television. Industry-wide, 57 percent of the programs surveyed showed some kind of violence. Premium cable stations alone offered violence in 85 percent of their programs, network television offered 44 percent and even PBS tallied 15 percent. Not surprisingly, American TV programming is the most violent in the world. America is also the most violent nation in the world, and most Americans believe that TV violence can lead to real life violence.

Media violence is a difficult issue, but one that you can profitably address with your children using the techniques of media literacy. In this chapter you will learn how different kinds of TV violence affect your children, what they learn from watching violence, what to look for in selecting and monitoring TV programs, and how to talk to your children about TV violence.

Why Is TV More Violent Today Than It Was When I Was Young?

Most of us don't remember our childhood TV being as violence-filled as it is today. Darren Stevens never beat Samantha. There were no grisly murders on *The Brady Bunch*, and the most harm ever inflicted on Gilligan was a whack with the Skipper's cap. Much of TV in the fifties and sixties was indeed violence-free. There were, however, some popular shows like *The Rifleman, Green Hornet, Gunsmoke, Batman, The Wild, Wild, West, The Three Stooges*, and many cartoons that contained violence.

But yesterday's violence was different. As we watch reruns of the old series, we notice that there are no gruesome double-figure body counts; very few incidents of sexual violence; and none of the fast action jolts-per-minute or high explosives that characterize today's violent TV. And, as we think back, our parents, teachers, and public officials weren't as worried about its effects. What changed?

The trend toward more, bloodier, and more dangerous violence on television began in the 1970s. After a somber decade of watching real violence on TV—Vietnam, civil rights protests, assassinations—Americans were less affected by images of brutality on their living room screens. We were living in violent times, and fictional TV, in its role as cultural mirror, reflected the violence in our society.

A new type of violent TV show emerged. Fast paced, urban, contemporary, and bloody, these shows were geared toward a younger audience, already numbed to and cynical about violence. Young, attractive heroes of shows like *Hawaii Five-O, Starsky and Hutch, The Rookies*, and *The Streets of San Francisco* replaced the crusty old cowboys of *Bonanza* and *Gunsmoke*. Dusty western towns became modern crime-filled cities, and fast car chases, shootouts, and pyrotechnics took the place of fistfights, shotguns, and roundups. Compared to today's shows they were tame, but at the time, they reflected contemporary tastes, seemed tremendously daring, and were very successful.

The networks discovered that audiences liked the new action-packed violent shows and so they made more of them. With shows like *The Six Million Dollar Man, Charlie's Angels*, and *CHiPS*, ratings soared and the networks made plenty of money; which, as we learned earlier, is the whole point of television. Producers realized that violence sells and people like to watch it. The violence trend had begun and viewers were hooked. So hooked, that by the mid-1970s, almost 60 percent of prime-time TV was violent, and people were happily watching.

Concerned about the rise in television violence, the Surgeon General commissioned a study of TV violence in 1972. The Surgeon General's report, showing surprisingly similar results to a study undertaken years later in 1996, concluded that there was too much violence on TV and that it was negatively affecting children. The report, however, had little effect on TV programming or viewers. Since 1972, the violence on TV has become more graphic and more disturbing and, with the rise of cable in the 1980s, more pervasive.

Dr. George Gerbner, Dean Emeritus of the Annenberg School for Communication at the University of Pennsylvania, has studied television violence since 1969. Dr. Gerbner believes that viewers of TV violence increase their tolerance levels over time, making once-acceptable levels of violence ineffective. In other words, as viewers get used to the level of violence they are watching, the producers must provide higher levels of violence to keep the viewers interested. As the viewer gets accustomed to the new level of violence, another larger, bloodier, more exotic dose must be administered. And so on, until viewers expect to see violence on TV and aren't satisfied unless there's plenty of it.

So here we are, in the 1990s, where what began as an "acceptable" level of violence on television has escalated to more than 100 channels of the bloodiest, most violent television on earth. Today, shows like *NYPD Blue* and *Cops* make *Starsky and Hutch* look like family entertainment. Even though our top-rated shows are typically nonviolent, violence and explicit sexual violence have invaded programs not generally regarded as violent, such as news programs, children's shows, and sitcoms. A large percentage of TV and theatrical movies are violent, and on regular TV programs there are almost five acts of violence per hour in prime time and more than twenty-five per hour in children's shows. Statistically, there is much more violence on TV than there is in real life.

We parents nostalgically remember when TV was not so dangerous, but we, unwittingly, are partly responsible for its present condition. Our generation's tolerance of and demand for greater levels of violence produced what is on our screens now, and our children have received our legacy: bloody, brutal, dangerous, and ugly.

However, our children do not remember the way it was and don't yearn for the return of "the good old days." Our children know only how it is, and today's television is their picture of the world. They are accustomed to it. Much of the TV violence we cringe over is familiar, even laughable, to them, just as our "old" violence is familiar and comfortable to us. As we continue to explore TV violence and its effects on

---

Where Is the Violence?

In a 1992 *TV Guide* study conducted by the Center for Media and Public Affairs, the highest incidence of violence on TV was found on cable television. In a survey of eighteen hours of TV, WTBS won the prize, with eighteen incidents of violence per hour, followed by HBO at fourteen per hour. MTV took third place on cable with eleven acts of violence per hour. Of the networks, Fox and CBS had ten incidents of violence per hour, ABC had three, and NBC and PBS were tied at two per hour.

Because cable television has fewer regulations than network television (Standards and Practices codes reduce violent content) and shows a larger number of movies, cartoons, and reruns, the numbers are consistently higher than those on network television. However, as the networks have tried to compete with cable for audience shares, their numbers have risen. In today's network prime time, it is easy to estimate that there are at least ten to fifteen incidents of violence per hour, with some of the highest rates appearing on news shows and so-called reality-based shows.

However, real life violence and TV violence have little in common. A *USA Today* study claimed that violence on TV far outstrips violence in real life in more than just the firepower. On TV, there are fifty-nine victims per thousand people, whereas in real life, that number falls to thirty-two per thousand. It's no wonder then that TV makes the world seem much more violent than it actually is.

---

our children, it is important to keep this perspective in mind and to accept that this "new" violence may not be nearly as upsetting to them as it is to us.

You don't have to like this new violence, though, and you don't have to allow your children to watch as much of it as they want, either. Violence of any kind affects children, so it is important to monitor your children's viewing and to recognize that although not all violence on TV is distasteful, even familiar violence can have harmful effects.

Activity: How Violence on TV Has Changed

Discussing how violence on TV has changed is an excellent activity for helping children become aware of TV violence in a critical and non-threatening way. It is also a good way to spend a constructive family TV night.

Check your local TV/cable guide or video store for reruns of an older series that you liked as a child. Schedule a family viewing night and share

---

Why Children Like to Watch Violence

Children have always been fascinated by violence, whether in fairytales or on TV. But why? Margaret Loesh, president of Fox Children's Network believes that children "love to be swept away" by watching action shows. Greg Weisman, a producer for Walt Disney Television, says that watching action-adventure programs is cathartic for children, and Jennie Trias, president of ABC Children's Entertainment says that "it's the basic good-versus-evil struggle and . . . I think that's important for kids to appreciate." Psychologist Bruno Bettelheim believed that violence helps kids come to terms with their own fears and aggressions.

Whatever the reason, it is clear that children derive some pleasure from watching violent action-adventure programs, or they wouldn't do it!

---

the show with your children. Explain to your children the reasons you liked the show. If the show has violence in it, use the opportunity to compare it to newer TV shows.

- Are there more acts of violence or fewer? Are they more graphic or less?
- How does the violence make you feel?

Discuss how TV violence has changed since you were young. Ask children to imagine how TV violence will look to their children and why they think it will be that way.

To conclude, ask your children to share one of their favorite violent shows with you next time, and repeat this activity, comparing the new to the old.

What Is Violence?

Violence means different things to different people. Some people consider a punch to the stomach violent, while others don't. Some people think one gunshot isn't really violent, but fifty are. Some people don't believe language can be violent, and others do. So, before we go any further, we need a basic definition of violence that is acceptable to most of us.

For the purposes of clarity, we will adopt the following widely used definition: *Violence is any action—physical or verbal—that hurts or kills or threatens to do so, and violence may be portrayed as live action or through animation.*

This is a broad definition, to be sure, but it serves our purposes well. Later in the chapter, you will have the opportunity to further define violence on your family's terms.

Are There Different Kinds of Violence?

There are actually two different types of violence on TV. I call them "mythic violence" and "reality-based violence." Each type of violence affects children differently, and we need to understand what is distinctive about each type and how to recognize them in TV programs.

Mythic Violence

It is night in a city of the future. Shadows fall on rain-filled streets, and a few hooded creatures huddle around a trash can fire. Ominous music plays. Suddenly, a large metallic being enters the frame. The moonlight glints from his steel features. Menacing looks shoot from his eyes. He raises his weapon, a futuristic laser-type gun and points toward the group of creatures by the trash can. Whoosh! The metal man turns as a superhero jumps into the street.

"Not so fast, Metal Man," our superhero declares. A laser light from his hand grabs the villain's weapon. Another laser light knocks him to the ground.

The superhero towers above the wounded Metal Man. "You thought you could win, didn't you? No one disturbs the peace and gets away with it!" Superhero turns and, with a last look at the villain, flies up into the night.

Mythic violence is similar to fairy-tale violence in that it is removed from reality and is metaphoric and instructional. The characters in mythic violence are larger than life and virtually invincible. They are frequently nonhuman; animals, monsters, superheroes, or aliens. Mythic violence takes place in a fantasy world not easily identifiable as a real place or time. The violence is not intended to be realistic; the weapons are fantastical or silly and the victims never die in a bloodbath. In mythic stories, violence is an integral part of the story and is often used for humor or to teach a moral lesson: If you took out the violence, the humor or moral point of the story might be lost.

Cartoons are the most common form of mythic violence on TV. In older cartoons, such as *Roadrunner*, *Tom and Jerry*, and *Bugs Bunny*, the characters and settings are unreal, and the weapons and violent actions are fantastical. Although there is a tremendous amount of violence in these cartoons, no one ever gets seriously hurt. There is no blood and no obvious pain. The violence is rarely traumatic.

Most of the older violent TV shows are also examples of mythic violence. Westerns, science fiction shows like *Star Trek*, and the original superhero series, like *Batman*, were violent, but the violence was an otherworldly, mythic type of violence.

Mythic violence is less disturbing and less harmful to viewers than other types of violence. We easily recognize it as unreal and therefore, unthreatening. Though children may imitate some of the violent actions they see on these shows, they are only playacting and usually understand that this violence is not real.

Reality-Based Violence

It is night in the city. Rain falls on the silent streets. We hear the sound of high-heeled footsteps approaching and see a woman huddled in her raincoat, walking quickly and looking around fearfully. Suddenly, a masked man jumps out from an alleyway and grabs the woman from behind. She screams loudly. We see her face contorting in pain and see the masked face of her attacker as he plunges a knife into her chest several times. The attacker picks up her handbag, wipes the blood from his knife, and flees the scene as the innocent woman lies dead in a pool of blood and rain. Credits run for the beginning of the show.

The other kind of violence on TV is what I call "reality-based violence." Reality-based violence is recognizable, representational, and sensationalistic. The characters in reality-based shows are distinctly human, TV versions of people we might see everyday—doctors, lawyers, police officers, waiters, clerks, criminals, neighbors, and friends. Most reality-based violence takes place in familiar settings, such as modern cities, small towns, or suburbs. Reality-based violence is usually set in the present or near future. The weapons and violence are realistic, even hyper-real, and although we may not see the true consequences of the violence, the victims are clearly, graphically wounded or killed. Unlike mythic violence, this kind of violence is not usually humorous or connected to teaching a moral lesson but is used to excite or thrill the viewer or form the basis for the story. If you took out the violence, there would be no story at all.

Most new violent nighttime dramas, cop shows, detective shows, reality-based shows like *America's Most Wanted*, and action-adventure programs are examples of reality-based violence. They all contain human characters, take place in identifiable locations and times, and exhibit realistic or hyperrealistic violence. The evening news is also an example of reality-based violence.

Reality-based violence is much more disturbing and harmful to viewers. We clearly recognize the violence as possible or plausible, even when exaggerated; the weapons and victims' suffering seem real. Since reality-based violence takes place in identifiable settings, we can more easily imagine something like it happening in real life.

Children of all ages are particularly disturbed by this kind of violence, and the more realistic it is, the more disturbing it is. Psychologist Ralph J. Garry discovered that preschool and lower elementary grade children were more disturbed by reality-based violence than by mythic violence, and Grant Noble, a researcher in Australia, found that older children play "less constructively" or imaginatively after viewing reality-based violence than after watching mythic violence. Other researchers have found that reality-based violence has greater long-term effects and that children are more likely to imitate reality-based violence by engaging in very harmful and destructive behavior.

Not all violent TV shows are exclusively mythic or reality based. Many shows combine elements of both types of violence. Although most cartoons tend to be examples of mythic violence, many of the newer cartoons have reality-based elements; sometimes the settings are realistic; frequently, the characters are human or behave humanly; there is even animated bloodshed. Some movies and video and computer games also have this mix of mythic and reality-based violence.

When choosing and monitoring programs, remember that children of all ages react more strongly to reality-based violence than to mythic violence. Although reality-based violence is rarely appropriate for young children, older children are drawn to it. When selecting programs for your children to watch, it is important to determine which type of violence is central to the show. Use the following guidelines to help you:

- Are the characters human, superhuman, or otherworldly creatures?
- Is the setting realistic? Does the story take place in an identifiable time?
- Are the weapons fantastical, real, or hyperreal?
- Are the victims of violence portrayed realistically?
- Is there a moral lesson of which the violence is a critical part?
- Is the violence only there to excite the viewer?

The Two Types of TV Violence

Mythic Violence:

- Unidentifiable setting
- Nonspecific time
- Nonhuman or superhuman characters
- Fantastic weapons
- Unrealistic violence and consequences
- Humor or moral lesson

Reality-based Violence:

- Realistic setting
- Recognizable time
- Human characters
- Realistic weapons
- Realistic or hyperreal violence and consequences
- Violence as sole reason for action

- If there is a combination of mythic and reality-based elements, is the show more one type than the other?

Activity: Identifying the Different Kinds of Violence on TV

Select two shows to share with your children, one of which is an example of mythic violence and another that is reality based. After watching both shows, ask your children to write down or describe what makes each show different from the other.

- Who are the characters? What do they look like? Are they human or humanlike?
- Where does the story take place? Is it an identifiable time and place?
- What kinds of weapons do the characters use? Are they realistic or fantastic?
- What types of violent actions are portrayed?
- What is the purpose for the violence? Is it part of the story or just added for effect?
- What would happen if the violence were gone?
- What are the consequences of the violence? Do you see them or not? Are they realistic?

> ## TV Producers and Violence
>
> Most TV networks have standards for children's action-adventure shows. Many networks operate under what they call "The Rule of Imitation," which says that they try not to depict anything harmful that children can try at home. Consequently, weaponry is usually fantasylike, actions are exaggerated, and producers are very careful about how they depict fire and water, because, as one TV executive said, "We have to remember that we're not programming for ourselves but for people who are still learning about the world."

Ask your children how they react to each show. Does one type of violence affect them more than another? In concluding, ask them to identify and list other shows they know to be examples of mythic or reality-based violence.

How Children Are Affected by TV Violence

After years of study, there is no longer any doubt that TV violence affects children, and more than anything else, parents are most worried about *how* their children will be influenced by the TV violence they see.

Research shows that children are affected by screen violence differently, depending on their age, maturity level, and ability to reason, as well as on the type of violence they've been exposed to. Research also suggests that these effects are more subtle than we think. Although watching violence on the screen will not *necessarily* make your child violent, it will cause your child to think and feel differently about violence in the real world.

Dr. George Gerbner has identified three primary effects of exposure to televised violence that are common to almost all children and adults: fear, increased aggression, and desensitization.

Fear

Darina's four-year-old-son, Bret, awoke frightened in the middle of the night and sat crying on his bed until she came in.

"What's the matter?" she asked him while she dried his tears. "Did you have a bad dream?"

"I'm afraid, Mommy," Bret whimpered.

"What are you afraid of?"

"The bad guys," he replied.

"What bad guys?" asked Darina, trying to coax the source of his fear from him.

"The bad guys that will come and hurt you and Daddy and steal me away!" Bret started to cry and grabbed Darina tightly. Darina explained that there were no bad guys, but Bret was inconsolable.

"I know there are bad guys," he wailed, "because they were on TV!"

Darina realized that he was right. There are bad guys on TV, and she knew right away what Bret was scared of. Earlier that night, Darina and her husband had been watching the news and the lead story was about a local kidnapping in which a child had been forcibly taken from his parents in the middle of the night. Although Bret had not been watching TV with his parents, he had obviously overheard the story from the next room where he was playing.

Recognizing the problem, Darina explained to Bret that there was in fact a bad guy who had done something terrible, but that no such thing would happen to him. He remained unconvinced.

Finally, feeling scared, alone, and helpless in the face of certain danger, Bret blurted out, "Mommy, who will protect me when the bad guy comes?"

Fear is the first and most common reaction children have to televised violence, and young children are especially prone to it. Children under the age of seven are easily scared by violence on the screen; they don't understand it and have no real context for it. Even if a young child has witnessed violence in real life, most televised violence—guns, murder, assault, and rape—is well beyond his or her scope of understanding.

Younger children are in the process of identifying their world—learning how it works, what to expect, and whom to trust. All televised violence, with its loud sounds and aggressive movements, disrupts this process and presents a very vividly disturbing picture of the world. Since younger children have a hard time differentiating between TV and reality, this TV version of a violent world quickly becomes their reality; they honestly believe in and are frightened by bad guys who might harm them.

Older children, between the ages of eight and twelve, have already been well exposed to the litany of televised evils, so it takes a different type of violence to frighten them. Already capable of discerning fantasy from reality, children over the age of ten aren't frightened by most forms of fantasy or mythic violence, the way younger children are. However, older children do express fear when the violence is reality-based, when it involves real people and especially children their own age.

Teenagers are rarely frightened by television violence. Many of my high school students tell me that they feel unaffected by most screen violence. They reveal that television and movie violence must appear very real and very possible to make them quiver. Reality-based sexual violence is most frightening to teens, and girls are more affected by it than boys.

Adults too can be scared by violence on television. Many of us harbor fears that the terrible things we see on TV could someday happen to us. Because of TV's emphasis on tragedy and crime, we lock our doors, buy security systems for our homes and cars, carry guns and mace, and avoid certain parts of town at night. We are afraid for our children's safety because news programs and TV movies show us unthinkable horrors. But for many of us, the experiences of our real daily lives are much less violent.

Since much more violence is portrayed on television than actually occurs in real life, viewers of all ages begin to feel overwhelmed and unsure. Dr. Gerbner calls this phenomenon the "Mean World Syndrome." He believes that people who watch a significant amount of violence on TV perceive the world as a more dangerous place than it really is and, therefore, feel more frightened and more vulnerable. The more we watch, the more afraid of the bad guys we become. Is it any wonder that our children are frightened of them too?

Increased Aggression

For the third time in one month, Susan was called to her son's school for a meeting with the principal and the counselor. According to them, her nine-year-old son, Will, was showing increased aggressive behavior in the classroom, in the lunchroom, and on the playground. He was often being disciplined for hitting, pushing, and using threatening language. Will was ordinarily a well-behaved, bright student, and the counselor and principal wanted to understand what might be causing this new violent trend in his behavior.

They asked Susan about the family's life. Was there any major change—divorce, death, et cetera? No, Susan replied, no changes. Was Will behaving aggressively at home? No, Susan said, She hadn't observed any aggression on Will's part. What kinds of TV shows did Will watch? Oh, cartoons, some movies, said Susan. Nothing different than any other kids.

Finally, the principal and the counselor detailed a recent example of Will's behavior for Susan. Apparently, Will had pushed a classmate out of his chair, claiming that the chair was his. The teacher had been surprised that Will had not used words to explain the problem but instead had instantly resorted to violence. Moreover, the principal explained that Will never seemed to understand why he was in trouble when he was sent to the office. He continued to maintain that he was doing the right thing by using physical or verbal violence to solve a conflict.

Despite this description, all three parties remained stumped. They couldn't fathom why Will would believe that violence was the best and most acceptable way to solve his problems. They hadn't looked hard enough at the messages of violence in the TV shows, movies, and video games that Will was exposed to.

Aggressive behavior is the most frequently cited effect of watching violence on TV. Nearly 3,000 studies have attempted to find a correlation between video violence and children's behavior. Some scientists have observed that children become more physically and verbally aggressive after watching a violent program on TV. Others note that children who watch violent cartoons exhibit aggressive behavior on playgrounds and in school yards. One scientist, Dr. Leonard Eron, who has been studying TV violence for more than thirty years, believes that children who watch large amounts of violent television are more prone to violent behavior as adults. Although these studies show evidence of a causal relationship between viewing violence and aggressive behavior, there is still debate as to whether or not watching TV violence teaches people to be violent. The real problem lies in the context of televised aggression and how children relate the TV aggression to real life.

On television, aggression is the way to solve conflicts. If you don't like what someone says or does, you hurt them or threaten to do so. Rarely are other methods of conflict resolution explored. Consequently, children who watch violent programs learn that violence is the way to solve problems. They might push or hit their classmates over a pencil or use aggressive and threatening language to intimidate others into submission. They may destroy furniture and belongings to express anger. Although parents might try to steer their children away from violent conflict resolution, the TV holds on, telling them again and again that violence is the way to get results.

More important, aggression on television is exalted. The character who is the strongest, has the best weapons, makes the meanest threats, or hurts the most people is the hero. On TV, the aggressor isn't punished for his actions but is instead declared the winner and is quickly rewarded with praise or love or money. Winning through violence and aggression is a strong message for children, and they have a very difficult time reconciling real life lessons of hard work, negotiation, and compromise with the powerful contradictory images on TV.

Young children who adopt aggression as a primary problem-solving tool run the risk of becoming violent as adults, unless the lessons from TV are counterbalanced by reality and parental example. At a young age, it is not too difficult to intercede and change behavior patterns, and it is uncommon for a young child to seriously harm himself or others.

The teenager who has accepted and absorbed the messages of violent conflict resolution and exalted aggression is another problem altogether. I recently read a news story about three seventeen-year-old boys who got into a shoving match over someone's girlfriend. Verbal threats were exchanged and two of the teens beat the third to death, stuffed his body in the trunk of a car, and dumped it in a vacant lot. According to news reports, neither of these otherwise well-behaved young boys actually blamed TV for their actions, but their passive acceptance of TV's examples of exalted aggression and violent conflict resolution might have contributed to the ease with which they carried out their brutal act.

Aggression is a complex social action. Many factors determine whether or not a person will behave violently toward others. As parents, we hope that our children learn the lessons of peacefulness and cooperation, but if children see people on TV behaving otherwise, it can be difficult for them to reconcile the differing concepts.

Desensitization

Nicky, Lillian, and Henry were laughing loudly at a cartoon on TV.

"Look at his face!" exclaimed Nicky.

"That's so funny the way he fell out of the window!" added Lillian.

"Hit him again!" called out four-year-old Henry. "Hit him again!"

One character explodes into pieces, and the three children break into uproarious laughter. The show ends with a scene of utter destruction—animated body parts fly in all directions while the children cheer, unaffected by the devastation they have witnessed.

"That was cool!" declares Nick.

"Yeah," agrees Lillian.

"I wanna see it again," exclaims Henry. "I wanna see him explode again!"

Desensitization, or numbness, to violence is the most pervasive and most dangerous result of exposure to televised violence, and to varying degrees, it happens to all of us. Sooner or later, the sight of someone punching or shooting another person on TV doesn't bother us too much. For some people, seeing 160 bloody corpses in an hour doesn't affect them. Still others, deadened by TV violence, are completely unmoved by witnessing a real life violent incident.

Children become desensitized to violence over time. While very young children are deeply affected, even traumatized, by viewing violence, teenagers are almost immune to it. By the time a child reaches the age of eighteen, he will have seen so much television violence in so many forms that it's no wonder he appears unaffected. The truth of the matter is that he *is* affected. He is desensitized.

The real problem of desensitization is twofold. The more violence a child sees, the more accustomed and immune to it he becomes, requiring even greater doses to provide the same thrill. This is similar to audience tolerance level increases that cause producers to raise the amount of violence on TV programs. Since children typically begin watching violence on TV around age two, by the time they are nine or ten, they have become so accustomed to it that watching violence has become a normal pattern.

It is this pattern of watching violence that desensitizes children and sends them seeking more and gorier violence, which explains the immense popularity of horror movies among teenagers. Desensitization also allows children to absorb and accept the messages of extremely violent programming without blinking an eye.

On the other hand, this psychic numbness to violence dulls children's abilities to respond appropriately to real violence. Children who are desensitized to violence might think violence is funny. A whack on the head in a cartoon makes them laugh. When a classmate whacks another on the head, a desensitized child looking on might find that funny too. If the child who has been hit begins to cry, the desensitized child who hit him might laugh at him or become angry or uncomfortable and react with even more violence.

The real consequences to victims of violence are rarely seen on television. According to the 1996 NCTA violence study, only 48 percent of the programs surveyed show actual harm to victims of violence. Fifty-eight percent of TV violence depicts no pain and 84 percent of TV violence fails to represent the long-term financial, social, or emotional costs of violence. Therefore, children who have been exposed to large amounts of TV violence are sometimes unable to recognize that violence really does kill or maim people, destroy their families, or cause harm to their communities. These children are less apt to identify with or feel compassion toward victims of real life violence. Desensitized children are also more prone to engage in criminal or violent action without feeling guilt or remorse. Since they can feel no empathy for their victims, they are unable to recognize the wrongness and brutality of their own behavior.

As adults, we also experience this desensitization. Violent movies are a staple of our weekends, and many of the TV programs we happily watch when the kids have gone to sleep contain violence. It doesn't seem to bother us much. For some of us, however, the numbness appears when we watch the news. A school administrator once told me that she felt deadened by the parade of body bags and crying relatives on the nightly local news. "I know I've reached the point where it doesn't affect me anymore. The same must be true for the kids."

It is important to remember, however, that not all children are affected in the same way by what they see. One child may be deathly afraid of something that another child barely notices. Boys tend to be naturally more aggressive than girls and therefore respond more aggressively to violence than girls do. Older children are affected differently by violence than are younger children. One thing is certain: The more violence your child sees, the more desensitized he will become to it and the more he will believe the world is a violent place, which increases the risk of fear and aggressive behavior.

Activity: Identifying the Effects of TV Violence

Since TV is often a passive activity, children don't always recognize their reactions, and so talking about what they feel is difficult. It is important that your children become sensitive to how violence on TV makes them feel, so that they will be better able to make choices about what they do or don't want to see on the screen.

Each time you watch TV with your children, make a point of asking them what reactions to the program they are experiencing, using the following TV-Talk questions:

- Does anything in the show make you feel afraid or worried?
- Do you feel unaffected by violence?
- Which violent acts or kinds of violence bother you more than others?

What Kids Say About TV Violence

"It always seems like people on TV aren't really hurt when they get hit or shot, but I think they are. It would really hurt if you got shot like they do. You would bleed and cry. My brother Jimmy doesn't think people bleed when they get shot, because no one in cartoons bleeds."

—Caryn, age 6

"All the violence on TV doesn't bother me. I mean, there is violence in real life, isn't there? So why shouldn't it be on TV too?"

—Thomas, age 15

"When I watch violence on TV, I usually have one of two reactions: either I think it's really cool and I get excited or I'm scared. If I'm scared, it's because it's like it could happen to me. It's real. I think the scariest show on TV is the news, because it's real!"

—Alan, age 16

"I think TV violence teaches us to hate other people. Everyone on TV always seems to be hurting other people and being mean. I never see people really being nice to each other on television. I don't want to hate people and I don't want to be hated, either. I especially don't want to be hurt."

—Maria, age 13

Begin a list of how your children are affected by certain forms of violence. This list will be very useful when you are selecting appropriate shows for them to watch.

What Do Children Learn From TV Violence?

• Children learn by observation and example, and we know that TV is a powerful role model, particularly when it comes to violence. Watching violence on television may teach children to be afraid of certain people or situations, to behave aggressively or to solve conflicts through violence. Children may even learn not to be bothered by violence, to think it is funny or to accept it as appropriate and even praiseworthy behavior.

Regardless of the form violence takes on the screen, children learn the *value* of violence. Most children believe that if something is on TV, it must be important enough or worthy enough to be there. After all, they don't put everything on TV. Since violence is so prevalent on television, it must have great value.

Sadly, the value of violence is all too often reinforced in our culture. Our nation is built on the idea of "might is right"; our history books and the news media teach war as a necessary and noble endeavor. Nonviolence or negotiation is often viewed as "wimpy" and a threat to use violence is almost as good as doing it. As a culture, we admire people who use violence to protect their country, families, or themselves and violence is revered as the only way to rid ourselves of the bad guys. In our society and on our TV, there always seems to be a justifiable reason to use violence, as long as the perpetrator is the good guy.

Justifiable Violence

Brothers Lucas and Shane were playing in the backyard one afternoon, when their mother, Cara, heard yelling and crying. She went outside to see what the problem was.

"He kicked me!" exclaimed Lucas as he writhed on the grass in pain.

Cara turned to Shane for an explanation. "Why did you kick your brother, Shane?"

"We were playing Ninjas. I'm the Ninja and he's the bad guy. I was defending myself," said Shane.

"Well, you didn't have to kick me, Shane! I didn't do anything to you," screamed Lucas.

"Yes, you did! You were about to poison the town," yelled Shane.

"Well, that wasn't hurting you!"

"So what? That's my job to stop the bad guys!" explained Shane.

"Yeah, but you didn't have to kick me, Stupid!" roared Lucas, and he lunged at his brother. Within seconds, both boys were in tears and Cara was beside herself. She pulled Shane out of the tussle and sent him to his room. Shane didn't know why he was in trouble. After all, he was just doing what a good guy does.

Children's cartoons are often a child's first exposure to the concept of violence as valuable and justified. In superhero cartoons, there is always a good guy or good guys (the hero) who must protect the inhabitants of their cities from the bad guy, who has harmed or is threatening to harm them. The hero struggles to confront the bad guy, and then, in a final fire fight, the bad guy is vanquished and retreats, promising to return and wreak havoc next week. The city and its inhabitants are safe, for a while.

There are no real consequences of the violence shown, and the untarnished hero is rewarded and goes home to rest up for the next battle.

Young children who watch these cartoons learn that there are two kinds of violence. There is bad-guy violence, which is never justified or rewarded, and good-guy violence, which is always justified and rewarded. Most children identify with the good guy, and so it is not uncommon to hear a young child defend a violent act by saying, "It's okay. He was the bad guy." This philosophy can translate into the real life belief that if you are the good guy, any violent act is justified and should be rewarded.

Reality-based TV shows and movies also provide many examples of "justifiable" violence. In these shows, the good guys are often police officers, vigilantes, detectives, or members of other law enforcement professions, and the very nature of their job gives them assumed permission to use violence. The bad guys are criminals of some kind—murderers, rapists, thieves, or terrorists. The very nature of their professions gives the good guys permission to clobber them. The plots of these programs are such that the bad guy has committed a crime for which he must be caught and punished and his victims vindicated or freed. For the remainder of the show, we watch the good guy struggle to find the bad guy and then, in a high-powered bloodbath, violently defeat him. The good guy is then rewarded for a job well done, and the bad guy is sent to his grave or to prison, only to return again in another form. Once again, the lesson taught and learned from these programs is that violence against perceived evil is necessary and justifiable. Since these programs are reality based, the message of justifiable violence appears more applicable to real life.

I am always amazed by how readily the message of justifiable violence is absorbed, accepted, and applied by children. Fairness and justice are important to children, and justifiable violence easily meshes with their notions of crime and punishment. It is very common to hear children of all ages remark that someone deserves to be beaten up or punished because they have done something bad. Young children might defend the punching of a classmate by saying, "But, he was hurting my friend!" Older children will justify an aggressive act by claiming, "If I hadn't knocked him down, he would have done something worse!" My teenage high school students overwhelmingly support vigilantism, war, and the death penalty. Most of them feel that unless violence is used against a wrongdoer, the problem won't be solved. Some of them carry guns and wouldn't hesitate to use them, if the need should arise. By their book, shooting a bad guy isn't really a crime.

Counteracting the powerful TV message of justifiable violence is critical if we are to teach our children that violence and aggression are not acceptable or appropriate acts. In order to do so, we must use all our media literacy skills and techniques. Parents need to monitor children's programs for examples of justifiable violence and talk to them about what they are watching. Children need your perspective on violence to balance against the TV. Without it, you are leaving them to interpret TV messages on their own and, consequently, will have little influence on what they learn and believe.

Pro-Social Violence on Television

Not all violence promotes negative values. Shakespearean tragedies, for example, are violent but use violence to express a moral idea. Nature programs are often violent, but the violence they show is a normal part of the natural world. Some other programs on TV use violence to show that violence itself is a bad thing. These kinds of programs are called pro-social programs.

Watching a violent pro-social program might disturb you more than other shows because unlike programs in which the violence is intended to thrill the viewer, the violence in a pro-social program is there to show the viewer how terrible violence can be. A program that expresses pro-social values of violence realistically portrays the short-term and long-term consequences of violence. Victims honestly express their feelings of loss, anguish, and anger. The audience may see very realistic portrayals of the physical tolls of violence. In these programs, perpetrators of violence are condemned, not rewarded. Violence is never condoned.

Children might be very disturbed by watching programs that portray pro-social violence because it differs tremendously from the entertaining violence to which they are accustomed. Consequently, it may confuse or scare them. However, they will not react in the negative ways we traditionally associate with viewing TV violence because it doesn't teach the same lessons. Pro-social programs teach children the valuable lesson that real violence is truly a terrible act with terrible consequences.

Unfortunately, there aren't many of these programs made for television, although you may find movies on videotape or on TV which use pro-social violence. *Schindler's List* and *Boyz 'n the Hood* are two such examples. When you do find pro-social movies or TV shows, it is important to let your older children watch them, if they wish, as they help to counterbalance the other negative violent programming they may see. It is also important that you watch with your children and try to answer some of the questions they may have about what they are seeing. And, of

---

What's "Real" About Reality-Based Shows

In recent years, there's been a rash of what are commonly referred to as reality-based TV shows (for example, *Cops* and *America's Most Wanted*). Cheap to produce and very popular, these shows contain some of the worst examples of justifiable violence on TV. Even more distressing, these shows portray this violence as "real."

Reality-based means just that: These shows are only *based* on reality; they are not actual, real life events. However, viewers tend to believe that what they see on these shows is real rather than a constructed *version* of reality, similar in many respects to a fictional TV program. Although the law enforcement officers and "criminals" who appear on these shows are real people, the scenes in which they appear are selected and edited for excitement and dramatic effect. A fight or a dramatic rescue are much more likely to make the show than the endless hours of paperwork most police officers do daily. Nonetheless, viewers—especially children—are fooled into believing that a real police officer's work is all about chasing and catching bad guys.

Beyond this "reality" problem, however, we discover the real trouble with these shows: If you count the number of violent acts on a show like *Cops,* you will find that the alleged good guys commit more acts of violence than the alleged bad guys. This is similar to any other program that promotes justifiable violence, except that these good guys are *real* people.

The belief that our law enforcement officers are always entitled to use violence is endemic in our culture. Although children need to believe that their police officers and firefighters are here to protect them, they also need to understand that law enforcement officials are subject to the same laws as everyone else.

---

course, it is a good time to discuss the other forms of violence on TV and teach children that not all violence is entertaining and that real life violence is both unacceptable and harmful.

Activity: Identifying Justifiable Violence

While watching TV with your children, ask them to pay attention to which characters are perpetrating violence.

- Who is the good guy? What does (s)he look like?
- Who is the bad guy? What does (s)he look like?

A Word About *Looney Tunes*

A frequently asked question about TV violence involves whether or not *Looney Tunes* cartoons, such as Bugs Bunny or Road Runner, are really violent. *Looney Tunes* and *Tiny Toons* cartoons do contain violence, but you must consider the type and context of the violence. Most of the violence in *Looney Tunes* and *Tiny Toons* cartoons is unrealistic—explosives, heavy objects falling—putting these cartoons in the category of mythic violence.

If you look closely, you will notice that, rather than resorting to violence, the protagonists—Road Runner, Bugs Bunny, Tweety—often use their wits to outsmart their antagonists. Although the results of the protagonist's actions are often violent—a gun exploding in Elmer Fudd's face—the actions themselves, such as ducking out of the way or turning the gun around, are not. Moreover, the protagonist's actions are often taken in self defense, to keep from getting caught, and not done for a justifiable purpose.

While these cartoons make violence seem funny and do not show realistic consequences of violence or the horror of real violence, their message is much less harmful than that of other cartoons, which depict justifiable or reality-based violence.

Have them count the number of acts of violence committed by each character and tally them on a piece of paper. Together, determine who has committed the most violence.

- Is the character defined as the good guy committing the most violence?
- Can you identify his motivation for the violence?

Try to name the motivation. Is it justice or revenge? Ask your children if they think his actions are appropriate. Together, notice if the perpetrators of violence are rewarded. If so, how? Is the reward appropriate? Do real heroes use violence?

Be sure to look for consequences to the victims of violence.

- Who are the victims?
- Are the consequences realistic?
- Whose victims seem to be in worse shape?

Share these observations with your children and discuss the consequences of violence in real life. Ask your children if they think using violence is ever OK. If so, under what circumstances?

Together, imagine an alternative version of the show you have watched, one without using violence.

- How would the characters behave differently?
- What nonviolent solutions to the problems might be used?

Encourage children to find nonviolent solutions to conflicts and reinforce any good suggestions. Together, come up with a definition of justifiable violence, then make a list of other programs that promote it or those that don't.

Will the V-Chip Help?

How often have you thought, "Aren't TV producers aware of how harmful TV violence is to children? Can't they come up with something safer to put on the air?" Have you ever wished for some magical device that would end the problem of TV violence once and for all?

According to *TV Guide*, more than 90 percent of adult TV viewers feel the same way about TV violence. For decades, parent organizations, doctors' groups, and children's television activists have been pleading with the TV and movie industries to lessen the quantity of violence on the screen. In some ways, the media have tried to respond. In 1968, the movie industry adopted a ratings system, helping parents to determine which movies may not be suitable for younger audiences. In the 1970s, when TV violence reached a peak, the television networks created a Code of Standards that, although general in nature, sought to control the use of gratuitous violence. More recently, some TV stations have included advisory warnings before programs that contain violence, and others have altered portions of their programming to comply with the *Children's Television Act of 1990*, which mandated that networks carry at least a minimum amount of educational programming for children. Clearly, however, these self-regulating measures have done little to curb the rising tide of violence on TV.

Spurred by a recent wave of public outcry against TV violence, President Clinton signed the Telecommunications Act of 1996, a section of which dictates that every new TV produced for sale in the U.S. be equipped with an electronic V-chip, capable of blocking violent programming from entering our homes. Along with the V-chip comes a voluntary industry TV rating system, similar to our current movie rating system, which is designed to help parents decide which shows are violent and should be blocked.

There is a lot of excitement about the V-chip and rating system, and many feel that the chip could be that "magical device" that will forever end the problem of TV violence. Others aren't yet convinced, claiming that the rating system and V-chip pose some difficult problems. The V-chip and TV rating system might, as President Clinton remarked, "Put the remote control firmly back in parents' hands." However, it won't happen without some help from parents and the industry.

Who Decides What Is Violent?

The V-chip is designed to work with a voluntary rating system, similar to the Motion Picture Association of America (MPAA) ratings system used for movies. Each program on television has a rating that can be read by your V-chip. You may "tell" your V-chip which ratings you wish to have blocked by your TV, and all programs that carry that rating will be barred from reception. Though it sounds simple, it isn't.

Let's look at our movie ratings for a moment. How often have you taken your child to a G-rated or PG-rated movie only to discover that it is actually quite violent? Have you ever gone to an R-rated movie and been shocked to find that, in your estimation, the movie should have been rated NC-17? Although the TV ratings may be more specific, TV-Y or TV-14, can you really trust a ratings committee of nineteen to twenty-five strangers to watch over 1,600 hours of programming each day and accurately determine what is too violent or potentially harmful for you or your children?

Jack Valenti, president of the MPAA, creator of the movie rating system and chairman of the committee that determined the ratings for TV says, "Ratings are only a guideline. People must decide for themselves what is too violent for them." If that is true, how can a TV rating system be truly effective? How do we know if a show that carries a certain acceptable rating won't contain anything we find offensive or inappropriate for our children? What kinds of violence are acceptable for a child-safe rating? How are pro-social violent programs rated? Is verbal aggression considered violent? What can be done with advertisements for violent shows? And what do the ratings do about sex, drugs, alcohol and other potentially harmful content? If we look at how vaguely the new TV rating system already handles these issues, we can understand the problems.

Only parents can make realistic decisions about which programs are acceptable for or harmful to their children. Once we have made decisions about what is acceptable for our families, it may be possible to use the TV industry's rating system as a "guide," but we must remember that the ratings are not necessarily based on *our* family's values and are not foolproof.

The New TV Ratings

The following ratings symbols now appear during the first few seconds of selected TV programs and in the TV Guide.

TV-Y   All Children. According to the ratings board, these programs are designed to be appropriate for all children. Examples: *Looney Tunes, Rugrats, Muppet Babies.*

TV-Y7   Directed to Older Children. According to the ratings board, these programs may include mild physical comedic violence, or may frighten children under the age of seven. Examples: *Ninja Turtles, Ren and Stimpy, Power Rangers.*

TV-G   General Audience. The ratings board believes that most parents would find these programs suitable for all ages. Examples: *Hee Haw, Biography for Kids, Gilligan's Island, Matlock.*

TV-PG   Parental Guidance Suggested. The board believes that programs with this rating may contain some material that some parents would find unsuitable for younger children. Examples: *Friends, Seinfeld, Singled Out, Law and Order.*

TV-14   Parents Strongly Cautioned. These programs may contain some material that many parents would find unsuitable for children under fourteen years of age. Examples: *NYPD Blue, Chicago Hope, Late Night with Conan O'Brien, Jenny Jones, Guiding Light.*

TV-MA   Mature Audiences Only. These programs are specifically designed for adults and therefore may be unsuitable for children under the age of seventeen. Examples: *Larry Sanders, Compromising Situations, Sex Bytes, Dennis Miller.*

Will Ratings and the V-Chip Make TV Better?

It has been speculated that the V-chip and rating system will finally force the TV industry to rein in violence. Some people believe shows that carry violent ratings will lose advertisers, thereby making violence less attractive to producers. Some major advertisers like General Motors are already leery of associating their company or products with controversial programs and feel that violent ratings on shows would most definitely steer them away.

Some advocates of the V-chip believe that the ability to block violent programs will deter producers from making them at all. Critics say that the ability to block violence will give producers carte blanche to make the most violent programming they can imagine. On the other hand, some industry executives, like Robert Iger of ABC, believe the rating system and V-chip probably won't affect their adult programming much. Michael J. Fuchs, the former chairman of HBO, says that "ratings will in no way influence the kinds of programs that get made."

While adult programs are unlikely to change and may even get worse, the TV rating system might have an effect on the producers of children's shows. Since no one wants to be accused of pandering violence to children, producers and broadcasters might be more careful about the children's shows they air. A violent rating on a kid's show could be financially and publicly devastating. Toy makers might pull advertising if the Saturday morning cartoons that feature their products are slapped with adult ratings. Watchdog groups might sponsor boycotts of advertisers and public campaigns condemning violent shows and their makers. Pressured, producers might have to change the shows to receive child-safe approvals.

But if history is any guide, not too much will change. We can already see that most children's programming, violent or otherwise, has been rated TV-Y, TV-Y7, or TV-G, and very few programs carry the TV-MA rating. As parents, our best bet is to keep track of the programs we have approved for our children to watch and those that may soon be of interest to them. Monitor these shows every so often and look for changes in the level or type of violence. If the violence get worse, reevaluate the program's appropriateness. Of course, if the programs change for the better, we can all be pleasantly surprised.

The Cookie Jar Syndrome

You have monitored your children's TV shows and have finally decided which ratings are acceptable and which shows will be blocked from your home. You've bought a new V-chip-equipped TV, programmed it and told your children that they will not be able to watch certain programs. Now what?

How often have you told your child he may not do something, which he then does behind your back? Most parents know that if you tell a child

---

What Americans Think About Ratings and the V-Chip

In a 1993 reader survey, *USA Today* discovered that nine out of ten adult TV viewers would switch channels if a violence warning appeared on a show. Sixty-eight percent of respondents favored a law that would force TV manufacturers to equip television sets with an antiviolence device. Ninety-six percent favored stricter guidelines on violence in the early evening family viewing programs, and 56 percent of those surveyed agreed that it was up to TV producers to control the amount of violence on TV. However, TV producers and lawmakers see problems.

Jack Valenti, president of the Motion Picture Association of America and chairman of the new TV ratings committee, says that controlling violence "is not an easy task. When you get into the details—how you frame a scene, how you write the dialogue, what you show and what you leave to the imagination—it gets difficult. It's not as simple as people think."

Senator Paul Simon, a leading congressional advocate for controlling media violence, says, "We're not suggesting that there be no violence on TV. We're suggesting that we eliminate glamorized violence." Of course, the big question is how does one define and rate glamorized violence and how will a V-chip know the difference between glamorized and pro-social violence?

---

he can't do something, it will be the first thing the child wants to do. Both experience and common sense tell us that prohibitive measures only serve to make the undesirable even more attractive.

The V-chip is a prohibitive measure. By preventing programming that children know exists from entering their homes, the V-chip simply makes that programming more attractive. If children realize that they can't watch those programs at home, they will find some other way to satisfy their increased curiosity.

Let's look at an example. Using your V-chip, you have blocked a certain undesirable program from your home TV. One afternoon, your child returns from school having heard about this program from his friends, whose parents have not blocked it. You inform him that he may not watch the program because it contains violence and it has been blocked from your TV. He now wants to watch it even more than he did before, so he goes to his friend's house and watches it there. Your V-chip has just been rendered ineffective. If a particularly desperate and inventive child can't get to a friend's house, he will figure out how to disable your V-chip, and it will be completely useless.

By attempting to ban violent TV from our children's lives, we simply make it more enticing for them. Even with the V-chip, not all parents are as diligent about controlling the TV as we would hope, and children have a way of talking to each other about what they see on television. Unless your child has no interaction with other children, he will know what is out there, and while your TV may have a chip, the neighbor's might not. Even while channel surfing or watching an approved program on your TV, your child may inadvertently catch a violent advertisement for another show. Advertisements, which contain the second-most-violent content on TV next to cartoons, cannot be blocked by a chip. One way or another, your child will be exposed to the very violence you seek to prohibit. More dangerously, he will see it without the benefit of your insights, questions, and responses.

What Use Is the V-Chip?

If the TV rating system is flawed and producers don't appear to be making an effort to lower the violence quotient and your child can easily circumvent the V-chip, what good is all of this?

The V-chip does have its benefits. By using it, we might be able to postpone the time when our children see certain types of violence. We might prevent very young children, for example, from being exposed too soon to confusing and frightening adult violence. And since children in homes with V-chips will not have uncontrolled access to TV violence, they might discover the value of programs which are nonviolent. They may even become less interested in or entertained by violence.

However, we cannot expect an electronic chip alone to miraculously protect our children from the dangers of viewing TV violence. The V-chip and rating system are devices, like other helpful appliances, which make a hard job a little easier. But like many other home appliances, they won't do the job for you. The V-chip and the TV rating system will only be truly effective when used in combination with the media literacy techniques you are learning.

The Violence Spectrum: A Family Rating System

We have already seen how differently people define violence. We have seen that we can't always expect our values and beliefs to be supported by a ratings board or a neighbor. Therefore, you and your family need to decide which kinds of violence and which programs are acceptable by creating a personal family rating system for TV violence to use as your guideline for the programs and types of violence you allow your children to see.

Building a Family Violence Spectrum

The following activity is one I use with my students and is also very effective at home. Give each school-age or older member of your family a piece of paper and a pencil and ask each of them to write their definition of violence at the top of the paper. Pre-school or young children may dictate their responses to you or another adult. On one side of the paper, below their definition, have family members describe actions that they consider to be violent, beginning with the most violent and ending with the least. Don't forget to include verbally aggressive acts, if you consider them to be violent. Use the listings to come up with a definition of violence, and a spectrum of violence that works for everyone in your family. Ask questions such as:

- Are there different kinds of violence? What are they?
- Is a show that depicts murder worse than a show in which people just hit?
- Is a verbal threat a form of violence?
- Are realistic programs more violent than fantasy ones?
- What do you think about programs that tell you that violence is OK?
- Is there any kind of violence that is acceptable?

Once you have come up with a common definition of violence and a listing of violent acts, turn the paper over and have children write the names or types of TV programs they consider to be violent, again beginning with the most violent and ending with the least violent. When this is finished, compare notes. Does everyone think that certain shows are more violent than others? If necessary, revise your list to reflect your family's attitudes. This is your family's violence spectrum, from which you will develop your TV rating system.

Sample Violence Spectrum

The following violence spectrum was compiled by a class of high school students. After discussing the different types of violence and violent acts, these students determined which TV shows were most violent and least violent.

Definition of violence: Actions that hurt or kill people or destroy prop-

---

What Kinds of Violence Bother Us?

According to *USA Today,* a poll of more than 71,000 Americans revealed that certain violent acts on TV are more offensive than others. Over 97 percent said that a scene involving a battered corpse offended them. Ninety-one percent told pollsters that a courtroom audiotape of a rape upset them. Eighty-three percent were bothered by cartoon characters hitting each other with a bat, but only 61 percent were angered by scenes depicting a detective involved in a fatal shootout.

Most people agree that reality-based violence is more upsetting than clearly fantastical images; however, a particularly bloody or brutal fantasy act can be disturbing to viewers. To many, the violence depicted on the nightly news is more frightening than anything Hollywood could conjure. And although the most violent TV programs are cartoons, which contain more than twenty-five acts of violence each hour, many people are not upset by them.

---

erty. Reality-based is worse than mythic. Glamorized violence is worse than pro-social violence.

Most Violent: Movie of the Week rape/murder/abuse stories
Death and crime stories on the news
Reality-based crime shows
Crime dramas and movies
Horror movies
Action-adventure movies
Soap operas
Talk shows
Cartoons
Sitcoms
Nature shows
Programs that talk about violence prevention

Least Violent: Certain how-to and educational shows

Developing Your Family TV Rating System

Based on the violence spectrum you and your family have built, you can develop a family TV rating system to use when selecting programs to include in your family TV menu. The process of rating programs may take a week or longer, depending upon how you approach it. Some programs may be very easy to rate while others may require that you watch an episode in order to give the show a proper rating.

To begin, choose a code—letters of the alphabet, numbers, colors, or any other kind of common identifiable classification. My family uses animals. Decide together which codes will indicate which level of acceptability. For example, in our code, the least violent programs are "Fish" and the most violent programs are "Lion." Write this code down.

There is no limit to the number of codes, or ratings, you may have. However, the more there are, the more difficult your code will be for children to follow. While you want to avoid being too general, you also want to avoid being so specific as to give each different program a completely different code. Work in categories. In our animal rating code, we have only four categories: Fish, Cat, Dog, and Lion. All TV programs that we watch are rated in this way. My son, Joshua, may watch shows that are rated Fish and Cat. Parental supervision is required for any Dog show and Lion shows and movies are off-limits for now.

You will have to decide how to rate certain programs yourselves. In addition to the broad categories, you might want to address the following issues:

- How will your family rate pro-social, reality-based programs?
- Is mythic violence more acceptable to your family?
- Do the ages of the main characters affect your decisions?
- What will you do about verbal aggression?
- What will you do about the news?
- What types of programs are strictly off-limits to children under sixteen?
- Is there any category that might be acceptable with parental supervision?
- Are any programs so offensive as to be off-limits to the adults in your household?

Once you have decided on your rating system, return to your violence spectrum and assign the most acceptable code to the programs you believe contain the least harmful violence. Then continue up the spectrum, assigning each new level of violence a new code. When you reach the top of the spectrum, or the most violent programs, assign them the final code name.

You are now ready to apply your rating system. Return to your family TV menu and determine which specific programs deserve which rating. For example, if your children have included *Looney Tunes* cartoons on their menu, assign it an appropriate rating from your system. Under my family's animal code, *Looney Tunes* receives a "Cat" rating, which means that although there is violence in the show, it is an acceptable kind. Do this with all programs that your children watch.

As new programs arrive or your children want to watch a program that hasn't been rated, you will have to determine a rating for it. In order to do so, you will need to watch the program with your children. This is probably a good idea anyway, as the occasion will give you and your children an opportunity to discuss issues as they come up and will allow you to make a joint decision about the suitability of the program.

You will discover that this rating process becomes both fun and educational for you and your children. Most children respond well to a personalized rating system, taking great pleasure in telling you exactly why a certain program should be a "Fish" or a "Cat" or a "Lion." It becomes a game to them. Children also tend to respect their own ratings more than ratings imposed by others and will be less likely to argue about not watching a certain show if they have had a say in its acceptability.

Educationally, the process of identifying violence and naming it is the first step toward understanding it and an important part of TV proofing. As you and your children go through the process of discussing, rating, and selecting appropriate TV programs and movies, you will discover that they are becoming more aware of what they are watching and are better able to make decisions about appropriateness by themselves. They might even surprise you by choosing not to watch any negative violent programming at all!

Sample Family TV Rating System

Mary Beth and Richard worked with their two children, Kaitlyn, six, and Ben, nine, to develop their family TV rating system for violence. They have four categories and coded them by color. Programs that are rated Black are off-limits to the kids, because they contain large amounts of reality-based, justifiable, or arbitrary violence. Red programs are acceptable only with parental supervision and include many violent movies. Blue programs contain violence, but it is mythic and/or pro-social, and Yellow programs contain no violence. The children are free to choose from the Blue and Yellow ratings but must have a parent watch with them for a Red show. Below are a few selections from their weekly family TV menu, complete with ratings.

Doug—Blue
The Simpsons—Red

Ghostwriter—Blue
Full House—Yellow
News—Red
MTV—Red
Looney Tunes—Blue
Other Saturday morning cartoons—Red

TV Talk About Violence

Violence on television is a rich subject and provides us with many topics for discussion. We can talk with each other and our children about how violence on TV has changed, the different kinds of violence on TV, how violence affects people, and what we learn from violence on the screen.

However, the most helpful thing you can do for your children is to talk to them about the distinction between violence that is a part of nature or the result of antisocial forces in a culture and violence that is there to entertain them. Talk to your children about real-life violence. Acknowledge that violence does happen in the world and explain why it happens. Describe the real consequences of violence—the pain, the loss, the financial and community tragedy it can cause. Explain how you feel about it. Then explain how TV violence works and why it is there. Make sure your children understand that TV is not always like real life and that TV violence and real-life violence are very different.

When talking to your children about TV violence, don't forget to point out the production techniques you learned earlier. They will help reinforce the distinction between TV and real life. Call attention to costumes and sets used in the shows. Describe the use of special effects and stage-fighting techniques. Illustrate how camera angles and sound effects can make things appear more frightening and more realistic. Explain that the guns don't use real bullets. Tell your children that the blood and wounds they see are created with makeup. Remind them that TV is a constructed reality, not reality itself.

As you and your children watch TV and movies together, remember the rules for TV Talk:

- *Respect* the fact that your children want to watch a particular show and might enjoy it.
- *Observe* the show quietly for points of interest and discussion.
- *Question* your children gently about what they think and about points you would like to discuss.

- *Listen* carefully and respectfully to what your children say about the show.
- *Reinforce* positive values and comments along with the positive aspects of the show.

As you talk about violence with your children, remain open to their responses and reinforce those that you support. If you continue the dialogue, you are likely to learn as much from your children as they learn from you. More important, you are both understanding that watching TV is not a passive entertainment but rather a learning activity that can stimulate questions, ideas, and critical thinking.

Discussion Starters for Kids

1. What is violence? Do you ever see people or animals behaving violently in real life? How does it make you feel? Do you feel different when you see violence on TV?

2. Why do you think TV producers put violence in their shows? Do you think people like to watch violence? Do you like to watch violence?

3. Are there different kinds of violence? What are they? Do the different kinds of violence affect you differently? Which kinds of violence make you scared? Angry? Which kinds of violence do you think are funny? Can people speak violently?

4. How is the violence in this program portrayed? Is it realistic or not? Why or why not? Could these things happen in real life? What would it be like in real life?

5. In this program, which characters are doing the violence? Are they good guys or bad guys? What is the difference between good-guy violence and bad-guy violence? If a good guy uses violence, is he still a good guy? Do good guys in real life ever use violence? What are real heroes like? Do you think it is OK to hurt people if you are the good guy?

6. Why are the characters in this show behaving violently? Is the violence being used to solve a problem? What is the problem? Do you think the violence is an appropriate response to the situation? Do you ever use violence to solve a problem? What other things could the character do that aren't violent and might solve the problem?

7. Are the people who use violence caught or punished for doing it? Should people who use violence be punished? How? What do you think should happen? What would happen to you?

8. How are the victims of violence represented? Do you see the blood? Do you think violence hurts? How do you think the victims feel? How would you feel if it happened to you or someone you know?

9. How would this program be different if there were no violence in it? Would you like it as much? Would it teach you the same things?

10. Is there ever an appropriate time for violence?

Sample TV Talk

Eight-year-old Jack and his father, Mitchell, have just finished watching an episode of Jack's favorite superhero cartoon, Batman. *Concerned about the messages of violence in the show, Mitchell decided to initiate a TV-Talk conversation.*

MITCHELL: You like that show, don't you, Jackie?

JACK: Yeah. Batman is cool.

MITCHELL: What makes Batman cool?

JACK: Well, he beats up on the bad guys and saves the people.

MITCHELL: Do you think that Batman uses violence to do that?

JACK: What is violence?

MITCHELL: Violence is any action that hurts people. Do you think that Batman hurts people?

JACK: Well, yeah, but they're bad guys. He doesn't hurt good guys.

MITCHELL: So, hurting bad guys is okay?

JACK: Yeah, Dad. Bad guys hurt other people.

MITCHELL: That doesn't seem right to me. To use violence to hurt people who hurt others. What's the difference between a good guy and a bad guy, then?

JACK: Bad guys go to jail, don't they? They're bad guys.

MITCHELL: And the "good guys" who use violence? What happens to them?

JACK: On TV?

MITCHELL: Yes.

JACK: Nothing?

MITCHELL: So, what message does that send?

JACK: That it's okay to use violence if you're a good guy?

MITCHELL: Do you think that's right?

JACK: That's how it is on TV.

MITCHELL: I know that, but what would happen to you, for example, if you shot someone that you thought was a bad guy?

JACK: I would probably go to jail.

MITCHELL: Probably. So what makes you, the good guy, any different from the bad guys who are in jail too?

JACK: I don't know.

MITCHELL: Neither do I. I wonder if there might be some other way that Batman could make the bad guys understand the problem, without using violence.

JACK: Maybe he could put them in jail?

MITCHELL: That's a possibility. What else could he do?

JACK: He could try talking to them. Have a meeting or something.

MITCHELL: That sounds like a good idea. Why don't they do that on the show?

JACK: 'Cuz it's boring, Dad! Who wants to watch people talking!

MITCHELL: Good point. So, do you think that they have violence on this TV show to make people watch it?

JACK: Yeah, sure. I watch it.

MITCHELL: Do you think that the violence they show is realistic? I mean, do the people that get hurt really bleed or anything?

JACK: Mm, not on *Batman*. Nobody bleeds on *Batman*. It's like they aren't really hurt.

MITCHELL: What about real life?

JACK: Yeah, I mean, if you get shot with a gun, it's gonna hurt and you're gonna bleed.

MITCHELL: So how come they don't show it?

JACK: Dad! It's TV! It's not real!

MITCHELL: That's very true, Jack. It isn't real. But somehow, we believe what it tells us, don't we?

JACK: Sometimes.

MITCHELL: So, what do you think we ought to do about that?

JACK: Not believe it?

MITCHELL: Well, at least think about it, like we just did with *Batman*. So, if someone asked you to tell them about what you think about *Batman*, what would you say?

JACK: That I like it, but it's not real.

MITCHELL: Maybe you could explain why it's not real, too. What should we watch next week?

JACK: Can we watch *Batman* again?

MITCHELL: Sure. And maybe we can even talk about animation and how
   it's done. Would you like that?
JACK: You mean how to make cartoons? Yeah!

Mitchell and Jack had a great beginning conversation about TV violence. Even though they didn't go into depth on each subject, Mitchell
was able to bring up a number of topics that made Jack think about what
he had seen and how it relates to violence in real life. I'm sure their next
TV Talk will go further.

8

"Sex, Drugs, and Rock 'n' Roll!"
Growing Up With Teen TV

MTV is more than just the first twenty-four-hour music video channel; it is a cultural force in more than two hundred million homes in seventy countries, with over $500 million in gross revenues. In the mid-1980s, the *Washington Post* declared MTV to be "perhaps the most influential single cultural product of the decade." Today, MTV determines the trends in youth culture, from the coolest music, clothes, and haircuts to the coolest causes, products, and political candidates. If it isn't on MTV, it simply isn't cool. And every teenager wants to be cool.

Beyond selling records, clothes, and ideas, however, MTV has spawned a whole new market in teen-targeted television. It was clear at its inception in 1981 that MTV had brought teenagers back to television and, recognizing the economic power of teenagers, producers began to bring TV back to kids. The MTV style invaded everything from commercials to programs, and each season new TV programs are unveiled for teens, who have become one of television's largest and most profitable demographics.

However, these Teen-TV shows aren't cut from the cute teeny-bopper Mickey Mouse images of yesterday. Today's TV teens and twenty-somethings are a sophisticated bunch, whose ideas about money, sex, fun, work, and friendship are powerful influences on your preteen and teenager.

This chapter discusses how teens are affected by MTV and teen-targeted programming and shows you how to use TV-Talk techniques to

TV-proof your teens against Teen-TV's messages about sex, drugs, alcohol, and responsibility.

A Brief History of the MTV Generation

In the late 1970s, a group of cable executives at Warner/AMEX got together to plan a new TV channel aimed at the lucrative, but then neglected, youth market. The founding fathers had a vision: they wanted their new channel to be something that would appeal to kids, and like traditional youth media, would speak to them and address their concerns. They wanted something different, something hip, irreverent, electric, and exciting; TV that embodied the spirit of youth and rebellion, the spirit of rock 'n' roll. And they wanted to make money at it.

Ever since the 1950s, youth culture has been a growing phenomenon created by and capitalized on by the media. Movies and music of the fifties targeted the wealthy, leisure-oriented post–WWII generation with Elvis, *Blackboard Jungle*, and *Beach Blanket Bingo*, setting them apart from mainstream culture and defining their role. In fact, the baby boomer generation was the first group of young people ever to be singled out as a target audience, and for two decades the music, television, and print media industries poured millions into reaching and appealing to them. TV shows such as *American Bandstand* were designed just for teens, and FM radio began to play rock 'n' roll just for kids.

But since the early 1970s, teens were considered hard to reach and were virtually written off by the networks. Although they were very dependent on media for information and entertainment, post 1960s teens watched less TV than their predecessors, read fewer newspapers and magazines, and were more or less hooked on radio. These kids lived and breathed rock 'n' roll. It was their culture. The cable industry saw an opportunity: Why not use the music and techniques of the Top-Forty radio that kids loved, but put it on TV, where commercials could be seen? So the pioneers at Warner/AMEX created MTV and went to the music industry for help.

In the late 1970s, the record industry had hit a slump. Teens, the largest group of record buyers, were turned off by disco music, and album sales were way down. The industry had to do something to increase sales. When executives from MTV contacted the record industry and told them about this new music television station that would show video clips of musicians to kids around the country, the industry saw a chance to increase sales by using the videos as commercials for records. MTV first aired in August 1981, and by 1983 the record slump was over. Kids around the country were so hyped by what they saw on MTV that record sales were at all-time highs. By 1984, the MTV virus had hit full force. MTV was available in millions of homes around the country, and those who didn't have it were clamoring, as MTV's advertising slogan put it, "I Want My MTV!"

Although kids were parking themselves in front of MTV all day and night and buying records and other products promoted on the channel, parent groups and legislators were wringing their hands over the rapid edit style, racy images, and violent scenes in some of the videos. Some educators were concerned that the fast-cut MTV style was shortening kids' already deficient attention spans, and The National Coalition on Television Violence started charting MTV's violent videos. Everyone jumped on the attack wagon: MTV was condemned for not showing videos by black artists; the AMA complained that rock music lyrics and images were bad for children's health; and even C. Everett Koop, the Reagan administration surgeon general, went on record denouncing MTV's combination of sex and violence as "highly dangerous to the emotional development of children."

These warnings fell on deaf ears; the kids around the country weren't listening to the adults. MTV was defining the new youth culture and kids by the millions were buying it up. A whole new generation was born— called, of course, the MTV Generation—defined by eighties-style excess, parties, fashion, fun, and zero responsibility. It was a generation that needed to be entertained; a generation that based its whole identity on name brands; a generation that bought into the message of MTV: Just have fun!

Then MTV changed. In the late 1980s, the all-music approach was losing steam, and so MTV altered its format to include programs that were more like regular TV. Teen talk shows, such as *Mouth to Mouth*, MTV News, and game shows, such as *Remote Control*, took over and music videos took a backseat. The new programs were just as popular, but they had an even greater effect on kids. Not only did they see their favorite music stars on TV, but they also saw regular teens, like themselves, doing things it then seemed to them teens should do! In shows like *The Real World*, added in 1992, teens and twentysomethings were hashing out problems of the day—AIDS, sexuality, drugs. They weren't just talking about these things, either, they were having sex, experimenting with drugs, risking AIDS. It was frightening stuff for adults, but kids responded in droves.

In 1992, MTV grew a social conscience and developed programs like *Rock the Vote*, designed to give the MTV Generation a political voice. It worked. After President Clinton appeared on MTV, his ratings among the younger generation soared. Political insiders credit his appearance on MTV as having influenced the swing vote of 25 million eighteen- to twenty-five-year-olds. In 1992, Tabitha Soren, a young, hip, political reporter for MTV, was better known among the twelve- to twenty-five age group than Dan Rather! MTV also began to air public service spots about AIDS, safe sex, the environment, and drugs and alcohol, telling an entire generation what they should be concerned about. What MTV said about politics or social ills mattered. And it mattered to one of the largest, most economically viable demographic groups in the country.

The MTV style and influence also spawned shows like *Beverly Hills 90210, My So-Called Life, Melrose Place*, and *Friends*, all designed to help the networks recapture a portion of MTV's audience for their own. These shows, which feature young heroes and heroines struggling with issues around families, schools, love, sex, friends, and work, have some of the highest ratings for the younger demographic and have developed loyal followings. Even network and cable sports shows have begun to target the MTV Generation with demonstrations of "X-treme" sports like downhill mountain biking and skateboarding. There are even whole MTV-styled sports shows just for kids!

Today, there are more than 30 million American kids between the ages of twelve and twenty-five who turn to MTV and the youth media for their definitions of how to be, think, and act. Fifteen years after its first broadcast, MTV and its offspring have given today's kids a TV authority they can call their own; one that defines and refines their tastes, purchases, attitudes, ideals, opinions, and actions.

Even children under the age of ten are affected by MTV, whether they watch it or not. Viacom, Inc., MTV's parent company, also owns Nickelodeon, the cable kid's channel, a favorite among the six to eleven set. Although different in content, "Nick's" irreverent, hip, punk spirit is MTV's first cousin and is responsible for channeling preteens toward MTV when the time comes. Nickelodeon even features a series of animated music videos for kids, featuring rock tunes like those on MTV!

Although many groups continue to blast MTV (and other Teen-TV shows) for their commercialism and their portrayals of sexuality, drug use, violence, and antiestablishment viewpoints, its influence on children, preteens, and teenagers around the world remains great. In the words of Bob Pittman, one of MTV's founding fathers and original shapers of its programming, "At MTV, we don't shoot for the fourteen-year-olds—we own them!"

As you explore the messages of MTV and other Teen-TV programs with your children, keep this in mind. More than anything else, accept that these shows are today's youth culture; your children like them and believe in them. As hard as this may be at times, try to understand these shows from their point of view.

What Kids Say About MTV

"I like some of the stuff they show on MTV. It really appeals to the things that concern me. From MTV, I learn about how I'm supposed to be and what I should consider important. It also helps me deal with problems I have at home, at school, and with my friends. And some of the shows are funny too."

—Amanda, age 15

"Without MTV, most of us wouldn't have a clue about what was hip or cool. I don't know how you older people managed. I personally would be lost without MTV telling me what music was hot and what styles were cool."

—Derek, age 14

"Sometimes I get tired of MTV defining my identity for me. It's like I can't be different than what MTV describes or everyone will think I'm a loser. We're all affected by MTV, and we judge each other according to its standard. Sometimes, I wish MTV had never existed. That way I could just be myself instead of competing with a TV channel!"

—Carter, age 17

"If I could say one thing about MTV and the shows it has created it would be that they scare me. They scare me because the producers of these shows seem to know us better than we know ourselves. It's almost like they can get into our heads. How do they know what we like and don't like? Or maybe we only like what they tell us to like. That's even scarier."

—Rachel, age 18

The Pied Piper

Many parents view MTV and other youth-targeted shows like the Pied Piper—the enigmatic stranger who comes into town, enchants the unsuspecting children with music and tricks, and leads them away. And in many ways, that metaphor is correct. MTV and other Teen TV shows do seem to capture the average teen's attention—through music videos and music-related imagery—and it seems as though teens are being led astray by the Piper. However, Teen TV leads teens not through tricks or enchantment but rather, unlike adult-targeted programs, through addressing their primary concerns: identity, peer relations, expectations, and values development.

Today's youth media taps into teen needs for independence and guidance, for a peer group and an identity. Rock lyrics address their concerns, fears, and desires, crossing the entire spectrum of teenage emotion. Movies and ads focus on the stories that dramatize their deepest feelings and tell them how they should act and react to the world around them. TV shows designed for kids provide comfort, security, and hope through the conflict resolutions of familiar characters. The whole of mass media gives them a forum through which to explore and define their lives, sponsored by products and companies interested in making a profit.

However, inasmuch as Teen TV serves as the guiding force for our young adults' development, it can distort their images of how young men and women should behave, what their ideals and goals should be, and what values are important. In the process of responding to teens' questions about themselves, each other, and their futures, it answers with destructive lessons about sex, drugs and alcohol, violence, and, of course, consumerism.

Growing Up Teen

A group of thirteen-year-old girls were huddled by their lockers before school, recapping the previous night's episode of a favorite teen show, which features characters in their early twenties.

"Oh, my God. He's such a jerk. I can't believe she would even go out with him!"

"He just dumped his other girlfriend, and he was sleeping with someone else too!"

"I think she should go out with him, anyway. I mean he's cute and he's got money and he has a great car!"

"Oh, my God. If I were her, I would just tell him to kiss off. I mean, she doesn't need that. She's got her stupid parents to deal with, anyway."

"You're such a liar. If you had the chance, you would go out with him, wouldn't you?"

"Well, it would just depend. I mean, I'd have to see what he had to offer!"

One of the biggest complaints about teens today is that they seem to be too sophisticated for their ages. They are having sex, drinking, and doing drugs much earlier than most of their predecessors; using guns; facing such adult issues as crime and AIDS; and discussing life in adult terminology. This is an accurate observation. Today's kids are much less innocent than their parents were at their age, and it's partly because of the TV programs they watch, which introduce them to adult themes, characters, and conflicts by age twelve!

Although most teen-targeted TV is geared to children ages twelve to eighteen, the characters, actors, VJs, and musicians are often in their twenties or even thirties. Since forty-year-old TV executives who create these shows know that children "view up," they purposely design shows in which the heroes and heroines are slightly older, more sophisticated, and more adventurous than the viewers. TV teens and twentysomethings have sex, drink heavily, discuss controversial topics, and behave irresponsibly. To the kid that is watching, unaware of this purposeful design, these young adults become the ideal, representing what one is supposed to be like as a teenager or a young adult.

In Teen TV, real adults are seen as bumbling, ineffective, idiotic, or simply nonexistent, adding to the already pervasive image of teens as the *real* adults. Although this trend began in the 1950s and is central to youth media, it has reached a new high. In his book, *Hollywood vs. America*, film critic Michael Medved claims that "teenagers . . . are portrayed as the ultimate source of all wisdom, sanity and sensitivity . . . [and] . . . the portrayal of parents as irrelevant—or outright evil—has become so pervasive in our popular culture that we have begun to take it for granted." However, Medved adds, this has a harmful effect on our kids. "We dangerously underestimate the impact of an omnipresent popular culture that repeatedly reassures kids that they instinctively know better than the tired losers of the older generation." With a message like this, is it any wonder that our teens are suffering from the "I'm grown-up!" syndrome?

More than anything else, teen TV provides young viewers with a fantasy version of what teen and young-adult life are like. It is an escape world of expensive goods, beautiful people, endless parties, no school or parents, and the freedom for kids to do things they could never get away with in real life. In 1988, *Seventeen* magazine commented that on MTV, "the world you'll escape to is a lot more fun. Here everything is geared toward fantasy. No one ever dies. There are no consequences for any action."

So, while teen TV appears to be addressing the concerns of young viewers, it is actually providing them with attractive, but unrealistic and dangerous, answers to their problems. It tells them that they can do things that they can't do, be things that they can't be, and have lives that only exist in TV land. Moreover, it creates the illusion that these answers are being offered by real teens, when in fact they are created and performed by adults with a specific agenda: selling them products.

Unfortunately, most young viewers don't recognize that Teen TV is more fantasy than reality. A high school student of mine once wrote that "if viewers don't see the falsehood of the realm presented, they are being entangled in MTV's notion of teenage escape."

In the fall 1996 new-show lineup, *TV Guide* listed eight new TV series aimed at the youth market. While none of these shows made it past a season, they exemplify the values that Teen TV provides each and every season.

Party Girl featured Mary, a twentysomething character who works in the library by day and parties all night. Executive producer Efrem Seeger is quoted as saying that the lead character "totally embraces her life and has fun doing it. Sometimes it gets her into trouble, but somehow she gets out of it and ends up a winner." In *Townies*, Molly Ringwald and her clan of twentysomething seafood-house waitresses "cope with dysfunctional parents and dream of the good life—or at least a good date." In *Sabrina, the Teenage Witch*, sixteen-year-old Sabrina Spellman, played by twenty-year-old Melissa Joan Hart, star of teen fave *Clarissa Explains It All*, uses her magic powers to gain the affections of boys and the attention of her peers. Executive producer Paula Hart says that *Sabrina* is "a show about a teenage girl coming of age." In one episode Sabrina tries to make a love interest jealous by creating and dating her ideal man.

Other new shows included *Lush Life*, about two broke but decadent young divas living life to the fullest. According to *TV Guide*, their antics include "getting drunk in the local bar and dressing up in outfits that would embarrass Elton John."

Another new show was a series version of the popular movie *Clueless*, featuring a number of wealthy Beverly Hills teens. Executive Producer Amy Heckerling said, "I hope this appeals to kids who want to take a fun look at what it's like to be a teenager in a fantasy world. And hopefully teens will like the hipness."

There were also three new teacher-student shows, including *Mr. Rhodes*, about a hip, sexy, young male teacher in a prep school. But perhaps my favorite Teen TV teacher is *Nick Freno: Licensed Teacher*, about a substitute teacher in an urban middle school. *TV Guide* describes Freno as an "anti-teacher, weaned on MTV and one developmental stage past puberty."

Activity: The Grown-up World

Helping teens understand the difference between the fantasy world of Teen TV and the real world is an important part of TV proofing. It is critical that kids realize that Teen TV is not made by teens but by adults, with a very specific agenda: selling products to the teen market. The following activity is a good one for introducing your teen to this concept.

While watching TV with your teen, pay attention to credits at the beginning and end of the show, and use the following TV-Talk questions to guide your discussion.

- Who produced this program? How old do you think they are?
- How old are the characters? Are they your age or older? How old are the actors?
- Why do you think that the producers use older characters and actors in shows that are meant for kids?
- Are there things that the characters on the show do that you can't do, because they are older than you are? Are there things that you wish you could do?
- What does the show say about real adults? How are they portrayed?
- What does the show say about how teens or young adults are supposed to behave? Is that accurate? Is there anything that is inaccurate?
- If the show were an accurate portrayal of teen or young-adult life, how would it be different? What would the characters do and talk about?

Sex Rocks!

Linda, Ruth, and Asa, all fourteen-years-old, were having a conversation in the girls' room after lunch. Ruth had recently begun dating Joe, sixteen, and the other girls were fishing for information on her love life.

"So, have you done it yet?" prodded Linda.

Ruth wasn't answering. She simply smiled and shrugged her shoulders.

"Of course, they've done it!" explained Asa. "They've been going out for at least two weeks now."

"That's true. But if they haven't done it yet, there's a problem." offered Linda.

"Besides, he's so cute!" said Asa. "If she doesn't do it, there are a million girls who'd love to. Me included!"

"And believe me, he'll go find them, too." agreed Linda.

At this, Ruth exploded. "Okay, okay. We've done it! Are you satisfied?"

An audible sigh of relief was heard. "Ruth," consoled Linda, "we were starting to worry that maybe something was wrong. I mean, everybody does it and, after all, you're fourteen!"

According to my students, the most common lesson of Teen TV is "Sex Rocks!" They say that MTV and the other programs tell them that sex is cool, sex is fun, sex is "grown-up," and if you're not having lots of it, something is wrong with you.

In the early years of MTV, one of the major complaints was that the videos were, so, well, sexy. Pelvic dance moves and half-naked bodies were everywhere. It wasn't an unfounded complaint. Sex is and always has been omnipresent in rock 'n' roll. Sex is also the primary concern of teenagers, whose unleashed hormones are running roughshod over their brain cells. The relationship is a natural one. And since sex is one of the surefire ways for a TV program to get an audience, is it any wonder that sexy music videos would be used to appeal to sex-crazed kids?

Beyond obvious concerns about wet, naked, writhing bodies, the complaints had merit in the way that sex was represented. In music videos and other Teen-TV shows, sex is often portrayed as harmless and fun, with no consequences or responsibilities. Everybody seems to be having it. According to a UCLA study from the early 1990s, almost half of the discussions in Teen-TV are about sex, with losing one's virginity being the number-one priority, and messages about abstinence are rarely heard. Even the safe-sex public service announcements on MTV are drowned out by the throbbing beat and sexy images urging kids to do it, anyway.

More disturbing is the way in which men and women and their sexual relations are stereotyped in music videos. In the majority of music videos, women are nothing more than objects, designed to fulfill male fantasies, fawning all over the guys with the guitars, willingly disrobing and dancing for men's obvious pleasure and enjoyment. Men, on the other hand, are adored and idolized, despite their penchant for destruction, harassment, and violence toward their video women. These stereotypes present a very sexist view of women and sexual relationships and are potentially damaging to teens' emerging sexual identities.

The messages of irresponsible, degrading, and stereotypical sexual re-

---

Dream Sex

That a station as influential as MTV continues to support the stereotype of women as sex objects is reprehensible to many people. Sut Jhally, professor at the University of Massachusetts and founder of the Media Education Foundation, produced a videotape in 1992 entitled *Dreamworlds,* in which he detailed the harmful nature of MTV's objectification of women in music videos. Jhally points out, through clips of music videos, that women are often portrayed as vacuous body parts, existing only to be looked at and fondled by the males of the MTV dreamworld or as willing victims of sexual and sadomasochistic violence. In the tape Jhally shows graphic examples of this treatment from clips of music videos and then relates it to male attitudes about women and sex in real life. It is a powerful and troubling video. So troubling, in fact, that MTV sued Jhally to force the tape out of distribution. It didn't work. Today, the tape is a standard in media studies classes around the country.

---

lations are prevalent on other MTV shows and youth-targeted programs. Today, MTV sponsors Spring Break contests, in which high school and college-aged boys act like idiots to get some equally idiotic bikini-clad babe's phone number, and features a cartoon in which two overly hormonal adolescents laugh insanely at the mere mention of the word *sex.* There is even an MTV version of *The Dating Game* called *Singled Out,* in which young male and female contestants ogle each other and ask off-the-cuff questions about bra sizes, sexual positions, and fantasies. The plot lines of Teen TV programs like *Beverly Hills 90210, Melrose Place,* and *Friends* consistently revolve around who is sleeping with whom, and advertising aimed at teens features half-clothed bodies in the process of removing the other half of their clothes!

Although my high school students claim to be unmoved by the fantasy messages of MTV and other shows, Teen-TV attitudes and stereotypes about sex do affect children in disturbing ways. Teenage girls and boys judge themselves and each other according to the sexual rules of teen TV, determining who fits in and who doesn't. The pressure to conform to this fantasy version of sexuality is high. Female students tell me that images that portray scantily clad, preening, sex-crazed young women as normal, acceptable, and desirable make them feel compelled to imitate what they see. Male students reveal that the promiscuous young men they see, surrounded by half-naked girls, seem to be the norm, and so

---

Sex and the Single Teen

According to recent polls, teenagers aren't as sexually active as the media would have us think. While it is true that there are isolated instances of pregnant thirteen-year-olds, that is not the dominant picture of teen sex in America. In a 1990 study by the Department of Health and Human Services, more than 65 percent of teen girls under the age of eighteen had never had sex. Of the girls ages fifteen to nineteen, more than 50 percent had never had sexual intercourse. Of the remainder, one in seven had had sex only once in their lives.

In a separate study conducted by *USA Today*, 54 percent of the teen respondents said that they heard "too little" about sexual abstinence in the media. Another study concluded that more than 80 percent of teenage boys feel that love is more important than sex.

While most teens admit that the pressure to have sex comes from the youth media, the trend is not to buy into the messages. This is a promising observation, because it points out that adult-generated media messages about sex aren't necessarily producing a generation of rabbits, but that kids do evaluate the validity of these messages and their applications.

---

boys behave promiscuously and expect to be treated the same way by the girls they meet.

Both genders are worried that the constant messages of sex might be edging them toward an acceptance of sexual activity that is more mature than they are. A study conducted by Children Now polled 750 kids between the ages of ten and sixteen and six out of ten said sex on TV sways kids to have sex at too young an age. However, a student of mine revealed that she thinks "it's good that they talk about sex on TV. I mean, our parents don't tell us about it, so how else are we supposed to learn?"

What is disturbing about this is that our teens are not only learning about sex from TV but are learning about it from a very adult and very commercialized perspective. It is important to remember that even though these shows appear to be "for kids" and have kids in them, they are produced by adults, whose adult ideas, fantasies, and experiences form the basis for the shows. The images that appear on the screen are not necessarily culled from teenage desires or experiences or needs but from adult ones, made to appear as though they belong to teens. Moreover, the use of adult sexual imagery and talk is designed to attract audiences and sell products, not to instruct.

Being sexual doesn't mean being a grown-up. Losing your virginity isn't the gateway to adolescence. Viewing women as sex objects negates their humanity. Conquering women is not the key to manhood. These lessons are the real keys to helping our teenagers grow into healthy, secure adults. We need to help our teens challenge the adult-produced sexual messages of Teen TV. One of my high school students once told me that "if all of us teenagers knew how we were being manipulated by TV into feeling like we had to have sex, we probably wouldn't feel forced into it and would be much happier, healthier and, in reality, more grown-up!"

Activity: Uncovering Sexual Messages in Teen TV

Helping teens see through the adult sexual messages in Teen TV is crucial to immunizing them against the potential harm of these messages. It is also not hard to do, and the following activity is useful and interesting.

While watching TV with your teens, ask them to keep track of any references to sex or stereotypical sexual representations that they find, whether in advertising or in the program itself. Follow up with the following TV-Talk questions:

- How many messages or references to sex did you see? Were they in ads or in the program itself?
- For whom was sex more important? Male or female characters? How could you tell?
- Is there a difference in the way that male or female characters approach sexual relationships? Why? Is there a difference in the way they are represented? How is it different in real life?
- Did the characters have a conflict about sex? What was the conflict? How was it resolved?
- Do you see representations of premarital or extramarital sex? Why? In what context? What is the message?
- Why do you think there is so much sex on Teen TV? Does it affect you?
- Do TV's sexual representations of women or men bother you? How?
- How important do you think sex is in real life? How important is it for you or your friends?
- Do you judge yourself or others according to the sexual standards of TV? How?

- How do you think the shows would be different if there weren't so many sexual messages? Would they still be interesting to you?

Let's Party!

Fifteen-year-old Robbie and his buddies were talking about their weekend party during a passing time in the hallways.

"I must have drunk a whole twelve-pack Saturday night. But I wasn't nearly as fried as you were, Dan; you drank all that vodka too! You were so wrecked that you were trying to convince us all to go get Nine Inch Nails tattoos on our butts!"

"Yeah, that was fun."

"Man, you guys should've seen Molly! She was so drunk that she was taking off her clothes in the kitchen! It was like some kind of beer ad!"

"Actually, she was taking off her clothes all over the house! I saw her!"

"Man, that was the most awesome party. When do your parents go out of town again?"

These days, it's hard to think about a teenage party without the presence of drugs or alcohol. In fact, terrifying real life statistics attest that kids themselves can't conceive of having a good time without using some form of mind-altering substance. Every year, in almost every city and town in America, a carful of teens are killed because they have been drinking or doing drugs and driving. There is shock, there is outrage, and there is grief, but somehow this sobering reality has little or no effect on teens in combating the lessons of drug and alcohol consumption put forth by MTV and Teen-TV shows.

Although you might never see anyone actually doing drugs on MTV or any other teen TV show, it seems to be an implied undercurrent, especially on MTV. Rock 'n' roll mythology is centered around tales of drug use and overdoses. News stories about musicians and heroin addiction appear in *Time* magazine as well as on MTV. Drug use always seems to be backstage at every concert or event, but it is never seen. While MTV can't be accused of *directly* promoting drug use—MTV has been careful to black out references to drugs on clothing and often denies airplay to musicians who glorify drugs in their songs—it can be said to glamorize drug culture through its very relationship to and idolatry of rock 'n' roll culture, and in how it makes that culture seem appealing to young viewers.

Alcohol use is seen often in teen-targeted shows. Virtually every party or gathering on these shows includes alcohol. It may be in the background of a scene or it may be in the forefront, but the message here is that no party is complete without it. On the rare occasion that a character has an alcohol problem, as happened on a recent episode of *Melrose Place*, it never seems to affect anyone else's ability to drink heavily. The character simply disappears for an episode or two for a stint at a rehab clinic and comes back cured.

Alcohol advertising is also prominent on teen shows. Beer ads, often featuring good-looking twentysomething men and women having a swell time with a beer in their hand, sell alcohol as a component of sex appeal. And in late 1996, the alcohol industry reversed its voluntary ban on hard liquor advertising on TV, setting the stage for even more advertising images of young people partying with alcohol.

My students have done several projects looking for drug and alcohol messages on Teen-TV programs and are always surprised at their prevalence. One group of kids watched an entire season of *Friends* and noticed that each episode had at least one scene in which characters were drinking or talking about going to get a drink. They also noticed that although the characters seem to drink a lot, no one ever had a hangover or spent the evening throwing up. Their conclusion was that the show said that it was okay to drink, there were no ill effects, and that drinking was what grownups did to relax and have fun.

Another group of students looked at MTV for a month and discovered that drugs were only talked about in terms of Kurt Cobain's heroin overdoses and subsequent suicide. They also noticed that there were a total of fifteen public service announcements telling kids that drugs weren't cool. Nonetheless, they noticed that many music videos still showed people who looked as though they had been doing drugs (staggering, dark circles, unkempt clothing and appearance, distant looks), and a character on *The Real World* mentioned getting stoned in the past. Their conclusion was that, although MTV tried hard not to show drugs, the message was that really cool people do drugs but don't talk about it. They also noticed that the station implied that as long as you don't have a drug addiction, it's okay.

Today, it seems coolness, acceptance, and adulthood are only possible through alcohol and drug use. As in the thirties, forties, fifties, and sixties, when cool adult-role-model characters smoked cigarettes, today's equivalents drink and do drugs. It is important to remember, though, that this message isn't as overt as it used to be. Whereas Humphrey Bogart made no bones about lighting up on camera, today's stars preach responsible drinking and saying no to drugs. But what they say and what they do are all too often at odds. And even though the networks and cable are more careful about what they show, owing to the kind of scrutiny they receive from parent and watchdog groups, the messages are still there for teens to absorb and accept.

My students tell me that, overall, the messages they receive from these programs have little effect on their actions regarding drinking and drug use. The greater influence, they say, is peer pressure. When I ask them where they think their peers get their ideas about drinking and drugs from, they all say TV. I suppose it's not cool to blame TV for making you want to drink or do drugs. It's much easier to blame your friends who watch TV!

Drug and Alcohol Use Among Teens

While most of the American government is running around hysterical about the statistical rise in drug use among teens, other surveys paint a very different picture of teen drug and alcohol use.

In one survey taken of more than 300 teens between the ages of fourteen and eighteen, more than 85 percent said that they had never used drugs. Conversely, more than 70 percent said that they *had* drunk alcohol, and a shocking 40 percent revealed that they drank on a regular basis!

As Jean Kilbourne, an expert on alcohol advertising and a popular lecturer, notes, the alcohol industry spends over $2 billion each year promoting its products, and that number is sure to go up when hard liquor ads hit the TV screens. The drug industry (which doesn't exist) spends no money on advertising. Doesn't this help explain why alcohol use among teens is a problem? Why aren't politicians complaining about this?

Activity: Detecting Drug and Alcohol Messages

According to health and substance abuse officials around the country, media literacy activities that help children become aware of media messages about alcohol and drugs are vital to eradicating early addictions and other problems associated with drugs and alcohol. A sobering activity for teenagers is to have them look for drug and alcohol messages in the shows that they watch and to examine how those messages affect them.

While watching TV with your teens, have them keep track of any drug or alcohol messages, either in advertising or in the program itself. Follow up viewing with these TV-Talk questions:

- How many drug or alcohol messages did you see? How many of these messages portrayed drinking or doing drugs in a positive way? How many were anti-drug or -alcohol messages?
- Were the messages primarily in commercials or did you see them in the program itself?
- Whom did you see using drugs or alcohol or talking about it? Were they teenagers? Young adults? Under what circumstances were drugs and/or alcohol being used or talked about?
- Did the users appear to derive a benefit from drugs or alcohol? What was it?
- Do you think those benefits are realistic? Do you know anyone who has received such a benefit in real life? Do you know anyone for whom the opposite is true?
- Why do you think alcohol is advertised or promoted on these kinds of shows? How do these messages affect you? What are your feelings about drug and alcohol use? Do you see alcohol or drug use as a beneficial thing? For whom is it beneficial?
- If you saw any antidrug or -alcohol messages, what were they? Were they effective? Why or why not?
- Do you think that alcohol and drugs should be promoted on teen TV shows? Why or why not? How would the shows be different without these messages?

I Buy, Therefore I Am

Eileen and her fourteen-year-old daughter, Christa, were having an argument about the clothes she was wearing to school one morning.

"Christa, that shirt is see-through. You cannot wear it!" Eileen insisted.

"Mom, everyone is wearing them! They're the fashion!"

"I don't care if they're the fashion; no daughter of mine is going to school dressed like a prostitute!"

"It's not prostitute's clothing! Mariah Carey wears this shirt on TV!"

"I said no and I mean it. Now go change." said Eileen, firmly.

"Fine, Mom. Then I'll just be hated by everyone and it'll be your fault!" Christa ran up the stairs in tears.

Today's media youth culture is about products; lots of products. The version of teenage rebellion sold by MTV and its brethren is a consumer rebellion, which tells its followers that in order to truly separate themselves from the adults, to define their individual identities, and to bond with other teens, they must buy, buy, buy. It is part of the whole TV advertising ethic, but it works in a uniquely revolutionary way.

MTV created a new style of kid-targeted advertising, which combined programming with advertising in a way that made the two inseparable and indistinguishable. Most of MTV's promos are for other media products—movies, TV shows, soundtrack CDs, of which kids are the largest consumers—but are presented in such a way that they appear to be part of the programming; they are highlighted in MTV News spots or made into videos from the movie soundtrack. So blurred is this line between advertising and programming that in 1983, MTV even went so far as to premiere a new commercial on the channel—Michael Jackson selling Pepsi—just as though it were a movie, complete with ads urging viewers to watch the premiere!

Between the videos selling records, news spots selling TV shows and movies, and the promos selling other media, are commercials hawking jeans, cars, stereos, and sodas that look like videos and include rock stars. In fact, this profitable blend of advertising and programming has prompted many people to refer to MTV itself as the longest-running commercial ever!

Teen TV shows have learned this lesson from MTV and also consciously smear the line between ad and program. Hot fashion designers scramble to get lead characters on popular shows to wear their clothes and other product manufacturers fall all over themselves for product placement of cars, drinks, and even cereals. A recent episode of *Friends* had a box of Captain Crunch clearly displayed on the breakfast table and a whole episode was devoted to discovering who had taken a can of Diet Coke! Music and movie stars also make frequent guest appearances on Teen TV in a thinly disguised commercial for their latest venture, and even soundtracks from TV shows are advertised.

Around the country, kids believe what MTV and the other Teen TV shows sell them and rush out to buy the clothes, makeup, records, snack foods, movie tickets, video rentals, acne medications, computer games, electronics, and cars that will help them define their identities, values, and peer groups and make the companies that advertise on these shows very rich.

The most fun I ever have when teaching kids about television is to talk to them about Teen TV and the consumer rebellion. I don't do it to burst their bubble: I do it to help them understand that their teenage-TV rebellion isn't unique and it isn't really much of a rebellion either, sponsored as it is by large businesses only interested in selling products. How much of a rebellion could it be to buy the same things that 200 million other kids buy? The real rebellion, I tell them, is *not* to buy these things! They get it. Being sensitive to manipulation of any kind, teenagers become indignant when they discover they have been duped. One high school class of mine even drew up petitions and sponsored an "I Don't Want My MTV Day" to teach other kids about the sham of the consumer rebellion. Another class had a (supervised) ceremonial ad burning; pulling ads from magazines by companies that also advertised on MTV and setting them on fire in a metal trash can.

Still another group investigated the number of products sold that have MTV, Nickelodeon, or other youth program endorsements and were appalled to discover that they were paying top dollar to advertise for these stations or shows by walking around in a *Friends* sweatshirt or carrying a *Beavis and Butthead* lunchbox!

While much of the American television ethic is based on consumerism, the Teen TV emphasis on buying products to solve the crises of teen identity and peer relations sets the stage for conflict. Whether we parents are upset because our kids spend their money on CD's with explicit lyrics, video games with violence, or clothing that is best left on the racks, it is important to understand why these purchases are made, what meaning the items carry for our kids, and how they are being affected by the consumer ethic of TeenTV.

As we look for ways to help our adolescents find meaning in their lives away from the messages of TV, we must address the way in which youth culture is packaged and sold to our kids and encourage them to question its validity and usefulness.

Activity: Discovering the Consumer Teen Rebellion

Helping children recognize the consumer messages in Teen TV encourages them to question the validity and usefulness of a product-based identity. The following activity is both simple and effective.

While watching Teen TV with your kids, ask them to keep track of the commercials they see, including any hidden commercials or "product placements." When the show is over, look at the list and try these TV-Talk questions:

- How many advertisements did you find? What kinds of products are advertised? Which products are advertised most frequently? Why?

One Hour of MTV Commercials

A few months ago, my students did a project looking at the commercials on one evening hour of MTV. The following are their results.

2 violent computer games
Nike sneakers mixed with movie preview
McDonald's
Tylenol
Sleepers—movie preview
Trident gum
Arrid anti-perspirant
1-800-Collect
Clothestime—see-through shirt
Mortal Kombat video game
Another movie preview
Shampoo ad
Car ad
Taco Bell with *Goosebumps* action figures (*Goosebumps* is a show on Fox)
Arizona jeans and cologne

- Do you purchase any of the products advertised? Which ones? Are certain products more appealing to you than others? Why?
- Why do you think the makers of these products choose to advertise on this show? Are they trying to reach a certain audience?
- What techniques do the ads use to appeal to you? Do they promise you that you will be attractive, popular, cool, athletic, et cetera? How?
- What do you gain from purchasing these products? Do they work the way the ads say they will?
- Do you think that advertisers should target teenagers? If so, how can they do it in a way that is less deceptive?
- What do you think would happen if kids didn't buy the products advertised on these shows? Would your lives be different? Would the shows be different?

What's Good About Teen TV?

By now, it may surprise you when I say that despite the negative messages put forth by many of these shows, I *like* MTV, Nickelodeon, and some of the other network teen-targeted programs. I think some of the visual techniques used in music video are wonderfully creative, filled with inventive uses of computers and special effects. I also think the way that MTV, Nick News, PBS's *In the Mix*, *ABC Afterschool Specials*, and other teen shows tackle issues of concern to teens—AIDS, sexuality, social and political issues—is vital to helping young adults confront and assess difficult and challenging questions. While the rampant consumerism promoted by these channels and some of the shows is hard to swallow, I believe children can learn a great deal about our consumer culture from thinking about the way in which products are sold to them. But more than anything else, I like MTV, Nickelodeon, and the teen-targeted network shows because they provide me, as a parent and as a teacher, with excellent TV-Teaching material.

The most effective TV Teaching I have with kids centers on these programs. This is *their* TV—they watch it, they know it, they like to talk about it. They get excited when we talk about advertising on MTV or value messages on *Friends*. They're involved in discussions about stereotypes in *Party of Five* or what cartoons on Nickelodeon say about violence. We can even discuss politics in the media through watching teen news shows. The teaching is relevant to their lives and their concerns. Although many parents claim that MTV is beyond them, Nickelodeon below them, and that network teen shows like *Melrose Place* are not interesting to them, I encourage parents to get involved in this part of their children's viewing if they want to know what their kids are learning from TV and how to combat any negative messages.

TV Talk About Teen TV

It's not always easy to approach teenagers about the messages of Teen TV. They are, understandably, extremely protective of it. It is their TV, and in their minds adults couldn't possibly have any idea what it is saying or what it means to them. Actually, they're right. While we can point out certain images and patterns in what we see, the only way we can hope to understand and talk about the difficult and challenging messages of Teen TV is to listen—really listen, without judging—to what our kids say about them.

As always, the best way to begin a TV-Talk conversation with kids is to start simply and slowly with a show that they are already watching. Ask if you can join them while they watch an episode, and, then, casually ask a few questions when the show is over. Don't force it, though. Build up to longer conversations and again, remember the rules of the game:

- *Respect* your child's desire to watch the show and his/her enjoyment of it.
- *Observe* quietly for points of interest and discussion.
- *Question* gently about your child's responses and opinions.
- *Listen* carefully to what they say.
- *Reinforce* any positive comments and positive aspects of the show.

TV Talk about Teen TV may be the hardest part of your TV Teaching. After all, you and your teen will be getting into murky waters and prickly areas when you talk about sex, drugs, alcohol, and issues of identity and peer groups. Be prepared for a little bit of resistance from older teens, who are especially sensitive to anything that seems like a lecture or judgment. If the initial conversation lasts only a few minutes, don't be alarmed or give up. Hang in there. As uncomfortable as it may feel at first, your teen will respect you for raising the issues. They want to talk about them. These subjects are important to them. They want guidance and reassurance. That's why they look to TV in the first place. Try TV Talk again in a few days, and soon your teen will be more willing and interested.

Try to view these discussions as part of an ongoing dialogue that begins with TV but is really a vehicle to help you and your teen get a better understanding of each other and the challenges of adolescence. As tough as these discussions may be, they are the most rewarding part of TV Teaching, and, in the long run, are crucial steps toward immunizing your growing adolescent against the potentially negative and harmful messages of Teen TV.

Discussion Starters for Kids

Although many of the topics raised by Teen TV—stereotypes, values, and consumerism—have been addressed in other chapters, there are a few specific Teen-TV topics that you can discuss with your teen. The questions below make good openers and can be modified according to your child's age and maturity level.

1. Why do you like this show? What does it tell you about how teens and young adults are supposed to behave? Do you identify with any particular character? Does it address any questions you have? Which ones and in what way?

2. Do you think that it is an accurate reflection of teen or young adult life? How is it accurate? How is it inaccurate?

3. Do you see any stereotypes? What are they? How are young women and young men portrayed? How are adults portrayed? Is there anyone that is not represented?

4. Are these stereotypes accurate? Do you know anyone in real life like the characters you see? Do you know anyone that is different? How do these stereotypical representations affect the way you view yourself or others?

5. What values does this show espouse? What is important to TV teens? To TV adults? To young TV women or men? Are these values accurate? Do you think they are important?

6. What does this show tell you about sex? What do TV teens and young adults think about sex? Is sex or sex talk common on the shows you watch? What is the message? Do you agree or disagree? Why is sex such a common element in teen shows?

7. Are there any sexual stereotypes? What are they? How are girls and young women most often portrayed? Boys and young men? Are these stereotypes accurate? If not, why are they there?

8. What does this show tell you about drugs or alcohol? Does it show people relaxing or having fun with drugs or alcohol? Is there a difference between girls and boys? Are there any ads for beer or liquor during the show? Why are they there, if kids can't drink legally? What do most teen shows say about drinking or drugs? Do you agree or disagree?

9. What kinds of products do you see advertised or used in the show? Why are these products advertised? Why are they used? Whom are they used by and what benefit is derived from their use? What products do girls use? Boys? Cool people? Do you find yourself wanting to buy products seen or advertised on these shows? Why?

10. Do you know who produces this show? Do you know why the show is on? What companies sponsor this show? Why do you think they sponsor it? Can you think of other programs that have the same products advertised?

11. If you could rewrite this show to be a more accurate reflection of teen or young adult life, how would it be different?

Sample TV Talk

Gina and her fourteen-year-old daughter, Kyla, just finished watching an episode of Kyla's favorite TV show, Melrose Place, *when Gina thought it might be a good time to talk about some of the issues the show raises.*

GINA: I can see why you like this show, Kyla. It seems like these young people lead pretty exciting lives, don't they?

KYLA: Yeah. I wish my life was as interesting.

GINA: In what way?

KYLA: I don't know. I wish I weren't stuck in school and could work and stuff.

GINA: Why do you think that would be so much more interesting?

KYLA: Well, you can go out and party with your friends any day of the week, you don't have homework and curfews, and you have your own money.

GINA: Kyla, do you know any young people who are out of school and working?

KYLA: Yeah. Kevin's brother, Pat, works at the health club. He's awesome!

GINA: Do you think that Pat stays out all night partying and then goes to work the next morning?

KYLA: Probably. I would.

GINA: Do you really think he does?

KYLA: Well, maybe not every night. But on the weekends, he does.

GINA: He probably does hang out with his friends on the weekends. No different than you do. But it's not every night, like the characters on TV, is it?

KYLA: I guess not.

GINA: Speaking of partying, what do the characters on that show do when they party?

KYLA: They go out drinking or something.

GINA: Does that mean that they're having a good time?

KYLA: That's what people do when they want to have fun!

GINA: Drink?

KYLA: Yeah, Mom.

GINA: Well, if they're always drinking, why aren't they ever drunk?

KYLA: 'Cause they're only drinking water in the glasses in real life.

GINA: So you're saying that if they were drinking that much in real life, they would be drunk?

KYLA: Probably.

GINA: In other words, you're saying that characters on TV can drink without getting drunk because they're not really drinking, but people in real life can't?

KYLA: Yeah.

GINA: So what's so fun about that?

KYLA: Mom, didn't you party when you were a teenager?

GINA: I did, but I used to wake up the next day feeling pretty awful. Partying may have been fun at the time, but the consequences weren't. I guess that's what concerns me about this show and some others. I never see anyone dealing with the real consequences of staying out and partying or any other action for that matter.

KYLA: What do you mean?

GINA: I mean that no one on *Melrose Place* ever spends the night throwing up or gets into a bad car accident because they were drinking and driving.

KYLA: So?

GINA: Well, I just think that the show is sending the wrong message, that's all. It's saying that it's okay to do these things and that there are no consequences for them. You yourself just said that there are consequences of drinking—getting drunk—that aren't shown.

KYLA: Yeah, but they do show consequences for some things.

GINA: Like what?

KYLA: Like if you cheat on your boyfriend or something and get caught.

GINA: Oh, sex has consequences?

KYLA: Yeah.

GINA: What are they?

KYLA: Your boyfriend gets mad and dumps you.

GINA: Any other consequences? Does anyone get pregnant or get AIDS or some other disease?

KYLA: Well, no, but everybody does it. Sex, I mean.

GINA: So, it's not a big deal?

KYLA: Sometimes it is. Lots of people are worried about sex.

GINA: Are you worried about it?

KYLA: Kind of. I mean, it seems like it's the only thing anyone ever thinks about.

GINA: It does seem to be pretty central on TV. Kyla, do you feel that the importance of sex on TV encourages you to engage in sexual relations?

KYLA: Kind of. I mean, I don't know.

GINA: I see that this is making you uncomfortable, so why don't you
    give it some more thought and we'll talk about it another time, okay?
KYLA: Okay.

Gina and Kyla did an excellent job of addressing the basic issues of
Teen TV, and although no one conversation can cover all of the topics,
Gina was able to get Kyla to think about some of the ways Teen TV
misrepresents teen and young-adult life. In many instances, Kyla didn't
agree with Gina, and Gina didn't try to convince Kyla of her views or
push the issue of sex when Kyla got uncomfortable with it. It is important to remember that TV Talk with teens can get sticky and if we want
our kids to really think about what they see and how it affects them, we
should approach these discussions as open dialogues with room for expression and disagreement on both sides.

9

"I Saw It on the News, So It Must Be True"
Navigating the News With Kids

"More Americans get their news from ABC!" is not just a clever jingle: it's a fact. More than 60 percent of Americans rely solely on television for their news, while only 23 percent read newspapers. Because of this, the last decade has seen a substantial decline in newspaper production, while the number of news and news talk shows on television has increased exponentially. Today, news or news-related programming—news talks, tabloids, talk shows and reality-based shows—account for almost 30 percent of network broadcast time, and entire cable stations exist only to provide viewers with twenty-four-hour news.

For adults and children alike, the news and news-related programming provide most of our information about the world around us. For children especially, who have few other resources for news information, TV news and news talks are extremely powerful influences on their developing opinions, ideas, and attitudes about the world they live in. And due to the sheer volume of news today, even very young kids are exposed to far more information than we ever were at their age. But unfortunately, the news, like all other TV shows, isn't an accurate reflection of the world; it is a highly constructed version of reality, subject to the same economic and commercial forces as the rest of TV and filled with the same kinds of problems.

Teaching children how to sort through the massive amount of information and watch the news with a critical eye is one of the hardest but most crucial jobs a TV teacher–parent has. In this chapter you will learn how to engage your children in thoughtful and critical discussions about current events and news programming and encourage them to use their critical TV-viewing skills to question the sources and validity of their information.

Let Me Entertain You

TV news wasn't always a circus parade of death reports, scandals, and movie promos. In the early days, it was a public service, necessary to fulfill FCC licensing requirements, which stated that TV stations had to provide programming that was "in the public interest." At the time, the news was seen as a necessary duty, and while not a money-maker, the news was respected and honored for the function it served.

Originally, this "necessary" TV news was only fifteen minutes long and consisted of one person seated at a table reading the news from a stack of papers in front of him. There were no fancy graphics, high-tech sets, coifed anchors, or video footage. There was no theme music or sports replays or silly comments about neckties and weather. There were also no commercial breaks. The news was simple, basic, and, to a large degree, useful to the people who watched it.

Then something changed. In the 1960s, when news about Vietnam, civil rights, and the space race was of vital importance to the country, TV news viewership increased dramatically. Audiences turned to TV for images of war, protest, and technological progress. Film footage became a crucial part of news reporting, and commentators, as anchors were then called, were some of the best known and respected of all public personalities. In the late 1960s, Walter Cronkite was deemed the "most trusted man in America."

News became a business, like everything else on TV. National news programs expanded to thirty minutes and then to an hour. Local news programs proliferated. Commercial airtime was sold. In order to attract the audiences necessary for advertising sales, news broadcasts developed more sophisticated production values. The anchors were hired as much for their attractiveness as for their journalistic skills. Sets became important design elements, complete with the sound effect of ticker tapes in the background. Music and graphics were added, and sports and weather, which interested a large segment of the viewing audience, became staple components.

The definition, context, and presentation of major news changed too. Gone were stories that required complex verbal explanations, replaced by stories that had dramatic video images to capture viewer attention. Political news took second place to emotional stories of individualistic heroics, fires, floods, crime, and social scandals. Local news became more sensationalistic than national news, but by the mid-1980s, both were making money hand over fist—billions of dollars annually. And in the late 1980s, when FCC licensing requirements were loosened and cable TV was deregulated, cable television stations—CNN, CNBC, C-SPAN, Court TV, and others—jumped in for their piece of the pie.

Today's TV news follows the news maxim, "If it bleeds, it leads." TV news directors define stories by their emotional appeal; a news director in Colorado even went so far as to say "a good story is one that brings a tear to your eye"! And although he doesn't espouse this notion, Robert MacNeil, a respected TV journalist, says that the idea behind TV news "is to keep everything brief, not to strain the attention of anyone but instead to provide constant stimulation through variety, novelty, action, and movement."

Tabloid programs like *Hard Copy* and *A Current Affair* set the pace for sensationalistic and scurrilous stories that win ratings and dollars, with network news not far behind. Our legitimate and once respected news programs are now filled with such fluff as the latest movie release or the E.Q. test, which enables you to determine your child's emotional intelligence by using marshmallows. And to further increase profits, news department personnel have been cut and stories are no longer always gathered by dedicated and hard-working investigative reporters but produced from news releases provided to the stations by politicians and businesses—complete with an outline of key points and made-to-broadcast video footage.

While our news content is being manipulated by profit-and-loss statements, the production values of news shows are being hyped to attract viewers. Hundreds of thousands of dollars are being spent redesigning sets and creating fancy computer graphics such as 3-D weather maps. Anchors and reporters are hired and paid according to their audience appeal, and whereas most of the lead national anchors are respected journalists and celebrity speechmakers, making millions of dollars each year, many of the newer and local reporters and on-camera talent are just that, talent (actors!) with nice hair, fancy clothes, and good tans. And to make sure the audience isn't bored for even a nanosecond, today's TV news stories are never longer than ninety seconds; in some markets, even lead stories are only fifteen seconds long! The average sound bite today is only seven seconds long! More and more, news outlets are relying on video, graphics, music, rapid-fire stories, and appealing anchors to convince viewers that their news is the most exciting show to watch.

Gone now is the idea of news as public service or as "serving the public interest." Today's news is pseudo-news, entertaining bits of fluff that lead viewers and citizens away from the really important information that truly affects our lives. In an effort to increase profits, TV news reporting has mostly become a circus sideshow, where the line between news and entertainment is so blurred that even the news outlets themselves can't tell the difference. *Time* magazine claims that "we've gone from the age of news to the age of entertainment," and revealed that "the public's attention is turning from substantive news to celebrity gossip."

Carl Bernstein, the respected Watergate journalist, recently bemoaned the state of today's news, saying that "lack of information, misinformation, disinformation, and a contempt for the truth or the reality of most people's lives has overrun real journalism." He argues that "today ordinary Americans are being stuffed with garbage" and claims the news media is in the process of helping to create "an idiot culture," in which average Americans know so little about the important workings of their country and the world that although we claim to be the most well-informed people in the world, we are possibly the *least* informed!

For children, this culture of infotainment can have a serious impact. Their developing worldviews are being influenced by a news industry that can't and won't provide them with real, full information on which to base their ideas. Instead, TV news insists fashion, trends, sports, and seven-second sound bites are important. We have already begun to see the effects of this "dumbing down" of news on our youth. Today, our nation's children don't know who their local politicians are or what is going on in Bosnia, Chechnya, Burundi, or even on their own city streets. They can, however, rattle off the names of all the recent movies, detailed sports statistics, or the social implications of people who wear underwear on their heads (or any other inane talk-show topic). My own students have commented that they are no longer sure what is important to know and what isn't.

Before we rush to condemn other forms of TV, we should look carefully at our news media and the effect they are having on our children's abilities to differentiate reality from fantasy, important information from distraction, and knowledge from fact gathering. Real TV-proofing begins and ends with the news media, and as parents it is crucial that we teach our children how to determine whether the information they are getting from the news is accurate and useful or merely infotainment designed to keep them watching until the next commercial break.

What Kids Say About the News

"I don't even watch the regular news. It's boring, and none of what they talk about has any meaning for me. I watch *The Week in Rock* on MTV or David Letterman if I need news. What's on those shows actually affects my life."

—*Craig, age 14*

"The only news I watch is sports or entertainment news. The rest of it is stupid. Who cares if Liz Taylor gets married again or if O.J. is guilty? And anything else they talk about on the news is just politics in some other place I don't know about or care about."

—*Jeff, age 15*

"I guess I never realized how much the news affected what I thought until I caught myself repeating something I heard on the news, word for word, as though it were my own belief."

—*Kathleen, age 17*

"I try to watch the news so I know what's going on, for school and all. I think I'm pretty well informed for a sixteen-year-old. I know what's important. I mean, if the news wasn't important, why would they put it on TV?"

—*Brianna, age 16*

Activity: Finding the "Show" in a News Show

It is important that children understand that news is an entertainment business, just like the other TV shows they watch, and that they begin to think critically about how entertainment values affect the kind of news that they receive. The following activity is an easy but effective way of helping children over the age of six recognize the difference between news and entertainment, and it can be repeated as often as desired with any kind of news, news talk, or tabloid show.

While watching the news, news talks, or tabloids with your children, have them look for entertainment elements in music, graphics, set design, costuming, lighting, scripting, and the like. Then follow up with these TV-Talk questions:

- What elements does the news program have that remind you of other TV programs?
- Why do you think those elements are there?
- What effect do they have on your thoughts about the news? Do the entertaining elements influence you to take the news more or less seriously?
- How do you think the anchors, reporters, hosts, and spokespeople look? What are they wearing? Does their appearance affect your ability to believe them? To like them? Do you have a favorite reporter or anchor? Who is it? Why do you like them?
- What does the set look like? Why do you think it looks that way? What impression are the producers giving you about the news? How does it affect what you think about the news?
- What do you like about the news? Which stories are more fun to watch? Which stories do you ignore because they are boring? Frightening?
- Do you think the focus on "fun" stories, video, graphics, and other production elements affects the news you receive? How?
- Does the news have to be fun and entertaining? Can you think of any news programs that don't include as many entertainment elements? Can you think of any that have more? Why are they different? How do the programs with fewer "fun" elements affect your understanding of the news?
- If you could produce a news program, what would it look like? What kinds of stories would you include? What would your anchors and reporters look like? What would be the purpose of your newscast?

Who Says It's News?

When I ask my students to tell me what they think is news, they often reply, "It's what's happening!" or "It's what the news says it is!" Media critic Neil Postman describes news as anything that the news producers think is interesting or important. While each definition is slightly different, they're all correct: News is what is happening in the world that is of import or interest to the consumer, and it is also what we know is happening, as told to us by the news businesses.

News is traditionally defined in journalism schools as information about events and occurrences that affect the lives and livelihoods of a specific population. That's a pretty broad definition, to be sure, and open to many interpretations. Determination of what is news, or news judgment, as it is called, varies from person to person. In the newsroom, the exact interpretation of what specific information is newsworthy each day is up to the discretion of the individual news directors at the individual stations.

Beyond this definition of news, there is another, unwritten definition of news that also affects news judgment: news is anything that people want to know about, anything that will make them want to watch the show. Consequently, there is a real conflict in the news business between news that is useful and necessary—news that news directors think people *need* to know about, even if it is unpleasant or difficult—and news that news directors think that people *want* to know about and will watch—no matter how inane or pointless.

Most legitimate news directors will try to balance their newscasts between the two types of news. Because of this mix, almost every newscast will contain some information that is not necessarily news you can use but is instead intended to lighten the mood or entertain the viewer. Most news outlets are veering more toward entertaining news rather than toward intellectually informing news, but the balance each day at each station is different.

The news judgment of the individual news director will determine what the lead story is and how much time or importance to give to any other stories. A half-hour network newscast only has about twenty-two minutes of program time, after commercials, and more than half of that is taken up with sports, weather, anchor banter, previews of upcoming stories, and what's referred to in the business as the "Happy Wrap"—the short, sweet little piece that concludes the program and sends everyone off to the next show in a good mood. Therefore, a regular network newscast has only about eight minutes of time to devote to real news.

What information goes into that eight minutes and how much of that eight minutes it occupies determine how important we think it is. Any crisis takes the lead, since it is what people want and need to know about, but other stories are placed in the newscast according to their news value and entertainment value. News and entertainment value are also determined in part by the kind of visual material—video footage—available on a story, since visuals are a great hook, and what kind of audience appeal there is for the information. If the president has just signed an important trade agreement, but the video is boring, it probably won't be the lead, or even get much more than a fifteen-second verbal mention, with a photo or logo in the corner. On the other hand, if there was a big fire in a local warehouse and the station can fly its helicopter over it, it will probably get the lead and at least a full minute of coverage. Why? The

---

Why Is It News?

To determine if a news story is important or has human interest, the
following criteria are applied by reporters, journalists, and news directors:

1. *Unusual.* If a dog bites a man, that's not news, but if a man bites a
   dog, that's news!
2. *Timeliness.* If an event happened three months ago, that's not news. If
   it happened this morning or is happening now, that's news!
3. *Local Interest.* What happens in a specific town is interesting to the
   residents of that town. What happens in this country is more relevant and interesting to us than what happens in another country.
4. *Importance of the People.* Nationally known figures—entertainers,
   politicians, sports stars—are more interesting than other people.

---

fire is more dramatic, more emotional, and will grab the audience's attention better than the story on the trade agreement.

By the end of the average local newscast, maybe four out of ten stories
will be real news, if you're lucky. A national newscast may contain more
minutes of real news but is also subject to the same demands for time,
video footage, and entertainment value as local news. National news also
has to compete with other national news shows, tabloid shows, and talk
shows for viewers. Consequently, national network news judgment is
often determined by what the other news outlets are showing and how
they present it.

The news judgment of news directors and talk-show producers around
the country affects what we know about the world: News directors and
news outlets are the gatekeepers of information, allowing only certain
information to be seen and heard by viewers, based on their opinions of
what we need and want to know. Since we assume that the information
they consider important *is* important, their versions of news dominate
our consciousness and our political debate, influencing everything from
public policy to our private lives.

It is critical that children understand how the decisions of national and
local news outlets shape their thoughts, opinions, and attitudes about
everything from politics to parties. Even if they never watch the news
themselves, children can see and hear the way the news affects others in
their own homes and schools. Parents and teachers often discuss current
events in the presence of children and often impart attitudes based on
news reports. Children need to understand that news doesn't just hap-

pen; nor does it always happen the way it is presented. The news is selected and shaped to sell to the audience, and this is why certain news stories make it on the news each night and others that are perhaps more critical are left on the newsroom floor.

What's on the News?

According to a study done by Jay Dover at the Center for Media Literacy, most stories in the news revolve around crime and murder, celebrity news, and what is called human-interest news—little stories about people and places with no real impact but with feel-good potential.

On one night of monitoring the 6:00 P.M. and 11:00 P.M. local newscasts in Los Angeles, Dover found that between 60 percent to 70 percent of the news stories involved crime, celebrities, or human interest, whereas 0 percent to 3 percent were stories involving economic or political news. The remaining 30 percent to 40 percent of the stories were about accidents or fires and issues of marginal interest.

Dover also did another survey looking at how children were represented during a week of local and national newscasts. He found that children were portrayed as criminals in 36 percent of the stories, as victims of crime in 32 percent of the stories, or as dead in 50 percent of the stories!

According to Dale Kunkel of the University of California, Santa Barbara, the news media does a terrible job of relating information that is pertinent to childhood issues and concerns to families—poverty, homelessness, child care, education—and that the "extensive coverage of crime and violence serves to displace other child-oriented coverage." In fact, many experts have noted that the number of crime and violence stories in the news not only exceeds the number of any other type of news story but is proportionately exaggerated compared to the amount of crime and violence in real life!

Activity: What Is News?

The following activity is excellent for helping children define news and learn to recognize the difference between news that we need to know and news that is only there to entertain viewers. Again, it is simple to do and only requires watching, talking, and listening and can be repeated as often as you wish, with any number of news-type programs.

While watching the news with your children, ask your children to make two lists—one consisting of stories your kids consider newsworthy

and another one of stories they do not consider newsworthy. Follow up
with these TV-Talk questions:

- Were there more news stories or non-news stories? Why do you
  think that is? What kinds of stories—crime, celebrity, et cetera—
  were most numerous? Which were least numerous? Why do you
  think that is so?
- How did you decide whether or not a story was newsworthy. Why?
- Do your criteria conform to the traditional definition of news? How
  is it different? Why?
- What criteria or definition of news do you think the news director
  and producers are using in this newscast?
- Why do you think the stories that appeared on the news were chosen? If there were non-news stories, why are they there? What
  effect do the non-news stories have on viewers?
- Were there any stories that should have been included, but weren't?
  What were they? How do you know about these stories? Would
  they be considered news or non-news? Why do you think these
  stories weren't on the news?
- What is the purpose of a newscast? Do you think that this newscast
  fulfilled that purpose? How do you feel about the news?
- If you were producing a newscast, what criteria or definition of
  news would you use to decide what stories to include or not to
  include? Would it be different from the news you already see?

How Accurate Is the News?

Most of us believe what we see and hear on the news to be true and
accurate as reported because the news appears to be up-to-date, authori-
tative, and run by experts. This is a fallacy. While the news industry
rarely fabricates news, it mixes facts with opinions, which can distort the
plain unadulterated truth.

Most of us believe that the news should report information objec-
tively. However, since pure objectivity is humanly impossible, the journalistic code of ethics requires only that reporters strive for balance and
accuracy in their reports. Unfortunately, many news stories are imbalanced nevertheless, presenting more opinion than fact, and while
opinionated news does not break any laws, it changes the way our information is presented and absorbed. Learning to distinguish between facts
and opinions in the news is crucial for helping children think critically
about the news.

Opinion Through Words

Anchor Voiceover: *"Bill Clinton today continued his triumphant campaign tour through Pennsylvania, Iowa, and Illinois, bringing his bridge to the future to the heartland of the Midwest. Cheering crowds greeted the president, who, only a week away from election day, still holds a commanding and almost unbeatable lead in polls against Bob Dole, who continues to stump in California, asking voters why they aren't outraged by the Clinton administration's ethical slips. Despite his forceful and sometimes bitter statements, however, Dole is facing an uphill battle in traditionally Republican California; voters there are simply not buying his message."*

Cut to: *Voter interview*

The most common way that opinions are expressed in the news is through the choice of words used to describe something. The way news reports describe people, places, and events, influences what audiences think and feel about them. In this example, taken from a real newscast on KNWS-TV, it is clear that the writer of the story was expressing an opinion through the words he used and thereby influenced our thoughts and feelings about Clinton and Dole.

Loaded words—adjectives and descriptive nouns—carry connotative as well as denotative meanings and are used frequently in news reports, talk shows, and other news programs. These words affect our opinions and, in some cases, actions. For example, on the nightly news, the leader of a country with whom America has a conflict might be described as an evil dictator, which justifies our anger and military hostility. An active protest might be referred to as subdued or rambunctious, either of which will affect how we feel about both the protesters and their cause. Words are a reflection of what a person thinks, feels, and observes, and journalists, just like the rest of us, are prone to choose subjective descriptive words when trying to express themselves. In their book *How to Watch TV News*, noted media critic Neil Postman and TV journalist Steve Powers say that because of the subjective nature of language, the TV news viewer "must never assume that the words spoken on a television news show are exactly what happened. Since there are so many ways of describing what happened, the viewer must be on guard against assuming that he or she has heard 'the absolute truth.' "

Helping children pinpoint loaded words and phrases in news reports is a good way to get them thinking about how language influences what they think and feel about current events. Encouraging children to locate and think about the use of language in news is also a great way to get them to pay attention to how language is used in other TV shows and commercials, too.

Opinion Through Pictures

What follows is a description of the videotape that accompanied the news story about Clinton and Dole.

Close-up of Clinton at rally—sunny day, flags and presidential seals are visible in the frame. Clinton looks impassioned and impressive.

Close-ups of cheering supporters—women, men, children, and minorities.

Long shot of a sea of Clinton-Gore signs.

Medium shot of Clinton with hands raised in the air.

Long shot of people applauding.

Close-up of toddler on father's shoulders, wearing a "Kids for Clinton" T-shirt and smiling broadly.

Cut to: Close-up of Dole at indoor rally. He looks dour and drawn, although animated.

Medium shot of passive supporters, some women, a man.

Close-up of male supporter looking upset.

The way in which people, places, and events are photographed for television news has a tremendous influence on our understanding of and reaction to what we are seeing. As we can see from the example above, the pictures alone give us an impression of a successful and well-liked Clinton, while Dole appears angry and unsupported.

Our thoughts and feelings about a person are affected by the way they are lit and filmed, and even by the setting in which they are photographed. For example, if we see someone photographed in low light, from a very low, extremely close angle, against a dingy gray background, we might not think that person is very trustworthy or even very nice. If, on the other hand, the same person were photographed close-up at eye level in bright but soft light against a colorful background, we might think that person was both nice and reliable.

The same is true of places. If, for example, we see New York City videotaped from a helicopter flying overhead on a crisp, clear night, filled with sparkling lights, we might think it to be beautiful, exciting, and important. If, on the other hand, we shot it on ground level, the same night, focusing on images of homeless people and steam rising from the subway gratings, we might think the Big Apple was a pretty dismal place.

Opinions about events can also be expressed and manipulated through the pictures we see of them on TV. A ten-person protest in front of the White House can be made to appear more dramatic and important by shooting low-angle close-ups of shouting individual people, signs, and reactions, or it can be made to appear insignificant by shooting it from the other side of the street, dwarfing the protesters and their cause.

Just as children learn to recognize the visual messages in other TV shows, they can learn to distinguish and dissect the way in which pictures in the news affect how they feel and think about what they are seeing. And since TV news is, more than anything, a visual medium, this skill is of vital importance. A fun way to get kids thinking about the visual meanings of images is to watch the news without the sound and see what the pictures reveal!

Opinion Through Editing

The second story in the news one night was about a local education issue— a vote as to whether a town should pay for students to attend the school of their choice, even if it is a private or parochial school. The story consisted of an anchor lead in, stating the problem, showing images of run-down public school buildings, crowded classrooms, and kids hanging out suspiciously on the playground, followed by an interview with a school board member, ineffectively explaining why funding shouldn't be taken from public schools, and three interviews with citizens. The anchor concluded with a brief statement about the upcoming vote.

Perhaps the most difficult forms of opinion to find are those expressed through editing. The simple process of selection and omission—deciding who and what will be shown—influences what we know and from whom we know it. For example, if a news station were doing a story on a local issue about education, like the one above, and the reporter wanted to get the opinions of regular citizens, she might go to a shopping mall and interview people. After an hour or so, she would have twenty interviews from which to choose. Which interviews does she choose and why? How does her decision affect what viewers think?

Let's say that the story is only fifty seconds long and thirty-five seconds are already taken up with reporter talk and an interview with a member of the school board. There are only fifteen seconds left in which to place these man-on-the-street interviews, which means that three very short interviews will fit. Out of the twenty interviews the reporter got, maybe ten are useless—either the people didn't articulate well, looked funny, or said virtually the same thing. So, there are ten good interviews from which to choose, and from those ten there are six women with children, two twenty-year-old shop clerks, a businessman, and a grandmother. The news team decides on one woman with two young children, the grandmother, and the businessman. The mother and the grandmother say that they agree with the issue, citing things like safety and educational advantage, and the businessman disagrees, saying something about the financial problems of the arrangement. What should we think?

The way the real story played out, viewers tended to agree with the issue because the mother and grandmother were more sympathetic and more believable than the businessman, who looked very uptight, uninformed, and spoke rigidly. In addition, the words and images used in the beginning of the story showed public schools in bad shape and implied that any alternative to crowded, deteriorating schools was better than the present situation. The school board member who spoke against the issue was not convincing. Was an opinion expressed by the news station through the editing process? Very much so. And since this story was the second story of the night, it is the opinion of the news director that it is very important, and so should be for us too.

This same process is applied in each and every news story. What do we show? Whom do we interview? What do we cut? Where does the story go? These are the basic conventions of journalism. And although many journalists and reporters aim to present balanced news stories, the problems of limited time, sources, human judgment, audience research, and oversimplification of information often create inadvertently imbalanced, opinionated reports.

While it is sometimes difficult for children to recognize opinions that are expressed through editing, it is important that they begin to look for them. As their own opinions about politics and social problems develop, they need to see how they are being influenced by the way in which news is presented and to question why they are being influenced that way.

Activity: Distinguishing Opinions From Facts

Although difficult for younger children, it is important that children over the age of nine or ten begin to discern fact from opinion. The following activity is a good one and can be accomplished simply through watching and talking. This activity can be repeated any number of times

The Camera Never Lies, or Does It?

Probably the most influential part of the news is not what is said but what is shown, and most people, children and adults, believe that the things that they see on TV news are both accurate and real because the camera never lies. Right?

Any camera person will tell you that the camera can not only lie, but it can also distort. A camera only records what the camera operator wants it to record; it sees only what the person behind it wants it to see. It is not omniscient or objective. Through composition, lighting, and angle, the camera operator can make things look different and even have different meanings. Decisions about *how* to shoot something can make a short person appear to look taller, a big gathering appear to look smaller. And decisions about *what* to shoot also affect what appears on the screen and what we know about what happens. For example, at a parade, the camera operator may choose to focus his lens on the cheering crowds, while ignoring the small group of protesters across the street. Is that a lie or a distortion? How does the camera affect what we know about the parade?

Additionally, in this age of public relations, many events are staged specifically for the camera to shoot and put on the news. In this case, while it is clear that the event happened, is it not a kind of distortion because it was staged and created especially to be photographed?

In their book *How to Watch TV News*, Neil Postman and Steve Powers say that the pictures on TV news shows can be as biased as the words and that a "reporter will direct the camera person to get shots that will tell the story *as the reporter sees it*" [italics mine], which means that although the camera may not actually be lying, it is only telling a certain version of the truth—the version that the reporter, camera person, editor, and news director want to tell.

and is sometimes easier to do if you can tape the news, then pause it and play it again to catch exactly what is said and shown.

Before watching the news, news talk, or tabloid show together, explain the difference between a fact and an opinion to your children and then have them pick one news story to follow in the newscast. Have them make a list of everything that was said or shown that was a fact and another list of everything that seemed to be an opinion. Follow up with these TV-Talk questions:

- What was said or shown that was a fact? What was said or shown that was opinion?

- How were the opinions expressed? Which words or phrases were "loaded"? Which pictures were used to make things or people appear a certain way? What effect did it have on the meaning of the story? What did it make you think or believe?
- Did you see or hear more opinions than facts? If so, why do you think that is? What would the story be like if you took out all the opinions? Can you think of any news stories in the broadcast you just watched that didn't have opinions?
- Why were certain people or places shown or interviewed? Were there any people or places that weren't shown or interviewed that might have changed the meaning of the story? Why do you think they were omitted? How does that affect the meaning of the story for you?
- Where was this story placed in the newscast? Why do you think it was put there? What does it make you think about the story? Is that an opinion?
- If you were going to rewrite this story, how would it be different? What would you show and say? Whom would you interview? What would you do to avoid adding your opinion? Is it possible to have a news story without opinions?

Talk Shows as News

There are many different kinds of talk shows on TV. There are early morning news-talk shows geared to women, featuring reports on dieting, food, health, exercise, parenting, entertainment, and an occasional political subject. There are daytime talk shows, conflict-laden free-for-alls in which the participants battle out the taboo social topics of the day. There are evening and weekend news-talk shows that pit experts against each other as they state their opinions about current events, and late night talk shows in which the hosts do a comic routine about something in the news, followed by interviews and performances by celebrities and authors, each of whom is pitching their latest work to the viewing public.

Talk shows are insanely cheap to produce, compared to fiction programs, and draw large audiences, as evidenced by the sheer number of them—at present writing there are more than sixty TV talk shows on each day! Although popular, many critics complain that these shows, especially the daytime talk-show circuit, are freak shows that bring all of society's tabloid news miscreants into the living rooms of America. Others claim that the evening news talks are nothing more than opportunities for pundits costumed as experts to get their opinion about the latest event firmly embedded in the national debate. Still others complain that daytime and late-night talk shows are only in the business of creating and manufacturing celebrityhood and support this statement by claiming that being on a talk show is the number-one goal of millions of Americans.

Whatever the complaints about talk shows, they are a vital part of our American information and news landscape. For many viewers, what is on a talk show is news—news about new products, new entertainment, new services and new ideas. It is news at ground level, providing millions of viewers with information that really affects their daily lives. In many ways, the news and information on talk shows is more important to the average American than what is happening in the halls of Congress or in some other country. It is certainly more entertaining.

Young Adults on Talk Show News

In a poll conducted by the Media Studies Center, only 22 percent of the population aged eighteen to twenty-nine claim to watch network news, while more than 40 percent say they get their political news from late-night talk shows. Moreover, only 15 percent of this population followed the 1996 elections in the news, and of that group, almost all of them relied on MTV's election coverage for their information.

As news, talk shows are subject to the same demands as regular news shows—brevity, excitement, and entertainment values. However, because the producers and hosts of these shows don't always claim to be hard news journalists, they are not required to present balanced reports or even to report on important subjects. They simply need to get audiences into the tent. This is as true of daytime talk shows as it is of "serious" evening shows like *Nightline* and *Larry King, Live!* Consequently, while many Americans get much of their news from these shows, the news they are getting is biased, sensationalistic, trivial, and in some cases, simply untrue. Even David Brinkley, a renowned journalist and one of the most respected talk show hosts of the last decade, admits in his book *Everyone Is Entitled to My Opinion* that his program, *This Week*, "isn't news. It's interviews and talk."

Regardless, these talk shows set the stage for what happens on the real news, providing both content and style to legitimate news programs and tabloid news shows. After all, the networks want to give the audience what they want, and if the news they want is what is on the talks, you can bet it will appear on nightly news too.

For children, who watch the talks more often than they do the real news, there are several dangers. Although the talks present some things in greater depth than does broadcast news, the subjects they cover are often trivial and sensational yet are treated with absolute seriousness. Hence, children come to believe that the latest fashion fad, celebrity scandal, or sexual deviance is serious business, more important even than what is happening in politics or economics. At the same time, the opinions expressed in these programs, and there are many, are accepted as truth by children who are unable to tell the difference between fact and opinion. Lastly, the emphasis on the entertaining quality of the news in these programs leads viewers to believe that all news should be emotionally gripping or entertaining, and that if it is not, then it must not be worth knowing.

It is important to note that while most of us would not encourage our children to watch these kinds of shows, they can have value in the process of teaching children how to think about news. On the talk shows, children can look for the more obvious entertainment values, question the validity of the information, look for how opinion is expressed, and discuss how they are affected by these programs.

Navigating Kid News

Everything we have already said about the entertainment values, selection of stories, and expression of opinions in news, news-talk shows, and tabloids also applies to kid news programs like *Channel One*, *Nick News*, and *MTV News*. The only difference is that these news programs have a greater influence on kids because they appear to be made for kids, by kids, and promote products that are marketed to children. Consequently, children are more likely to watch them but less likely to analyze them.

On kid news shows, stories are chosen for their appeal to youngsters and are frequently told from kids' perspectives, with interviews and images selected to express kids' opinions. For example, *Channel One*, the controversial school news show whose set looks almost identical to MTV's basement hang-out, features two nineteen- or twenty-year-old anchors in jeans and T-shirts and a twenty-one-year-old star reporter, Anderson Cooper, who travels from Bosnia to California talking about issues that are important to kids. Sometimes the stories cover current events in other countries, as well as domestic issues, but each week there

---

A Day in Talk-Show Land

The following topics and celebrities were featured on a selection of talk shows one fall day in 1996.

Today—Oprah Winfrey; Tips for Indian Summer Vacations
Good Morning America—Dealing with pain
This Morning—Actress Fran Drescher (*The Nanny*); preview of fall 1996 movies.
Kids These Days—Discussing death with children
Regis and Kathie Lee—Fran Drescher
Maury Povich—Bosses and miserliness.
Rosie O'Donnell—Dan Aykroyd, Bette Midler, Bryan Adams, and Sean Nelson appear
Jenny Jones—Makeovers; disapproving of a family member's mate.
Home and Family—Talk show hostess Sari Locker
Montel Williams—Presidential candidates' views on juvenile crime; violence and teen dating
Larry King, Live!—Whoopie Goldberg
Prime Time Live—Sarah Edmonston and Ben Darras, a real-life Bonnie and Clyde.
Jay Leno—Brooke Shields and Miss America
David Letterman—Bill Cosby

---

are several stories on the latest movies, TV shows, music, and trends, all selected and designed to appeal to kids and their pocketbooks.

Nick News, one of the best kid news shows, created and hosted by respected journalist Linda Ellerbee, often pits kids as young as ten against adults in debates about screen violence or other issues that directly affect kids. Recent specials have centered around kids and guns, elections, children's body images, and even welfare reform from a kid's perspective. Nonetheless, even this great news show features occasional kid-entertainment stories, such as interviews with child movie stars. *MTV News*, on the other hand, is much less focused on real current events, unless there's an election, and concentrates almost exclusively on music, fashion, sports, and entertainment news, with a recent week being almost completely devoted to Madonna's baby.

There is controversy surrounding news programs for kids, particularly concerning *Channel One*, which is shown daily in over 4,800 school districts and 12,000 schools around the country and features ten minutes of news interspersed with two minutes of commercials. *Channel One* is produced by Whittle Communications, a unit of Time-Warner, and provides subscribing schools with thousands of dollars' worth of free TVs and a satellite dish on the condition that the news program be shown each day. Several states, including New York and California, have banned *Channel One*, claiming that it exploits children and school districts. National public interest groups like UNPLUG! call for already subscribed schools to oust *Channel One*, saying the news it presents is not only biased but irrelevant and is really nothing more than an excuse to market junk food and sneakers to a captive daily audience of schoolchildren.

Channel One isn't the only TV news station marketing to kids in their classrooms. CNBC, CNN, and many other news outlets also produce school news programs for kids. Although informative, these programs also include advertising, much of it hidden inside shows that claim to be "commercial free." For example, CNBC has a program called *Smart Living*—a consumer-reports-like show for kids that features stories about "how to shop for jeans"!

Despite the controversy, kid news shows have value—both for kids, in exposing them to current events in a way that is understandable and meaningful, and also to parents and teachers, who can use these programs to teach children about news itself. Sometimes these programs themselves address problems with the news, helping children think about the purpose of news and its effects. *Nick News* often features stories about the media, including a special on how TV talk shows affect children!

If you have the opportunity, watch a kid news show with your children and be sure to point out the entertainment features, discuss hidden commercials, and ask your children about the importance and accuracy of the information presented. It's a terrific way to get kids started thinking about the news without being threatening or overwhelming. Of course, a great activity would be to have children write and produce their own kid news show for a real inside look into what makes the news and how news is made.

How the News Affects Kids

We have already seen that TV is always teaching and that children are prone to accept its messages, especially when those messages are cloaked in the appearance of authority, legitimacy, and reality. There are three primary ways that children are affected by news, depending on their ages and the kinds and amount of news they watch. But even if they don't

---

Channel One's Educational Goals

According to *Channel One* spokespeople, each daily newscast—10 minutes of kid-friendly news and two minutes of commercials—tries to meet five educational goals: To enhance cultural literacy; to promote critical thinking; to provide a common language and shared experience; to provide relevance and motivation; and to strengthen character and build a sense of responsibility.

Whether or not programs like *Channel One* achieve these lofty goals is debatable. Many of the 8 million school children who now receive *Channel One* report that the daily broadcast is virtually ignored by students, except when the commercials come on. Teachers also report mixed feelings about the program's academic usefulness, saying that while it may bring current events alive to children, it presents them in a simplistic and commercial way. A marketing expert had this to say about *Channel One*'s real goals: "School is the ideal time to influence attitudes, build long-term loyalties, introduce new products, test markets, and above all, to generate immediate sales!"

---

watch news at all, they can be affected by the news and its influence on others.

Fear

Shelly was trying to get her eleven-year-old daughter, Jenna, to come with her to the mall to do some Christmas shopping, but Jenna wouldn't go.

"Jenna, you like the mall, especially during the holidays—with all the lights and the big tree. Come on," pleaded Shelly. "Maybe we'll see some of your friends there."

"No. I'm not going. I don't want to go to the mall."

"Since when do you hate the mall so much?" asked Shelly.

"I don't hate the mall, I'm just scared," Jenna replied.

Shelly couldn't figure it out. "What are you scared of at the mall?"

"The news said a lady got robbed at the mall yesterday and they didn't find the robber and people are supposed to be careful," Jenna explained. "I don't want to get robbed, so I don't want to go until they catch the robber."

Children of all ages react strongly to the grisly reality-based violence on the news. The violence that is shown on the news has a more intense effect on children than the "fictional" violence in other TV shows and movies, and children often react with greater fear, increased aggressiveness, and deeper desensitization to the barrage of real violence they see on the news. Young children are easily frightened by the nightly assault of kidnappings, terrorist acts, robberies, rapes, and murders, and may react with nightmares and irrational fears, while older children are more susceptible to Dr. Gerbner's "Mean World Syndrome," discussed in chapter 7, and believe the world to be a more violent and mean place than it is. Even teenagers can be deeply frightened by the news; my high school students have commented that they think the news is the most frightening thing on TV.

In addition, the emphasis that the news places on scandals, crimes, and corruption among adults reinforces children's fear and distrust of adults. Many kids I know are afraid of adults, particularly those in positions of power—police, government officials, and even parents—in part because they have seen and heard on the news how mean, harmful, and vindictive they can be. My own son said it best one day when he saw me talking to a friend who is a policeman. "Mommy," he asked, "why are you talking to him? Policemen are bad. They beat people up!" Having never witnessed or experienced police brutality in real life, the only way my son could have learned such a thing was from TV.

Confusion

Ali and Natalie were discussing a current events project, for their ninth-grade history class, in which they were supposed to follow a news story about the Middle East for a week and make a report. Although both kids were honors students, this assignment was difficult for them.

"Did you watch the news last night?" asked Natalie.

"Well, sort of," replied Ali. "I watched it for a little while, then I switched to see the scores on the football game, and when I came back to the news, the only thing they said was that some important guy had said something, but they didn't say what he said. And then they showed some pictures of people throwing stones. So I switched to another station and they said something about people being killed, but they didn't say who killed them, and they showed the same pictures of kids throwing rocks. And on a talk show, they had some other guy talking about water rights, whatever that means!"

"I didn't understand it either," Natalie moaned. "So, what do we say in class today?"

Ali threw his hands in the air. "I have no idea. I'm totally confused."

In this era of twenty-four-hour, instantaneous, satellite-transmitted news, it seems like everywhere you turn there is new information to be processed and absorbed, a new crisis to be followed, another health hazard to be on the lookout for, or a new trend to be aware of. With so much news, it's difficult to know what to focus on, and for children of all ages it is mind-boggling. Kids are simply confused. Which information is important? Which isn't? What should I be concerned about?

While adults frequently follow news stories over a longer period and even read in-depth reports about the causes and effects of events in newspapers and magazines, children are left with partial stories, disconnected video shots, seven-second sound bites, and pat explanations. Younger children, who don't have the history background or the language skills to understand what is said or the context of events, are completely lost by news reports.

Students of all ages have told me that the news makes no sense to them, that it never answers their questions about events. It only throws some images and words at them, expecting them to understand. The result, my students say, is that they rapidly lose interest in the news. Probably the most telling example of this kind of reaction came from a fourteen-year-old student of mine who once asked me, "Why does the news matter, anyway? I mean, I never understand what they're talking about and there's so much of it; it can't all be important. Or is it? No one would ever be able to keep track of everything that happens. It would make you crazy! I'm lucky I can keep up with my classes, let alone what's happening in the world!"

Disinterest

> *Gavin and Adam were sitting in the back row of class listening to their teacher drone on about the upcoming presidential elections.*
>
> *"This is so boring!" Gavin whispered across the desk.*
>
> *"I know," replied Adam. "It doesn't matter, anyway. It's not like we can even vote! Like I really would, anyway."*
>
> *"Why can't he just tell us what the news says and stop analyzing it? He must be mistaking us for people who care."*
>
> *"Yeah," agreed Adam. "I'd much rather hear him talk about the World Series. Now that matters!"*

Around the country, scholars and political commentators have bemoaned the lack of voter participation and civic concern among the younger generation. While many attribute this decline in social responsibility to our failing educational system, it may also be fostered by the news media's lack of attention to and trivialization of important information. When the younger generation is being fed sensationalized news about O. J. Simpson or the newest action-adventure movie, why should they be interested in political or social events that are far less entertaining or dramatic?

Even before children reach voting age, this disregard of vital information has a negative effect on their emerging social and moral consciousness. When the news reduces information to entertaining seven-second sound bites and video clips, how could children possibly have enough information to think about the issues at hand? Moreover, since most adult news doesn't focus on issues or events that interest kids or are about kids, why should kids be interested in the news enough to struggle with an idea or an issue that is raised?

Cynicism about political and social issues also takes root during these years and again is fostered by a news media that focuses on scandals instead of real issues. What twelve- or thirteen-year-old could possibly have much faith or interest in the government or its leaders when all they hear on the news is who their leaders are sleeping with or some other scandal that makes the government and its leaders look bad? Many preteens and teens express a great distrust for our elected officials and their ability to govern because of what they hear and see in the news. Most of these kids also believe corruption is rampant in the government and that their own participation has little, if any, effect. Who can blame them? My students once told me the news has very little effect on them because they don't watch it and they don't care about it, and even if they did, they couldn't change anything, so why bother?

Hopelessness

Nat and Ellie were making plans to go to the movies on Sunday night, but Ellie was hedging, claiming that she had a big test first period on Monday and needed to study.

"Study? Are you kidding? What for?" asked Nat.

"Well, it's the second big math test this semester and I only got a C– on the first one. If I don't study, I'll fail geometry!" Ellie was trying to convince herself of the importance of studying, as much as she was trying to convince Nat.

"Look at it this way, Ellie," Nat reasoned, "if you go to the movies and don't study, is this test going to have any effect on your real life?"

"Well, no. I mean, it doesn't matter if I do well in school, anyway.

*There aren't any jobs that pay anything, and who knows, I might get
carjacked tomorrow and I will have wasted my last night studying for a
stupid math test!"*

*"There you go," Nat was on solid ground now. "And besides, it's not
like the world is going to change if you pass geometry or not. You don't
have that much power, and neither do I. So what movie are we going to?"*

The combination of fear, confusion, and disinterestedness results in a
feeling of hopelessness that pervades much of this younger generation.
While some of this despair is caused by deteriorating social conditions
in communities around the country, a great deal of it comes from the
disparaging and depressing news media, which consistently send the ominous message that the nightly murders, bombings, scandals, and problems are just "the way it is." The implication for kids who are already
scared, confused, and disinterested by the news is that if that's the way it
is, I give up because I can't change it.

Hopelessness is perhaps the most vicious of all the effects because it is
circular: if I can't change it and it depresses me, then I won't watch it, so
I will be even more afraid, confused, and disinterested than I was before.
After a short time on this downward spiral, your average teenager will
become a disinterested, depressed, and disillusioned young adult. I know
many such eighteen-year-olds, and it is not encouraging.

This feeling of hopelessness reaches beyond political action; it creeps
into youngsters' attitudes about school, work, relationships and even lei-
sure activities. What's the point of working hard at school if you can get
shot standing on a street corner? Why get a job and pay taxes if you
don't get anything in return but an uncontrollable deficit, potholes, corrupt police, and bad schools? Why get involved in relationships when
people are crazy and malicious and your girlfriend or boyfriend might
beat you or give you AIDS? Why do anything but party? Why ask why?

It's a formula for disaster but, fortunately, this vicious cycle can be
mitigated through the TV-Teaching techniques you have learned. Even
the most jaded teenagers can begin to develop a critical awareness about
the news media and how it affects their attitudes, beliefs, and opinions
about themselves and the world around them. Younger children, whose
ideas and ideals have not yet been deeply influenced by the news, can
benefit from learning early to question the news media and to look beyond the ads and the movie reviews to discern the important information.

If one of the goals of media literacy is to help children become truly
informed citizens of a democracy, we must help them see through the

messages of TV news and question not only the information and its usefulness, but also its sources and meaning for themselves and the country.

Kids' Reactions to News

According to a 1994 study by the advocacy group Children Now, more than 50 percent of the children surveyed said that they felt "angry, sad, or depressed" after watching the news. For young girls, that statistic jumped to more than 60 percent, and 71 percent of the children agreed that they "get sick and tired of seeing so much negative news on television." Sixty-six percent believe that "there is a lot of violence and crime . . . [and] the news media is just reporting what is going on."

Most significantly, a majority of children reported that they would like to see more stories about kids "doing good things" instead of as victims or perpetrators of crime, drugs use, and violence and better reporting on teen-related issues.

TV-Talk About News

Although schools often use the news as a supplement to the study of social studies and history, they rarely analyze the news for opinion, entertainment value, or how it might affect their students. Parents are still a child's best guide when it comes to navigating the news, helping them understand what information is important, why it is important, and how it is presented. No matter what your children's ages, talk to them about current events in a way they can understand. Answer their questions. Guide them to other sources of information and encourage them to watch different news shows to compare and contrast. Ask them about the news they watched in school and, most important, watch the news, news-talk, and tabloid shows with them and discuss what you see.

Generally speaking, children under the age of six should have little or no exposure to the news—it is too confusing and too frightening. You might consider saving your own news viewing for those times when very young children aren't present. From the ages of six to ten, children are better able to handle the news, but they should have limited exposure, preferably with parental supervision or with programs like *Nick News*, which are geared to children that age.

While most of your TV Teaching about news will be with children over the age of ten, even children who are not yet old enough to watch the news on their own will benefit from your early instruction and discussions. However with younger children, it may be quite a while before you can get to the deeper issues. Be content to get your kids thinking about the news in any way possible. Older children also need to start slowly, but with time, they will be navigating the news like pros.

As always, it's best to begin any TV-Talk conversation simply and with a sense of humor, focusing your initial questions on such obvious aspects as production elements and leading up to the more difficult questions about opinion and effect. Since children often have a hard time keeping up with the furious pace of a typical newscast, it is sometimes best to focus your conversation around one memorable story and build to the newscast as a whole. Another suggestion is to tape the news, so you can play it back and pause when necessary. And since everything that we have already discussed—commercials, advertising, stereotypes, values, and teen issues—applies to news, it is a great vehicle for TV Teaching about anything that pops up. Just stick with it, remember the rules of TV Talk, and you will initiate a conversation that will last a lifetime—both yours and your children's.

Discussion Starters for Kids

The following discussion starters can be modified for the ages of your children, but generally speaking, news and news shows can be discussed in depth only if your children are old enough to watch the news and to understand the words that are used. If you would like to begin discussions with younger children, start with something like *Nick News* or another kid-news show.

1. What is news? How do the news producers decide if a story should be on the news or not? What do you think is a good way to decide if something belongs on the news?

2. What is the purpose of news? What purpose does it serve for you? What purpose does it serve for others? What is the purpose of news for the TV stations that produce it?

3. How is news like other TV programs? What production elements or decisions affect the entertainment value of news? How do they affect the content of news, news-talk, and tabloid shows? How do they affect you?

4. What effect do the news-talk shows and tabloids have on real news? On people's understanding and concern for real issues? On you? How do these shows differ from broadcast news?

5. Do news programs have a responsibility to communicate information in a balanced and unbiased fashion? What does that mean? Do you think the news does that? If not, why is the news unbalanced or biased? What creates that impression?

6. Are facts more prevalent than opinions in news? Which shows are more opinionated? Which are more factual? How can you tell that an opinion is being expressed? Do you find loaded words or pictures? How do these opinions affect you? Others? Should news be factual only? Is it possible to eradicate opinion from news?

7. What issues are important to you? Do you see these issues discussed in the news? Where and how? What issues don't you see? Why do you think that is?

8. What stereotypes or values do you see most often in the news? How are women and minorities portrayed? Who are the anchors and spokespeople? What things seem to be most important, according to the news? Who and what are left out? Do you see hidden commercials in the news? What about the regular commercials?

9. How do you feel when you watch the news? Does it make you sad, angry, afraid, confused, or depressed? Why? Which kinds of stories bother you the most? The least? If you are confused, why are you confused?

10. If you could produce your own newscast, what would it be like? What would it look like? What stories would you include? What criteria would you use to determine newsworthiness? Would you present fewer stories in longer segments? How would you deal with opinions? Who would be your anchors, reporters, and spokespeople? Would you have commercials? Would this be news for kids or adults? Would you show it in schools? What would be the real purpose of your news show?

Sample TV Talk

Twelve-year-old Alicia had been studying Africa in her social studies class, and one of the assignments was to watch the news to follow the story of recent problems in Zaire and Rwanda. Alicia's father, Jerry, chose to

watch with his daughter one night before dinner. After the news, Jerry
decided to try a little TV Talk while they prepared dinner.

JERRY: Well, did you see anything about Africa?

ALICIA: I think so. Is Burundi in Africa?

JERRY: Yes. It's a small country in central Africa, next to Zaire.

ALICIA: Then they said that there were people killed in Burundi.

JERRY: Did they say which people were killed or why they were killed?

ALICIA: I don't know. Are Hutus people?

JERRY: Hutus are a tribe of people, yes.

ALICIA: Oh, I remember. Then they killed the Hutus and some other people had to leave.

JERRY: Who killed them?

ALICIA: I don't know.

JERRY: You know what, I don't either. They didn't say, did they?

ALICIA: How come?

JERRY: That's a good question, they didn't have time to explain it. And you know what else? They didn't tell us why they were killed, either, did they?

ALICIA: Nope. Dad, how am I supposed to learn anything about Africa if they don't tell you anything on the news?

JERRY: Well, you'll probably have to do some reading about it. Alicia, can you think of anything that you did learn from the news tonight?

ALICIA: Umm, that the guy who test-drives the fastest car in the world almost got hurt.

JERRY: And what else?

ALICIA: That moms are talking to each other on the Internet.

JERRY: Anything else?

ALICIA: Yeah, a building fell down with some people trapped in it.

JERRY: Do you remember where the building was?

ALICIA: No.

JERRY: It was in Cairo, Egypt.

ALICIA: Egypt's in Africa!

JERRY: Good! Tell me something else. Do you think that any of those things you learned from the news tonight were important things?

ALICIA: Ummm . . . important how?

JERRY: Important in that they affect your life.

ALICIA: No. Well, except for the Africa stuff, 'cause I need to know that for school.

JERRY: Okay, so if nothing except the Africa story was important, why is it on the news?

ALICIA: Because it's interesting?

JERRY: Probably. What do you think the purpose of news is? What is it for?

ALICIA: I don't know. Maybe to tell you things that you need to know?

JERRY: You're right. Why do you think the news has so much stuff on it that isn't important to know?

ALICIA: Maybe so you'll want to watch it?

JERRY: Exactly! So the stations can make money. Alicia, what kinds of things do you think should be on the news? What do you think is important to know?

ALICIA: Ummm . . . the weather, like if there's a hurricane or something coming.

JERRY: Good. Anything else?

ALICIA: I guess if there's some kind of danger—a war—or if someone I know is in trouble.

JERRY: Do you see those things on the news?

ALICIA: Sometimes. The weather, I do. Wars, I do.

JERRY: So, you're saying that the news doesn't give you all the important information you need, right?

ALICIA: I guess. Yeah.

JERRY: And most of the stuff it does give you is interesting, but unimportant, or important but incomplete, like the Burundi story?

ALICIA: Yeah.

JERRY: So how would you change it?

ALICIA: Maybe make the news shorter, so it only deals with the important stuff but tells you more about it.

JERRY: Good! You know, news used to be like that. There was no video, no music, no fast stories.

ALICIA: What happened?

JERRY: Oh, well, lots of things. The stations realized they could make money selling advertising if they made the news more entertaining for people to watch. So they added all that showbiz stuff, shortened stories, and added stories about things that they thought people would find interesting.

ALICIA: Oh, is that why they have all the stupid stories about movie stars and the guy who talks about slime in the ice machines?

JERRY: Exactly. I'll tell you what. Let's go look up some stuff on Zaire for school, and next time we watch the news, we'll look for other entertaining elements like the slime man, okay?

ALICIA: Okay.

Jerry and Alicia were able to touch on many subjects in this conversation—What is news? What is entertainment? Why is the news filled with non-news?—and even addressed the important idea that to be truly informed, you have to use a number of sources for information, not just the TV. Maybe next time they can address how the news makes Alicia feel.

PART III

SAFE AND HEALTHY SCREENS BEYOND TV

These days, television sets are used for many things beyond watching TV shows. Movies, videotapes, video games, and even the Internet all consume a large amount of time on our TV screens. In many homes, computers have become a new source of screen images. With all these other uses of screens come problems, ranging from excessive time spent in front of them to harmful messages about sex, violence, stereotypes, and consumerism.

The TV-proofing techniques you have already learned can be successfully applied to all screens and their uses. The information in the following chapters will help you tackle problems with movies, videos, video games, computer games, and the Internet to make all of your children's screen time safe and healthy.

10

Managing Movies and Videotapes
How to Encourage Selective, Critical Viewing

Many parents in workshops express special concern about the movies and videotapes that their children see. Movies seem to be even more violent, more inappropriate, and more unpredictable than television, and their influence on children is harder to monitor and control. Parents cite newspaper stories that tell of children committing unthinkable copycat crimes because they "saw it in a movie," and many are petrified of exposing their children to Hollywood's negative authority. Parents recognize that movies and videos have great appeal to children but wish that either the movies would somehow change or that their children would be less affected by them.

Like television, movies and videos are here to stay, and the best way to deal with them is to use your TV-Teaching skills to help children become more selective and critical of the movies and videos they see and to make all of their screen time safe and healthy.

Are Videos Better Than TV?

Today, more than 85 percent of American households own VCRs, and the average American family rents 2.3 videos each week. In an attempt to capitalize on America's video mania, more and more companies are producing videos for the home market. From recently released blockbusters to classics, TV-show reruns to documentaries, almost any kind of videotape is available for rental or purchase at your local retailer. For most of us, this growing market ensures that there is more variety in our average video store than on our TV each night, providing us and our children with ever-increasing viewing options.

Many parents, frustrated and frightened by the programs offered for children on TV, are taking advantage of the number and variety of children's videotapes available as a useful alternative for viewing times. There are a number of excellent children's videos on the market, particularly for preschoolers. For young children, these well-made videos are preferable to commercially televised programs.

Many children's video producers work closely with child development experts to create tapes that are developmentally appropriate for young children and are both entertaining and educational. Some of these tapes are based on children's educational TV shows and many are adaptations of popular children's books or children's stories from around the world. There are a number of quality children's videos that are nonviolent and stress the important values of ethnic diversity, equality, friendship, and peaceful resolution of conflict. Most of these tapes are free of advertising and ancillary marketing, so children won't be exposed to commercials for toys or sugary foods. With these tapes, parents can feel confident that their children are spending their screen time positively, while avoiding the pitfalls of early, harmful TV messages.

In addition to the obvious content benefits of these videotapes, using videotapes as an alternative to TV helps children learn selectivity in viewing. Many families keep a video library of children's tapes, and when children want to watch TV, they are given the chance to choose a specific video. Young children easily develop attachments to certain videos and will ask to watch them again and again. This can be very useful, as repeated viewing allows children to better absorb the material while offering parents an ideal opportunity to do some valuable early TV Teaching. However, just as with TV, it is important not to use videos as a time filler or a baby-sitter.

Where Can I Find Good Videos for My Kids?

While there are many good high-quality videotapes for children on the market, finding them can sometimes be frustrating. Most video stores carry only a few titles, and then they are often rented out by the time you get there. Sometimes, it seems as if there are no good children's videos anywhere and your only choices are cartoons, Disney, or the latest action-adventure release. Actually, there are many great tapes for children beyond the children's section in the video store.

Check the family section and you will find classic family films—

Sounder, Mary Poppins, The Sound of Music, or *The Love Bug,* to name a few. You will also discover a wide range of family films you might never have heard of. Family films are excellent choices for a family viewing night and provide perfect TV-Teaching time. The travel and documentary sections also contain a number of child-appropriate videos, like National Geographic nature and travel videos or tapes about different animals and habitats. Most children like these films; one of my son's favorite video activities is to "go on a trip" with a travel documentary about a foreign country. Older children might enjoy a video biography of a favorite athlete or performer, or even an occasional historical documentary.

The classics section offers tapes of classic TV shows, some of which are appropriate for older children, as well as classic cartoons and movies. Older children might enjoy a classic film or an episode or two of an early sitcom. The music section has a variety of tapes featuring classical, jazz, and children's live concerts and musicians from other countries. Young children love music, so a video from this section might interest them while at the same time exposing them to a wealth of musical styles and traditions. Even the how-to section contains videos that might be interesting to children. A tape on building a birdhouse or cooking might stimulate a project or encourage an experiment in the kitchen.

So even if your local video store seems devoid of any good children's videos, explore the other aisles for variety and encourage your local video store to purchase more quality children's tapes for the future. Remember, many video stores are able to special order tapes, so if there is a particular video you would like to rent or own, ask your video store to order it for you.

While looking for tapes, don't forget about your local library. People are unaware that libraries often have video collections and are able to order tapes that aren't available to the general public. You can often find some terrific children's videos in their collections, and a trip to the library for a video gives your child a great opportunity to check out a book to go with it!

Finding good videotapes does take a little more time than just picking up whatever is on the shelf at the video store, but the effort is worth it. A well-chosen, well-made video will provide your child with a positive TV experience, give you a good opportunity for TV Teaching and at the same time assure you that your child is not being exposed to any harmful screen messages.

Choosing Videotapes for Children

A trip to the video store can be a daunting task for parents. With so many videos claiming to be child safe, how can a parent choose a quality tape? What do you look for? How do you find the good ones? Below are a few suggestions to help you discover the better videotapes for your children.

Invest in a video guidebook. There are several very good video guidebooks on the market, and some deal specifically with movies and videotapes for children. Many of these guides offer detailed reviews of children's videotapes and are very useful when selecting from both popular and unknown titles. Take the guide with you to the video store to help you select tapes. These guides are also good resources for ordering tapes that aren't carried at your local video store.

Check the rating. A rating of G or PG is a good place to start, but remember that a rating is only a guide and not a definitive seal of approval for your child. You must still check out a video's particulars. Many children's videos aren't rated, however, so referring to your videoguide is an excellent way to check the tape's content and appropriateness.

Check the length. A two-hour video is too long for young children: They simply can't concentrate for that amount of time and will become fidgety and fussy. Generally, forty-five to sixty minutes is a good length for children under five. Most children's features are under ninety minutes, and most good videos for preschoolers are forty-five minutes long, at most. Decide if your child has the attention span for these tapes before renting them.

Use your videoguide and look for positive elements.

- Does the video contain anything that might frighten or upset your child?
- Does the video contain age-appropriate stories, characters, and conflicts?
- Does the video present positive, nonviolent conflict resolution?
- Does the video portray women and minorities in positive, nonstereotypical roles?
- Does the video contain child-appropriate humor (no sex jokes or insults)?
- Does the video offer an interesting cultural or educational experience?
- Does the video move at the appropriate pace for your child?
- Does the video encourage positive values and behavior?

The more positive elements, the better the tape.

Avoid "toy movies." Some children's videos are really no more than long commercials for the toys that go with them. Unless you intend to make a trip to the toy store after watching the tape, try to avoid these videos. Frequently, these videotapes contain ads for the products before the show starts and after it is over, so if you must get one of these tapes, fast-forward to the start of the movie and turn the tape off when it ends. Look instead for videos that are based on popular children's books and take a trip to the library afterward. For older children, remember that a video that may be appropriate might contain ads for videos that aren't. Take care with previews.

Ask friends for their suggestions and reviews of videos. Most kids' movies make the rounds, and within a few weeks or months all of your child's friends will have seen a particular movie or tape. If your child hasn't yet seen a video or movie, ask other parents for a review. You might also ask other parents for their suggestions on appropriate movies and tapes. You never know: they may have found a great one that you didn't know was out there!

If you are unsure of a video's content or appropriateness, preview it before showing it to your children. You are the best judge of what is appropriate for your children, so if you are still not sure about a particular movie or tape, rent it and watch it by yourself before deciding whether to show it to your children. After all, there's nothing more distressing than playing a tape you thought was fine and discovering that the first five minutes are filled with graphic violence!

Surviving the Video Store Scramble

With so many videos to choose from, it's no wonder that parents and children walk into a video store and instantly become confused. Often, everyone scrambles around, looking for something that they wouldn't mind watching that night, then eventually settle on whatever happens to be on the shelf. More often than not, most of us leave the store without the video we wanted to see but with an armful of other videos, some of which may be of questionable quality or simply not suitable for our kids. Older children, who are making their own video selections, are particularly prone to this, but all of us get easily overwhelmed when faced with a warehouse full of tapes. Here are a few tips to help encourage video selectivity in older children and avoid the video store scramble for all of your kids.

*   *   *

The Toy Chest

Does your child's toy chest look like the backlot of a Hollywood studio? Do TV- and movie-inspired toys, books, and clothes top Christmas and birthday lists? If so, you will be interested to know why that is.

Merchandise sales of TV and movie products make up a large percentage of the profits for producers and studios. In 1993 alone, character- and merchandise-generated sales reached $15.8 billion in the United States and Canada. In recent years, that number has almost doubled, thanks to increased efforts by Disney and TV producers. Licensing and merchandising do not just encompass toys, however. Videotapes, books, CDs, clothing, snack foods, and even dinnerware are all part of the licensing and merchandising blitz.

TV and movie executives are very interested in licensing and marketing, and the sales potential of ancillary products can often determine whether a movie or TV show gets made. Roger Strode, a licensing and merchandising executive in Hollywood says that "merchandising has become a much larger part of the formula for studios. When someone comes to the studio with a script, they're looking for merchandising opportunities."

So next time you take your kids to see a new movie or let them watch a new kids' TV show, prepare for the onslaught of "buy me's." After all, the studios are going out of their way to make sure your children's toy chests, wardrobes, and even diets are licensed and paid for!

Read your videoguide. Before going to the video store, sit down with your children and the videoguide. Ask them to tell you which video they are interested in renting and read about it. Familiarize yourself with the videos that are available and read reviews, if they are too recent for your guide. Don't go to the store unprepared or you will end up being talked into a movie you aren't sure of. If in doubt, take the videoguide with you to read up on tapes before renting them.

Have a specific video in mind when you go to the store. Most people go to the video store to get a movie, any movie, depending on what is available. To avoid the video store scramble, have a specific video and one alternative in mind when you go. If the store doesn't have the video you wanted, go with your alternative. If the store has neither videotape, go home empty-handed. It may take awhile to get used to this, but it prevents you from renting a video no one really wanted to see or which may be questionable.

Rent only one video at a time. An armful of videos is a perfect setup for a fight about TV time use, and helping children learn to bring home only one video is a valuable lesson about selective screen use. If you have more than one child around the same age, encourage them to compromise on one movie. If your children are of vastly different ages and developmental stages, allow each child to select only one video. If you are planning to stock up on videos for a long weekend or vacation time, allow each child to select only one tape and compromise on a family video. Setting limits on video rentals and sticking to them is an important step in managing the amount of time your children spend in front of the TV set and making all screen time safe and healthy.

Go the video store less often. The average American family rents videos two to three times each week. That means that most people are not being very selective about the videos they rent or the time they spend watching them. Try to limit your trips to the video store to no more than twice a week and work toward going only once a week. More time between video rentals helps encourage selectivity and gives both you and your children a chance to think about what you have seen and would like to see.

Going Out to the Movies

Everyone loves going out to the movies, but going to the movies today is not nearly as simple or carefree an activity as it used to be. Cineplexes and multiplexes present parents with some very challenging situations. Since many of today's movies are simply unsuitable for children, despite their rating or advertising, an unprepared trip to the movie theater can be a recipe for disaster. Insuring that your children's movie outings are positive screen experiences requires just as much diligence as helping your children choose a video movie or TV show for the evening.

Choosing Movies Safely

Movie producers, just like TV producers, keep their jobs by aiming their products at the largest possible audience, and, consequently, they fall victim to the same formulas and themes. Sex, violence, and insulting humor are standard fare in today's movies, even in children's films, and, therefore, a movie that claims to be child safe may not be. Below are some suggestions to help you and your children be more selective about the movies they see.

*   *   *

Movies on TV

It has been noted that movies of all kinds tend to have more extreme violent and sexual content than regular TV shows. In fact, the worst offenders of violence and sex on the small screen are the premium cable movie channels. HBO, Cinemax, the Movie Channel, Showtime, and the satellite movie services show first- and second-run feature films from theaters that have almost twice as much violence and sex as network TV. Many parents have addressed the problem by flocking to TV and satellite locking devices, like the one offered by DSS, but another solution is to make a special effort to seek out alternatives to cable and satellite fare. Helping children learn to choose videotapes of movies selectively is your best defense against unwanted and unplanned screen nasties and provides you with ideal TV-Teaching time.

Use movie ratings as a guide only. Movie ratings can be deceptive and should not be the only way you determine if a particular movie is appropriate for your children. The MPAA ratings board comprises a group of individuals whose job it is to decide if a movie is suitable for certain ages and their decision is essentially based on standard public-tolerance levels. The MPAA board looks at the type and amount of violence shown, sexual content, or how much foul language is heard to determine what might be least offensive to the majority of people. The ratings board does not look for positive things. They do not base their decisions on whether or not a film portrays minorities and women accurately, if the film contains examples of nonviolent conflict resolution, positive values, or child-appropriate humor. Even board members admit that a movie's suitability is often determined by what might upset parents, not by what is good for children. And they aren't necessarily the same thing.

When looking at a movie's rating, remember that ratings are only a guide, not a definitive child-safe seal of approval. You must look beyond the rating to determine not only if the movie is potentially harmful but if it might contain something positive for your child.

Read reviews. Movie reviews are good sources of information regarding a particular film's appropriateness and appeal and a good way to help you and your children select films. Although a review is simply one person's opinion about a film, reviewers often go into greater detail than the thirty-second ad, preview, or poster for the movie does. Reviews will warn you of possible problems and will tell you about climactic scenes, performances, and thematic content so that you can be prepared when you and your children see the film. It's a good exercise in critical thinking to also have children read reviews and discuss their accuracy after they see the movie.

Look for positive elements. From reading reviews, seeing ads, and talking to other people who have seen the movie, try to determine if the movie has any positive elements.

- Does the movie portray minorities and women in non-stereotypical ways?
- Are there examples of positive, nonviolent conflict resolution?
- Is the humor funny without being insulting or sexual?
- Does the movie encourage positive values or behavior?
- Is the movie well made, with interesting production elements?
- Does the movie offer your child opportunities for follow-up activities that don't include buying a toy?

If the positive elements outweigh the negative ones, you have probably found a good film.

Ask friends for their opinions about a movie. Sometimes another parent's opinion about a movie is an ideal way to determine if the movie is safe for your child. Ask questions. Did they think it was too violent? Did it encourage any positive values or behavior? Was there bad language or inappropriate sexual content? How did their children react to it? Ask other children what they thought about a movie too. They will tell you if they didn't like it or if it frightened them.

When in doubt, preview the movie before your children see it. Once again, you are the best judge of what is best for your children. If there is a movie that your children are desperate to see but you are still unsure, try to see the movie first. Although this is a time-consuming, expensive option, it can mean the difference between a negative movie experience for you and your children and a positive one. If previewing the movie is not possible, see it with your children and be ready to help them understand anything that might be upsetting or harmful. If at all possible, try to delay until the movie is released on video, so you can rent it, watch it together, and talk about it in greater detail.

Avoiding Multiplex Madness

Not long ago, parents and children went to the movie theater to see a specific movie, and usually, only that movie was playing at that theater at that time. If there were other films showing, they were at vastly different times: Children's films often played in the afternoons and early evenings, with more adult fare reserved for later in the evening. With such limited choices, it was easy for parents and children to avoid the temptation to see an inappropriate film or even a preview for one.

But today, most theaters are maddening multiplexes, conveniently showing up to 20 movies at the same time, ranging from the potentially child-safe to the absolutely unsuitable. With so many movies to choose from, all attractively advertised outside and inside the theater, it is not uncommon for parents and children to find themselves sitting through a movie they never intended to see or one that is inappropriate. Older children who go to the movies on dates or with a group are often tempted by ads and wind up seeing a movie that you would probably dislike.

Below are some helpful suggestions for avoiding multiplex madness and helping your children make the most of their movie experiences.

Don't use movies as a time filler or baby-sitter. Using movies as a time filler or a baby-sitter is just as harmful as using TV inappropriately. Don't go to the movies for "something to do," but rather because there is a specific movie you or your children want to see. Help your children become choosier about what they see and when they see it by making moviegoing a selective and conscious event.

Choose movies before going to the theater. Waiting to choose which movie to see until your arrival at the movie theater is a surefire formula for a disappointing or potentially detrimental experience. Check your local listings for what's playing and when and have a plan before you go to the theater. Read a review or two before choosing a particular movie. Encourage older children to read reviews and make conscious choices too. It's hard to be unpleasantly surprised if you know what you're going to see.

Go to the movies with your children. Whenever possible, go to the movies with your children and talk to them about what they see. Use the movies as teaching time to discuss characters, stories, production elements, and themes. Encourage your children to think about what they see at the movies, not just eat candy and popcorn.

Try a foreign film or a museum film. After years of multiplex Hollywood movies, it is easy to think that all movies are alike—big stars, big explosives and predictable stories. For variety, check out your local museum or alternative theater which shows foreign or independent films. Look for animation specials and appearances by filmmakers, which may be of interest to older children. If there is something appropriate, treat yourself and your children to a different kind of movie experience and use the opportunity to expose your children to film as art, rather than as sheer mass market entertainment.

Go to the movies less often. As your children become more selective about the movies they see, a naturally limiting effect occurs. You will discover that they go to the movies less frequently, but when they do, they get more from the experience. Until this new way of going to the movies sets in, try to limit your children's movie outings to twice a month. Since movies generally stay in theaters for two or three weeks, even if your kids only go to the theater every other week, they won't miss any film they really want to see.

TV Teaching With the Movies

Movies and videotapes offer you some of the very best TV-Teaching opportunities, whether it is a lesson on selective viewing or one about stereotypes or justifiable violence. Movies on tape allow you to pause, rewind, and fast-forward to particular scenes if you want to talk about them. And, because of the preplanning involved in choosing movies and videotapes, you and your children will have lots to talk about while watching.

Before going to the movie or watching the tape, choose something to look for. You might decide to look for stereotypes, how conflicts are resolved, or certain production elements. You could even plan to discuss the accuracy of the movie ad or review. Refer back to the sections in this book that deal with certain types of programs to gather ideas for discussion. And once again, remember the rules for effective TV Teaching:

- *Respect* your child's desire to watch this movie or video.
- *Observe* the movie or tape for points of interest and discussion.
- *Listen* to your child's comments without judging.
- *Question* him gently about his responses to the movie and the things you see in it.
- *Reinforce* the positive comments your child makes and the things that are positive about the movie or videotape.

Even a bad movie or video choice can become a great lesson in critical viewing. It might seem a little awkward at first, but helping your children use movies and videotapes consciously and critically reinforces the idea that all screen time is a conscious, critical choice and can be a safe and healthy activity.

11

Challenging Video Games, Computer Games, and the Internet
New Media, Old Messages

Children today spend as much or more time playing games on their TVs as they do watching programs, videotapes, and movies. A recent survey showed that children in homes with Nintendo or Sega systems spend an average of three hours each day playing and that young boys between the ages of five and fifteen make up 60 percent of the players. Video games are the most popular "toy" in America today, topping many children's Christmas and birthday lists, and the video-game industry posts sales in excess of $7 billion from purchases of games, video-game-themed breakfast cereals, action toys, clothing, cartoons, magazines, and even whole cable stations devoted entirely to game playing!

In addition to the voluminous video-game market, the proliferation of home multimedia computers has created a market for computer games, which are, in effect, little different than the video games that already appear on our TV screens. While there are many wonderful video and computer games that are educational or nonviolent, studies reveal that children prefer the violent ones, and statistics show that children who play computer games at all spend an average of three hours playing them each day.

Concern about the prevalence and content of video and computer games led to a 1982 ruling by Surgeon General C. Everett Koop, who said that video games were producing "aberrations in childhood behavior." While many parents and teachers complain about the way children are affected by video and computer games, some researchers claim that video and computer games are wonderful teaching tools, helping to promote growth in children's self-esteem and other developmental processes. Other researchers have been looking into the effects of violent video games on children's behavior, but have found no conclusive evidence that video and computer games cause aggression or violence.

As computer technology develops, concerns about children and the Internet have surfaced among parents and teachers. Citing news reports about pornography on the Net, parents have started using blocking devices, which claim to keep children who surf the Net from finding Web sites that are dedicated to illicit and illegal subjects. Since the Net is the fastest growing media technology in the world, accessed by millions of children in homes and schools, other concerns about the Net and its implications for children are, justifiably, surfacing.

Many of the TV-proofing techniques you have already learned will help your children use video games and computers constructively and safely, and in this chapter you will learn how to apply them to make all of your children's screen time conscious, selective, safe, and healthy.

Why Do Kids Like Video and Computer Games?

Parents around the country complain that their children are like little addicts when it comes to video and computer games; they simply won't stop playing, and the goal of reaching the next level is almost obsessive. What is so great about these games, and why do our kids like them so much?

Several studies have been done searching for the answer to why kids like video and computer games and the results have been revealing. Study after study indicates that children like these games for the following three reasons:

- Skill attainment and reinforcement, in which children easily and quickly advance to higher levels and are rewarded for their actions.
- Vicarious power, in which children identify with strong and powerful characters through emotionally appealing fantasy.
- Control, through which otherwise powerless children can manipulate and affect their environment.

Children are also attracted to the visual and aural elements of games. Researcher Patricia Marks Greenfield says that "video games are the first medium to combine visual dynamism with an active participatory role for the child." In other words, video and computer games take the appealing

---

What Makes Video and Computer Games Fun?

In the 1970s, researcher Thomas Malone identified three elements of video and computer games that make them fun to play.

- *Challenge*—in which there are multiple clear goals and variable degrees of difficulty.
- *Fantasy*—emotionally satisfying fantasies, such as the fight against evil or the rescue of a victim. Fantasies enable children to become emotionally involved in the outcome of the game.
- *Curiosity*—hidden information, surprise elements, and visual or aural elements that keep the child interested in playing.

If you examine your child's favorite video and computer games, you will probably find each of these elements to be present.

---

elements of television—the fantasy visuals and sounds—and allow the child a measure of control over the outcome, which TV doesn't do. Video and computer games are essentially interactive television, with a few other surprises.

Children also like video and computer games because of the promise of perfection that is offered. Figuring out how to "beat the game" or get the highest score are a large part of the games' appeal to kids. According to researcher Sherry Turkle, the promise of perfection—even immortality—is alluring because nothing else in a child's world promises such an ideal. Although achieving perfection in a game is difficult, the games are designed to make it seem easy by providing children with little reinforcements and encouragements along the way. Turkle also claims that this is perhaps the most "addictive" element of the games, since attaining perfection requires the child's undivided attention over a long period of time.

Perhaps the most appealing aspect of video and computer games is that they have hard-and-fast rules, which give children a badly-needed sense of consistency and structure and promise simple solutions to problems. In a video or computer game, actions are clearly spelled out. You can only move this way or that way, and if you make the right move, you will solve the problem, whether it is beating up your opponent and winning the game, or finding the coin that will help you unlock the answer to the mystery. Sherry Turkle believes that this "rule-governed world" is the holding power of all computer and video games and provides children with a predictable and controllable environment.

Knowing why our kids like to play video and computer games will help us understand the pull these games have and the importance of monitoring their use, but equally as important, and in many ways of greater concern, is knowing what our children are learning while they play and teaching them how to question those messages.

What Kids Say About Video and Computer Games

"My favorite game is Super Mario Brothers. It's fun to make Super Mario jump and fly. I like to get points. Someday, I'm going to get the most points of everyone and be the champ!"

—Evan, age 5

"I like to play videogames even more than I like TV because with video games you have control over what happens, instead of just sitting there. Besides, you can't win on TV."

—Christopher, age 8

"Whenever I play Nintendo I feel strong. Sometimes, when I come home from school and I've had a bad day, like some kids were picking on me or something, I play for awhile and I feel better."

—Dean, age 9

"My friends and I like to play video games to compete with each other and see who can get the highest score. We keep track, and every week we have a competition. I've won most of them, so it kind of makes me the best of all my friends!"

—Isaiah, age 14

What Do Children Learn From Video and Computer Games?

Video and computer games are a form of mass media, and as such they contain value messages that teach children about the world. Like TV shows, different video or computer games teach different lessons. Violent video games, for example, teach that violence is the way to solve problems, that violence has few or no real consequences, and that violent behavior is justified in the name of good. Other video and computer games teach lessons about gender and occupation stereotypes. Some educational games can actually help children learn about specific subjects such as reading, math, or science, and many games teach lessons about perseverance.

Regardless of the content of a game, all video and computer games teach the same lessons about problem solving, competition, winning, and success; lessons that may seem positive on the surface but which can actually be detrimental to a child's progress in learning to relate to the real world.

Success

The world of a video or computer game is a very concrete place—there are specific rules to follow and prescribed ways to win. This rigidity is necessitated by the fact that the technology—the computers and programs that run the game—has clear rules about how it can work. You must click on this object to make it do something or make these moves to advance. If these rules and patterns aren't followed, the player cannot achieve success. On the surface, this message about rules and formulas can be interpreted as a positive one—we all have rules to follow—but the underlying message is actually quite harmful: Following rules and instructions is the only way to success.

While it is true that there are rules in the real world, there are not always clear paths to success. In his book *Video Kids*, researcher Eugene F. Provenzo Jr. says that children who spend a great deal of time with video and computer games are prone to accept the rule-driven, ordered world of the game as true and that when they try to apply its techniques to the real world, they are frustrated by the absence of hard-and-fast formulas for success. Other researchers argue that the preprogrammed nature of the games only supplies children with an illusion of control and freedom, while providing no real opportunity to experiment and no skills with which to evaluate real-life situations. I know a ten-year-old boy who was so frustrated by the variations of the real world that he asked his mother to create a rule book for him so he would know exactly how things worked and what he had to do to get what he wanted! Now, wouldn't such a thing be useful to all of us?

Problem Solving

While the makers of video games insist that their games teach positive problem-solving skills, researchers have argued that the skills games require are inadequate for solving problems beyond the game, and rely too heavily on instinctive behavior rather than on thoughtful decision-making.

For example, one of my son's computer games requires the player to solve certain problems—finding a key, acquiring moon rocks, and purchasing parts to rebuild a spaceship—in order to get home from the moon. On the surface, it appears that this could be a challenging game for a six-year-old, but the problems and their solutions are actually quite simple and unrealistic. The game tells you exactly what you have to do to find moon rocks or buy engine parts and some of these actions include playing hide-and-seek with a moon creature, who gives you the rocks if you win, or going to visit the man in the moon, who pulls out spare parts from his garage! These problems have little or no relationship to problems in the real world, and these solutions are not exactly thought provoking—or even real solutions! Once the player has gone through the game once, he knows how to solve the problems and all he has to do is repeat what he did the first time. This is problem solving through rote memorization. Some challenge!

The effects of these messages are actually dangerous to a child's development of problem-solving skills. In the real world, problems aren't solved by a quick karate chop or by swinging from a vine to rescue the stranded baby elephant! And, in the real world, the same action doesn't always produce the same result. Eugene Provenzo says that "the games do little or nothing to help the child develop an inner culture, a sense of self, an awareness that while the world provides challenges and problems, resourcefulness and the use of one's imagination and knowledge of self are an important part of being able to confront those challenges."

Competition and Winning

Almost every video and computer game is based on the idea of competition; either against an opponent, the clock, or oneself. Winning, which can be accomplished any number of ways, is the desired result. The danger of this emphasis on competition and winning is that it reduces all challenge and achievement to black and white; either you win or you lose. Children who frequently play these games often have trouble with competition and winning in the real world.

My neighbor's son and his friends are avid video game players and winning is very important to them. If one child loses a game, he immediately falls into a depression, feeling as though he is inadequate. Rematches are constantly demanded, and fits and punching fights on the living room floor are not uncommon. When this attitude takes itself into another activity, it wreaks havoc. Not everything needs to be competitive, but these little boys are so fixated on winning and losing that even a simple game like catch becomes the Super Bowl.

Another way this win-lose mentality affects children away from the video or computer game environment is seen in classrooms around the country. Teachers have reported a substantial increase in competitiveness in elementary classrooms, even when the class is designed to be noncompetitive! Concerns about who got the best grade or who made the best drawing erupt into arguments and tears! Even more alarming, a first grade teacher once told me that she overheard a group of kids discussing a cooperative project as though it were a video game, setting rules for competition, defining characters and levels, and explaining what actions would result in winning the project!

Stereotypes and Values in Video and Computer Games

While many video and computer games appear to be teaching important life skills, such as perseverance and problem solving through the attainment of specific goals, many of the goals pursued have little real significance outside the game and, while the goals may reflect certain values and beliefs, they are not necessarily admired or even acceptable.

Studies of video and computer games reveal that the most popular games contain messages about the value of violence and deeply offensive stereotypes of women. Researcher Terri Toles found that out of 100 video games, 92 percent had no female characters, and of those that did, 6 percent portrayed them as sexy victims of abduction or assault who had to be rescued as part of the game. The 2 percent that showed women in roles of power portrayed them as evil metal-breasted amazons who had to be defeated through violence.

Social psychologist Philip Zimbardo believes that many of the stereotypes and value messages of video and computer games "feed into masculine fantasies of control, power, and destruction," and since the primary players of video games are young males, these messages and stereotypes are potentially dangerous.

Game-Proofing Your Kids

Video and computer games, like TV, are not going away anytime soon. Nor are they likely to become free from any objectionable, violent, or value-laden messages. While we can ban the use of video or computer games in our homes, it is a prohibitive measure that will not help our children learn to use video and computer games consciously and critically.

The best way to make video and computer games a healthy and safe activity for your children is to use the same techniques you have already learned for TV proofing. If your children are playing video and computer games too often, help them learn to use them for a conscious purpose, not out of habit or boredom, which will cut down on the time they spend playing. If you are concerned about the negative messages of video and computer games, work with your children to select appropriate games and discuss their messages, just as you would with TV, videos, and movies.

The following guidelines will help you and your children learn to make video- and computer-game playing a conscious, selective, and healthy choice in your home.

Determine when video and computer games are being used unconsciously or out of habit. Fill out the Family TV Use Chart for video and computer game use. As with TV, pay careful attention to why the games are being played. Mark each time that the games are played unconsciously or out of habit and strive to eliminate those times, just as you have done with TV. Avoid using games as baby-sitters or time fillers. If children want to play a game, ask them what game they want to play and why they want to play it! If they can't answer with specifics, deny the request.

Determine appropriate times for game playing. As with TV, it is important to decide when game playing is a choice in your home. Set some guidelines. In our house, the computer game rules are the same as for TV. No games until homework and chores are done; no games after 7:00 P.M. on school nights; no games on good-weather days or when friends come over to play. These guidelines help to lessen the amount of time children can play and eliminate a lot of unconscious game playing.

Make selections of appropriate games. Research shows that many parents are unaware of the content of their children's video and computer games. However, it is important that you treat video and computer games just as you would TV shows and make an effort to be informed about their characters, themes, and messages so that you can help your children select games that are appropriate and acceptable in your home.

Video and computer game magazines can tell you a great deal about a game's characters, actions, themes, and goals. It's not a bad idea to pick up a few magazines and read about games before purchasing or renting them. Also, every video and computer game comes in a box that will tell you about the game. Read the box. Look at the pictures on the box. Check games for age appropriateness and content. If you are going to limit violent games, decide what level of violence is inappropriate and, before purchasing or renting a game, determine if the game contains inappropriate violence. Try to choose games that are less competitive and more cooperative. Stick to your choices and don't buy or rent games that go against your decisions. Require children to ask before purchasing or renting new games and to show you what the game is about and how it is played. As with TV, if you are unsure about a game's appropriateness or content, do some research; rent the game before buying or ask other parents or the retailer before you or your children bring it home.

Talk about the content and messages of games. If you are concerned about the messages of violent video and computer games, talk to your children about those messages, just as you would if you were talking about a violent or stereotypical TV show. Watch your children play their games; offer to play with them. Get involved in what your children are learning and ask them how it makes them feel and what they think about the violence, the stereotypes, and the value messages. Talk to them about problem solving, competition, and success in the real world. Help them learn to think critically about their games. As always, remember to follow the rules for TV Talk: respect, observe, question, listen, and reinforce.

Should your children have a video or computer game that you really dislike, talk to them about it before you jump to conclusions. I know one parent who was ready to throw her son's Mortal Kombat video game in the trash until she played it with him and talked to him about it. She was pleasantly surprised to learn that although he liked the game, he was very aware of how violent, unrealistic, and stereotypical it was. He was also willing to acknowledge that it made him feel stronger, more in control, and more competitive, yet he was willing to limit the amount of time he played with it. Armed with that reassurance, she let the game stay but made him promise not to buy any more violent video games without talking to her about them first.

Kids and the Internet

The Internet is the fastest-growing communication medium in the world right now. There are over 30 million people accessing the Internet, and America Online, the largest access provider in this country, boasts well over 2 million subscribers. More than 50 percent of the nation's teenagers are now on-line, and the numbers of schools, businesses, and individuals on the Net increases daily. A new home page is added to the Net

---

Video and Computer Game Checklist

Bruno Bettelheim said that children's games should provide children with room to play, to experiment, to try out ideas and roles, and to grow in developmentally appropriate ways. Many video and computer games on the market today do not provide children with these opportunities. When selecting video and computer games with children, it is important to keep Bettelheim's idea in mind and to use the following checklist to determine if a game is safe and healthy for your kids.

1. Is violence the main purpose or action of the game?
2. Does the game promote negative or offensive stereotypes?
3. Does the game teach realistic problem-solving skills?
4. Does the game provide intellectual challenge through multiple goals, variable outcomes, and different skills needed for success?
5. Does the fantasy world of the game provide children with opportunities to experiment with roles and actions that are related to those in real life?
6. Does the game promote cooperation rather than competition?

---

every four seconds! In classrooms around the country, children are being taught how to use the Net for research and for communication with other children around the world. It's an exciting medium, filled with educational possibilities and opportunities for building a sense of community on a global scale, but it is also rife with potential dangers for children.

The 1996 Telecommunications Act carries provisions for the arrest and prosecution of adults who provide pornography to children over the Internet. This is of great concern to parents, whose children may be surfing the Net for other activities and information but can accidentally stumble across a pornographic Web site. Another concern comes from stories of adults who "pick up" children in "chat rooms" on the Net and make attempts to meet those children for illicit or illegal activities.

While there have been isolated cases of each of these situations, they are by no means normal occurrences. Parents and children need to be aware of them, but there is no cause for undue alarm. However, there are some other problems with the Net and its effect on children that don't make the headlines but about which parents and children need to be cautious.

The Internet is filled with advertising. Some on-line services carry ads for products and services at the bottom of each screen or when the user first signs on. Many Web pages are really nothing more than advertisements for merchandise, such as cars or stereo systems; media products, such as movies and CDs; or services, such as computer help or restaurants. Many of these advertising Web sites make advertising into a game, wherein the user-consumer is entertained into purchases. This poses a problem for children who are unaware of what advertising is and how it may affect them and calls for parental awareness and guidance.

The Internet also carries photos, video clips, news items, and magazine articles. In this regard, the Net is a lot like television and can carry messages about stereotypes, values, and what is important to know. One of the most difficult challenges posed by the Net is helping children learn to sort through the enormous amount of information available and make decisions about what is important or useful information, and what is simply trivia. Again, parental guidance is vital.

Despite the negative aspects of the Internet, it does offer a wealth of valuable information to students of all ages. The Net has access to libraries and museums around the world, as well as to databases, bulletin boards, and Web sites about almost every subject. On the Net, kids can talk to Nobel prizewinners, scientists, writers, and other adults who have something to share. There are homework help sites, kids-only chat rooms, and even Internet pen pal Web sites!

The possibilities for the Net are endless, but so are the complications. The key to making the Internet a child-safe, positive, healthy, and useful tool is to teach our children to use the Net consciously, selectively, and critically, just as we do with TV.

Net-Proofing Your Kids

There are several Internet screening programs on the market, but these devices, like the V-chip and other TV-locking gadgets, are prohibitive measures that neither truly prevent our children from accessing unwanted sites nor encourage them to be conscious, selective, and critical of the information that is available. In addition, much of the Internet safety software requires parents to program and monitor it. It can also be bypassed pretty easily by a computer-savvy kid. The surest way to make the Internet a positive and healthy choice in your home is to use the same TV-proofing techniques you have already learned.

*   *   *

What Kids Say About the Internet

"I just discovered the Internet, because I needed to find some stuff on the space program for school. It took me eight hours to find what I was looking for, but I also found some other stuff. Do you know that Smashing Pumpkins, my favorite group, has their own Web page? You can buy concert T-shirts and bootleg CDs and all kinds of stuff! I'm psyched! I know where I'll be hanging out!"

—Keesha, age 15

"In my school, we use the Internet to send music and pictures to other kids in a different state. I got some neat music and a photo from my pen pal in Indiana. We've also used the Internet to talk to the astronauts on the shuttle! That was amazing! I think the Net is cool."

—Tommy, age 11

"My parents keep telling me that there's all kinds of bad stuff on the Net—pornography and people trying to talk me into things—but I've never found it. I guess you have to know where to look. Most of what I've found is ads. It seems like every company has their own Web page to sell you things. I think it sucks. All I want to do is find the stuff that I need for school and the model-airplane bulletin board. I'm really into model airplanes."

—Andre, age 14

"I spend most of my time on the Net sending E-mail to friends I've met in the chat rooms. We talk about all kinds of things—parents, school, our favorite music—I've actually learned a lot! One of my best Net friends is a girl in Germany. She's teaching me German and I'm helping her with her English!"

—Tonya, age 15

Set rules for purposeful, selective use of the Internet. There are many reasons for getting on the Net; to do research, to stay in touch with friends, to follow a news story, or to keep up with a hobby or special interest. Just as with TV, we want to encourage our children to use the Net for a constructive purpose and to avoid "surfing." Together with your children, set some on-line rules. What are good reasons to get on the Net? Research for school? To keep up with a hobby? To E-mail friends? To connect with other kids? When are appropriate times to be on the Net? Once you have established rules for Internet use, you need to stay firm. Abuses of the rules need to result in consequences.

Establish guidelines for Net behavior. You need to explain the potential dangers of the Internet to your children and to establish some guidelines for safe Net behavior. Have your children promise not to make purchases via the Net, not to give their address, phone number, credit card number, or any other personal information to anyone on the Net, and never to arrange to meet people they talk to on the Net without parental approval and accompaniment. Remind children that people on the Internet use code names and may not be who they say they are. Other guidelines might concern E-mail, the use of certain kinds of language and images, and hacking (illegal entrance to sites). Once your guidelines are set, stay firm. If children can't abide by the guidelines, revoke Internet privileges for a period of time. Remind them that being on the Net costs money, and that if they abuse it, it may cost them!

Learn what is on the Net and guide children toward useful and appropriate sites. There is so much to discover on the Net, and everyday there are new Web sites, discussion groups, and community notices posted. It is impossible to know everything that is available. But it is important for parents to have a working knowledge of what is out there in order to guide children toward specific sites that are both useful and appropriate. Check the index of your on-line service, which will provide you with the names and addresses of kid-friendly sites. Invest in an Internet guidebook, which gives addresses and descriptions of many sites that may be of interest to children. Use the guide and the index to suggest sites to your children and create your own index of appropriate sites. Post your list near the computer or enter it under your Web browser's "favorite addresses" file. And, of course, be with your children while they are on the Net to offer guidance and help.

Talk about what you find on the Net. Everything we have learned about TV also applies to the Net, particularly in the area of news, talk shows, and advertising. Use your TV-Talk skills to encourage your children to question the information they receive on the Net and to look for news judgment, opinions, and advertising tricks. Since the Net can also transmit photographs, video, and sound, you can also use the opportunity to discuss the meanings and messages of the visual images and aural output. You might also discuss things that are specific to the Net, such as who is posting the notices, what their purpose is, and how the Internet works. Encourage your children to share their Internet discoveries with you, and together you will find the Net to be a positive, safe, and exciting choice in your home.

The Net as Ultimate Infotainment

Web sites on the Internet are becoming increasingly sophisticated and already blur the lines between ad and entertainment. In 1996 the movie industry began creating Web sites promoting new films, but these sites were more than just ads. Incorporating 3-D graphics, virtual reality, and other high-tech elements, Web sites for movies like *101 Dalmatians* and *Star Trek: First Contact* were more like advanced video games. According to James Ryan of the *New York Times,* the *101 Dalmatians* Web site enabled visitors to play an interactive game to find lost puppies, and on the Web site for Sylvester Stallone's *Daylight,* visitors could play a game in which they rescue damsels in distress! Even more interesting, the Web site for *Jerry Maguire* offered on-line advice for the lovelorn and an interactive soap opera, while the site for Woody Allen's *Everyone Says I Love You* allowed viewers to download pictures of the movie's female stars dressed in negligees or wrapped in a sheet!

Sites for major motion pictures won't replace trailers or TV or print ads anytime soon, but Alan Sutton, vice president of publicity for Universal Pictures, says that although a Web site can be costly, between $50,000 and $100,000, it allows the industry to "romance your audience more directly" than TV or print ads. Since Web sites for major movies now entertain more than 100,000 visitors a day, it's not a bad way to target potential ticket buyers.

Many in Hollywood are excited about the possibilities for a marriage between movies and the Internet. Brent Britton, a film industry Web site designer, envisions a future in which movies will be "a trailer for an extensive entertainment service on the Web." In that sense, the Internet will become the ultimate infotainment, blending video games, movies, TV shows, and ads to create one full-service interactive screen! All the more reason to begin TV-proofing for all screens now!

The Future

We do not yet know what the future will bring in terms of new media challenges for parents and children. Possibilities for the near future include 500 channels of TV; telephones, computers, and TVs all linked together; the ability to order movies on demand; the creation of personalized newspapers! Nicholas Negroponte, director of the MIT Media Lab says that in the future, "mass media will be redefined by systems for transmitting and receiving personalized information and entertainment," and new technologies, as well as new products, will emerge. As media corporations continue to merge, cross-fertilizing each other, there is no telling what may appear on our screens. All we know is that our already media-saturated culture will be even more so.

While we may be unsure of the specific nature of our new media products, one thing is certain: the TV-proofing techniques you have learned will be necessary and vital in the coming years. It is important that children learn to make all media experiences—whether with TV, computers, newspapers, magazines, radio, or movies—conscious and selective and that they learn to think critically about the information they receive, no matter what form it comes in. If we teach our children now about how the media work and the messages they carry, we can rest assured that our children will use the media in positive, safe, and healthy ways for the rest of their lives.

12

Kid TV
Making Media Literacy Come Alive

Since 1986, I have been teaching children of all ages to understand television and movies by creating their own shows and movies. My students tell me they enjoy the process immensely and that they learn a tremendous amount about how TV shows and movies work and affect people. They also develop a deep appreciation for the time and work that go into making a movie or TV show, and, consequently, look at them more critically. This kind of hands-on learning, advocated by media literacy experts around the world, is the best way to solidify concepts of critical thinking and media awareness.

Kid TV is a very good way to teach your children something positive through TV. The best part is that you don't need any fancy equipment. Any child with access to a simple family camcorder can do it. With very little help on your part, you will be amazed at what they can produce. Just give them some ideas, along with the camera and a tape and watch them go. You may even have a budding TV writer or filmmaker on your hands, who, with his or her new knowledge of TV and movie messages, might change the face of TV to a positive one!

Getting Started

In most homes, the family camcorder sits on a shelf gathering dust until there is some special occasion or event that needs to be videotaped for posterity. Then an adult gets the camera and starts shooting. Rarely do children ever get to use the camcorder, though most would jump at the chance to help you record those family events. And since most home camcorders are relatively simple to use, it's an accessible and safe activity for even very young kids.

Next time you get ready to videotape a party or family gathering, ask your child if he would like to record a little bit. Show him how to push the record button to start and stop and leave him alone for a few minutes. It's as simple as that. Don't be upset if your child misses the "big moment" and you wind up with two minutes of grandma's feet. Your child had fun and it's part of the process of learning.

When you watch the tape with your child, point out the section your child shot and gently ask him if what he sees on the tape is what he was trying to capture. If it isn't, ask him what he would do to make it better. Comment on how well he did this first time and ask him if he would like to try it again. He'll probably say yes, in which case he'll be ready to hear your ideas for Kid-TV projects.

For a younger child, you might suggest making a commercial for a favorite toy or a short animated piece using favorite action figures. A younger child might also be interested in making a video letter to send to a friend or relative. Older children can begin with a music video of their favorite song or their own version of a sitcom, drama, or talk show. Some children might even enjoy taping an everyday activity like making dinner or creating a family news program or even recording the people, places, and things in the neighborhood. Whatever you suggest, start short and simple and save the epics until your child has a better grasp of the techniques. Once an idea triggers an interest, you only have to help your children write the script or do the storyboards and they are on their way.

Scripts and Storyboards

Scripts and storyboards are blueprints for a movie or TV show, describing what the shots look like, where each shot goes, and what the actors say. Every movie or TV program uses them in some form or another, and while most professional scripts and storyboards are very elaborate, children can create simpler ones that do the job just as well.

Before beginning a script or storyboards, have your child tell you the story of her movie. Talk about the characters, if there are any, and help her make decisions about what the characters should look like, what the setting is, and what is said by whom. Try to encourage her to imagine what the final movie or TV show should look like, being as specific as

---

Kid-TV Video Ideas

The following ideas for Kid-TV programs are similar to those I have created for students of all ages. Suggest one or let your kids choose!

- Video letters to friends and relatives.
- Video news of family, neighborhood, or school events.
- Commercials for imaginary products or realistic commercials for old ones.
- Public service announcements on current issues.
- A new version of a favorite sitcom or cartoon.
- A video of a short story, poem, folktale, or play.
- A music video for a childrens' song, folksong, or other musical selection.
- A video recording of family history through interviews and photographs.
- An original screenplay or cartoon.

---

possible. Once the details are ironed out, she can begin to write the script.

Take a piece of paper and draw a line down the middle. On one side of the page write the heading, "Video," or "Pictures," and on the other side write "Audio" or "Sounds." Have your child write what will be seen, shot for shot, in the Video column, and any corresponding sounds, music, or words in the Audio column. Work with your child to be as specific as possible. Refer to the glossary of production terms (Appendix B) to help your child make decisions about what kinds of shots to use. Once the script is completed, it should look something like this script for a short movie about a boy who wanted to be a basketball player, written by a ten-year-old.

Video	Audio
1. Long shot of boy from behind, playing basketball in driveway.	1. Sound of basketball dribbling.
2. Close-up of boy's face as he prepares to shoot.	2-4. *Voice-over—boy:* "I'd always wanted to be a basketball star. I
3. Medium shot, low angle of ball going toward hoop.	dreamed about it all the time. About the NBA finals and how in
4. Close-up of ball going through hoop.	the last ten seconds of the fourth quarter, I'd make a three-pointer and bring my team the

	championship. I can hear the voices of the crowd, cheering and calling my name. . . ."
5. Medium shot, arc of boy raising his arms.	5. Cheering sounds and calling "Johnny, Johnny!"
6. Low angle, tilt up of boy standing beneath basket. Stop at close-up of face as he drops his head.	6. *Voice-over—boy:* "Someday, I'll play in the NBA, but only if I grow some. Who wants a four-foot basketball player?

Storyboards are drawings of what will appear on the screen, drawn as a sequence of frames in succession almost like a comic strip. For younger children or those who prefer to draw rather than write, storyboards will work as a script. On a piece of paper, draw a series of two-inch squares, in rows across the page. In each square, have your child draw a picture of each shot, in order, as it would look if you saw it on the TV. Stick figures work just as well as highly detailed drawings, but encourage your child to be as specific as possible. Beneath each square, write the words or sounds that go with the picture. When completed, the storyboards should be something like these for the same basketball movie.

When the script or storyboards are finished, your child is ready to begin videotaping her TV show or movie. But even if you don't have a family camcorder, writing scripts and drawing storyboards are very good tools for teaching children how TV shows and movies are made and can be good rainy-day substitutes for actually watching TV.

Basic Videomaking for Kids

When your child has finished his script or storyboards, he is ready to begin putting his ideas onto tape. To begin, explain the basic functions of your camera to your child, showing him the record button and the zoom control. To make your child's first videomaking experience less frustrating, turn off all other controls, title makers, or special effects or leave them on automatic. Try to simplify the process as much as possible.

Next, explain to your child that he will be shooting his movie in sequence, since editing is not something you have the equipment to do, and that he needs to follow his script, remembering to push the record button to stop recording when he is finished. Remind him that the camera will record sounds at the same time as it is recording the picture, so he needs to be aware of what is being said while he is taping and to speak loudly near the microphone if what is said is to be heard.

If you have a tripod, you may want to show your child how to use it, so that he can stabilize his shots or even be in the movie himself. If you don't have a tripod, another stable, adjustable object, such as a chair, can be substituted. If necessary, your child can get someone else's help to shoot a difficult scene, but encourage your child to do as much as possible alone.

Since he will not be editing, encourage your child to think before he shoots, minimizing the possibility of outtakes. If, however, he needs to shoot a scene again, he may. Simply rewind the tape back to the beginning of the shot to be replaced and record over it with the new shot.

Younger children may require your supervision during the shooting process, but you will be surprised to see what they can do without you. Older children can be left alone with the manual, if they have questions. In either case, helping them learn to make their own movies and TV shows is a rewarding and positive activity.

Editing the Easy Way

Learning about editing is a wonderful way to teach children about how TV shows and movies are edited for the screen, and it's easy to do if you have a camera and a VCR. Simply plug your camera to your VCR through the audio- or video-in outlet. Use the camera as the source tape and rerecord desired segments onto the master tape in the VCR by pressing record and pause, the way you do when recording audiocassettes. Consult your VCR and camera manuals for specifics, but the basic process is the same for all cameras and VCRs.

For more advanced editing, your home multimedia computer may have the software needed. Consult your computer manual.

Animation and Other Video Techniques

Animation is a favorite technique for children, and it is easy to do. Based on the theory of persistence of vision, animation involves recording objects as they are moved in small increments, so that when shown at full speed, they appear to be moving naturally. Almost anything can be animated—action figures and other toys, clay figures, cutouts, even food. The only limit is your child's imagination. Animation is usually done on film, one frame at a time, but it can also be done on video, although the movement will appear jerkier. It makes little difference to children; as far as they are concerned, they are making their own cartoon!

Most home video cameras come with a remote-control attachment, which allows you to record without touching the camera. If your camera has one, you will want to use it when making animation movies, but even if you don't have a remote control, you can still do animation.

Just be careful not to move the camera when you press the record button.

Set the camera up on a tripod or some other stable object facing a table or flat surface. Zoom the lens all the way back, so that the camera is recording the largest possible area of the surface and mark the boundaries of the viewing area. This is where the action will take place. It is important not to move the camera from its location while shooting as this disturbs the illusion of animation.

Once the camera is set and the playing space is delineated, your child can move the objects within the space, one small movement at a time, recording each movement for the count of three. For example, if a car is crossing the table, your child will move the car forward a small amount, remove his hand, then record for three seconds, stop recording, move the car a small amount again, and record again for three seconds, until the car has crossed the table. The smaller the movements, the less jerky the final sequence will appear. Remind your child that his hands need to be out of the viewing area when recording or he will be seen in the movie.

Animation can be as simple or as complex as your child wishes. It can be only one moving figure or many. Backgrounds and sets can be drawn or constructed, clay figures can be made, and music and voices can be added. Before you know it, your child will have created a cartoon or animated movie by himself!

Music and sound effects add an exciting, professional touch to children's videos, and even without editing equipment, this is easy to do. Most home camcorders are equipped with audio-dubbing capabilities. Audio dubbing is simply the process of recording new sound over the picture, without affecting the picture. Your video camera manual will explain the specific method for your camera, but usually, audio dubbing involves cueing up the picture, pressing the audio-dub and pause buttons, releasing the pause button, and recording music from a stereo or voices in time with the picture. When you want the music or sound to stop, simply press stop. You can record as many times as you like, adding sounds and music in different places or adding a narration, if desired.

Another easy way to add a professional touch to children's videos is through titles and credits. Most children thrill to seeing "Produced by" above their name on the screen; it gives them a real sense of pride and accomplishment. Even if your video camera doesn't have a titling function, your child can make titles by writing them on a piece of paper or cardboard and shooting them at the beginning and end of their movie. Titles can be very creative; they can be done on a computer or even animated. Once again, the only limit is your child's imagination.

As your child becomes more and more adept with the camera, her projects may get more complex. If she really takes to videomaking, there are videomaking books for kids that can give her more information and ideas. And if you have a home multimedia computer, your child can actually do some complex editing with special effects. Who knows? With your help and encouragement, you could have the next Steven Spielberg in your very own living room!

TV Teaching With Kid TV

No doubt your child will want to show you the fruits of his videomaking labors, and when he does, it is a great opportunity to do some valuable TV Teaching. Even before the big premiere, however, your guidance and encouragement will go a long way toward making the experience a positive and educational one.

From the time you suggest a project, you can guide your child toward critical TV awareness. If, for example, you observe that your child is easily influenced by commercials, you might suggest making a commercial, which will allow him to address the problems of what will be said about a product and how it is shown. If your child is having difficulties with violent TV shows, you might suggest a video project that addresses problems of justifiable violence or the consequences of violence. If your child is obsessed with music videos, let him make one. If news is a problem, let him try his hand at a news story. Whichever project you suggest, you will be giving your child an opportunity to observe firsthand the primary lesson of TV Teaching: how to recognize the difference between TV and reality. By going through the process of scripting and shooting, your child will understand that TV shows and movies are constructions of the imagination, not real life.

As you work with your child to script and storyboard his video, you can raise important questions about stereotypes, values, and behaviors. Ask your child why a character looks or dresses a certain way or why he behaves in a specific manner. Ask about the setting or the theme. Lead your child to think about why he has chosen to tell the story this way and what he thinks its messages are. Guide your child to think about production elements, such as composition, lighting, or sound and how those elements affect the meaning of the movie.

What Kids and Parents Say About Kid TV

"I had always wanted to make my own cartoon, but I never realized how hard it was and how much work it took. Now that it's finished, I really had fun and I learned so much. I know how to shoot and how to write a script and how important it is to think about what you are putting on the screen so that people don't get the wrong messages about what you are trying to say. Even though it took six hours to make a one-minute cartoon, I can't wait to do it again!"

—*Casey, age 10*

"My friends and I made a documentary about homeless people, and I learned so much. Not just about homelessness, but also about all the decisions, imagination, and hard work that go into making a movie or TV show. And the best part was that other people saw it and liked it and said that it changed the way they thought about homeless people, for the better!"

—*Ross, age 16*

"My son and daughter made a family history video over the summer. They interviewed everyone in the family and found out all kinds of things that I didn't even know. The video is a family treasure, but it is also important in another way: I have never seen my kids work so hard and so eagerly on something. They feel great about it, and their feelings have affected almost every other aspect of their lives!"

—*Dana, mother of Ariel, age 11, and Grant, age 12*

"Through making a video I began to look at TV differently. I began to see the good commercials from the bad ones, good TV shows from bad ones, and even good movies from bad ones. Even though my video wasn't perfect, I have a great sense of accomplishment and achievement. And I'll never watch TV the same way again!"

—*Maisie, age 15*

Once the shooting is all finished, bring out the popcorn and watch the final product together. After the showing, ask questions, just as you would with any other TV show or movie. You may find that your child has developed quite a good sense of production techniques and how messages are conveyed on the screen. He may surprise you with some very critical comments about his own TV show. Once again, remember the rules of TV Teaching, and above all else, be proud of your child and praise his or her efforts. He has done something that required a lot of planning and work and has learned a positive, safe, and healthy use of the TV screen in the process.

13

Ten Tips for Positive Screen Use
Creating a TV-Proof Home

Now that you know how to combat the negative aspects of TV, movies, and video games, how do you make screen use a more positive experience in your home? Here are a few easy-to-follow tips that will help you manage screen time while encouraging your children to make better choices in their viewing and playing.

Determine how screens are being used in your home. Before you can tackle the seemingly huge task of managing your children's screen use, you must determine how screens are being used and whether or not they are being used for a specific purpose or simply to fill time or baby-sit.

Look at when and why your children are watching TV or playing video and computer games. Pay careful attention to *why* the TV or computer is on. Determine if they are being used to fill time, baby-sit, or calm children or if they are on for a specific purpose or program. Remember, the goal is to make all screen use a conscious, planned activity, not a habit or something to do when bored. Flag those times when screen use is not an active choice. If you notice that the TV or computer isn't on to watch a specific program or movie or to play a game for a productive purpose, turn it off and encourage your children to turn it off too.

Centralize TV viewing and game playing in your home. Experts agree that a TV in a child's room is a very inviting distraction that isolates children from the rest of the family—and keeps them from concentrating on their homework. More important, a child's TV is one that you cannot control.

While locked in his own room, a child can watch or play anything he wants, without your knowledge or consent. The same is true for computers. Moving the TV and the computer to a centralized location allows parents to monitor their use and forces children to make selective choices when watching or playing games. It also encourages family TV viewing, which is beneficial toward building critical thinking skills.

If your child already has a TV in his room, consider moving it to a den or playroom and to use it only for watching videos or playing games. Better yet, put it in storage and only use the TV in the family room. If you have more than one child, each with his or her own TV, have them choose a common location for one TV and get rid of the rest. Learning to compromise on which TV program to watch or which game to play will help children make more selective choices.

Experts also agree that placing the TV in a centralized location where it can be closed off or concealed discourages children from being distracted by the ever-present blank screen and the urge to turn it on. Closing cabinet doors or throwing a blanket over the TV reinforces the message that screen time is over and removes the temptation.

Select appropriate viewing and playing options with your children. Treat the TV Guide, movie reviews, video guides, Internet, and game guides as menus for your children. Consult them and, with your children, select appropriate options. From the TV Guide, you might select several age-appropriate TV programs that are on each week, as well as special programs that offer variety or educational opportunities. From videoguides and movie reviews, choose appropriate movies and videotapes to rent or see. Use the game guides to study new games and only buy or rent video and computer games that are suitable. Use the Internet guide to pre-select Internet sites that are useful and kid friendly.

It is helpful to write down TV and video options and post them near the TV set, or make lists of appropriate Web sites and post them near the computer. Let children make their own choices from the options you have presented. If none of the options is appealing, the TV or computer isn't turned on. If they do choose a program, video, Web site, or game, make sure that the TV or computer is turned off when it is finished.

By pre-selecting screen choices with your children, you are not only assured that your children are watching programs, movies, and games that you approve of, but you are also reinforcing the idea that all screen use is a selective, conscious activity.

Watch TV or play a game with your children at least once a week. Once a week, select one program or movie that you and your children might enjoy and can discuss together. It doesn't have to be educational; any appropriate show or tape will do. Use the opportunity to talk about what you are watching. Discuss the characters, the story, or specific thematic ideas. Point out TV and movie production techniques. Don't forget to discuss the commercials! To reinforce information from the program and your discussion, plan for follow-up activities, such as reading, field trips, or creative play. Once a week, play a video or computer game with your kids and talk about it.

Watching TV shows and movies or playing games with your children creates the ideal situation for TV Teaching. It is this valuable interaction between you and your children that helps them develop the critical skills they need to make responsible screen choices on their own.

Encourage your children to talk back to the screen. Most of us view TV and movie watching as a passive activity, and so we tend to sit quietly in front of the set, accepting its messages without thinking about or commenting on what we see and hear. However, one of the most important things you can teach your children is that the TV screen can be wrong and that it is acceptable to question or disagree with it. When you watch TV or movies with your children or play a videogame, point out things that are inconsistent with your values or are untruthful. Tell the TV that it is wrong and why it is wrong. Although talking to a TV set may feel strange at first, it is crucial to teaching children how to use screens critically and actively, not passively. Besides, the TV can't hear you, so you can say whatever you want. It can even be fun.

If your children are online, encourage them to post comments at each site they visit to express their feelings and ideas about what is on the screen, even if they disagree. It's the same as talking to the TV, but someone will actually read what they say and may even take it to heart.

Agree with your children to limit before- and after-school use. Most teachers will tell you that children who watch TV or play video games before school or while doing homework suffer greater academic and behavioral problems than those who don't, and teachers unanimously agree that it is in a child's best interest to limit before- and after-school TV, video, and computer games.

To help your children focus on their schoolwork, encourage your children to choose other activities before and after school. If there is a specific program that your children want to watch at those times, agree to tape the show so they can watch it later, when their homework is completed. Set game-playing guidelines that state that games cannot be played until homework is finished. Have the children do their homework in a location that is not near a TV, so there won't be any temptation to turn it on.

Many doctors have determined that eating while watching television leads to poor nutrition and obesity, as children tend to snack while watching and reduce their exercise time. Limit TV watching and game playing during mealtimes to help your children get the best from their meals.

Don't use TV or video games as a reward or punishment for academic performance. Many parents use TV watching or video-game playing as a reward for good grades or as a punishment for poor ones. Although TV watching or game playing can impinge on academic performance, TV or games as incentives for good grades discourages motivated learning and deters children from making critical choices, while making TV or video games more important than they should be.

Instead of threatening to take away TV or game time for poor academic performance, consider another alternative. Promising an exciting activity in return for better grades would be a solution. For example, if your child likes ice cream, you might suggest that an A on the next report card would earn her a trip to the ice-cream parlor. Older children might be encouraged with an outing to a nearby amusement park or a concert. In any case, it's best to leave the TV out of it, or you will be giving television and games more power over your children than you want them to have.

Discuss tips for screen management in the home with other parents. It is a good idea to share your helpful tips with other parents, particularly with those whose children are your children's playmates. Many parents have heard new and promising ideas about screen management from other parents, and what works for another family might also work for yours. Sharing screen-management ideas with other parents, caregivers, and relatives is also a good way to insure that your children will not be using TV or computers inappropriately at a friend's or grandparent's home.

Organize a meeting of your school's PTA group to discuss screen management. Some very successful ideas have come from PTAs. For example, some PTA groups have joined together to ban their children from wearing or bringing Power Rangers clothes and lunch boxes to school in an attempt to lower the incidence of Power Rangers–type behavior on the playground. Other PTAs have brought in speakers to discuss the effects of TV and video games on children. Some have organized their own TV-critic workshops for children in their schools. Joining forces with other parents can help to make screen use a positive activity for the community as a whole.

Plan a meeting at your children's school to discuss TV viewing and screen use with teachers and administrators. As hard as you work to improve your own children's screen habits, all your efforts can be undermined if schoolmates and teachers don't reinforce your goals. Encouraging your child's school to find and effect common solutions for home and school will help children understand that selective viewing and critical thinking about TV, movies, and video games is not just "Mom's weird idea" but is supported by all adults in authority positions. Many schools around the country are already beginning to incorporate media literacy education into their curricula. Some schools offer classes in media literacy; others organize special TV-Awareness Weeks. Encourage media literacy education in your child's school.

Be a good model. Children learn many screen habits from their parents. Children will watch the same kinds of programs their parents watch. If you watch lots of violent programs, your children will assume that violence on TV is acceptable and will not understand when you tell them they can't watch. If you watch the soaps or sports or sitcoms, your children will too. If you play video and computer games, so will your children. Moreover, if you come home, turn on the TV or computer and leave it on all night, so will they.

Look closely at your own screen habits. Are they what you would like your children to have? If not, make the effort to change your own screen use to encourage your children to change too. Everyone's old habits can be broken and replaced with newer, healthier ones, if the effort is made.

Conclusion
Answers to Frequently Asked Questions

Q: We watched a lot of TV as kids. Why weren't we affected badly?

A: Actually, we were affected. Our opinions of the world and ourselves were affected by TV's stereotypes and values too, but not to the same degree as what is happening to our children.

There is a lot more TV available now than what we were exposed to—more channels, more variety—and because of a change in audience tolerance, social mores, and network profit levels, what we see on TV today is much more extreme than it was when we were kids. Images and techniques that would have been considered outrageous in the 1960s or 1970s are now perfectly acceptable and even necessary to win large audience ratings and profits. Sex jokes, which were very subtle or nonexistent in our time, now show up blatantly in family sitcoms. We rarely saw disfigured or brutally maimed corpses during our prime time, but high body counts and extreme gore are commonplace for our children. Even the values TV depicts have changed, as characters show more selfishness and little compassion toward each other. Consequently, even though our children may be watching as much TV as we did, they are exposed to things that may influence them more strongly. And as the Information Superhighway approaches, TV producers, struggling to compete for audience share, will dish up even more extreme fare for our children's viewing.

Q: How much TV should my children be allowed to watch?

A: The average American child watches four hours of TV each day, but the American Academy of Pediatrics and other health organizations recommend that children watch no more than two hours of television each day. While many approaches to TV management stress time limits, the approach presented in this book does not. To my mind, one hour spent passively in front of a terrible TV show can be too much TV, while two hours spent watching and discussing a good program might be just fine. The amount of time spent watching is less important than what is being watched and how it is watched. By focusing on selective and critical viewing, the TV-proofing method guarantees that the time spent in front of the TV set will be naturally limited and more constructive.

How often you let your children watch television is up to you, but remember, if you tell a child how much they *can* watch each day, that's how much they *will* watch. You are setting them up to watch anything, for however long you will let them. Setting a time limit does not necessarily encourage selective viewing. You want your children to watch TV if, and only if, they have a specific program they want to see or a constructive purpose for watching.

Watching TV should not be your children's only recreational activity. It should be balanced with outdoor activities and creative play. If, however, TV watching is as selective and conscious a choice as other activities, you can feel confident that your children will not be watching too much TV and that the time they spend watching TV will be productive.

Q: I have been so lax about TV management in the past. Will it be impossible to start now?

A: The earlier children begin to view TV critically and selectively, the easier it is, but it's never too late to start! Just remember that your children will have to break old habits at the same time they learn new ones. You may therefore encounter some resistance with older children and may have to do a little more explaining. Be patient. Don't overload your family with everything at once. Go one step at a time, adding something new each week.

First, inform your children and spouse that you are going to try a new way of watching TV and ask for their help. Ask each member of the family to give their thoughts on TV use and recommend possible alterations. Put those ideas into practice and wait a week.

Then choose one show to watch together and discuss it afterward. This is the hardest part, so expect some funny looks from your kids. After all, talking about TV is not something they know how to do.

Go easy this first time and then wait a week before you try something else.

Slowly, you can select programs from the TV Guide and add more discussions. Just remember to give it time; you can't undo in one week what took years to do. But if you stick with it, your children will get the hang of it and will soon be selecting and discussing TV all on their own.

Q: Won't my older children rebel when I try to limit their TV watching?

A: Because this approach does not focus on limiting TV watching but rather on making TV watching a selective and constructive activity, your children will be less likely to perceive it as a parental limitation, like curfews, which demands rebellion. While your older children may think your new approach to television is a bit strange, they won't necessarily be uncooperative. Remember to tell them that you are not trying to "take away their TV" but are interested in finding a new way to watch it. Make it fun, enjoy your discussions, and with time, your older children will recognize the value of critical viewing and will take pride in their ability to analyze their favorite TV shows or pan a really bad show.

Q: Does your method mean that my children can only watch educational shows?

A: Absolutely not. While watching an informative documentary about whales may be valuable, your child can learn just as much from a sitcom or cartoon. Remember, to a child, everything on TV is "educational"; they learn from whatever they watch. Your job is to help them become more selective and critical of their TV curriculum and to direct their learning in a more constructive, positive way.

If you follow this method, your children will learn as much from a discussion about justifiable violence or animation techniques while watching cartoons as they will from a discussion about bird migration while watching a nature program. Remember, it's not just *what* is being watched that is important, but *how* it is being watched. Although you want to steer your children away from programs that are not age appropriate or contain too many negative aspects, even the problems inherent in those programs can be neutralized through critical discussion and awareness.

Q: What do I do if my child insists on watching a TV show or a movie that I disapprove of?

A: If your child insists on watching even after you have explained your position, use the opportunity to do some serious TV Teaching. First, ask your child why he wants to see the show or movie. If he doesn't have a good reason, deny the request. If he tells you that all his friends have seen it or that he heard it is good or funny, offer to watch the program or movie with your child by saying, "If everyone else thinks it's good, I'd like to see it too." If he refuses to watch with you, deny his request. If he really wants to see the show, he'll let you watch with him.

Watch the show or movie with your child. After the program, point out things that upset you and explain why, but be careful not to flat-out pan the program or you will anger your child and defeat your purpose, which is to make your child think critically about what he has seen. Use your own analytical skills. Ask questions. Use the ideas for discussion topics provided in this book to generate discussion. Tell him your thoughts on the program.

Finally, ask your child if the program was as good as he expected. Ask him to tell you why he thought it was good or bad, and ask him what he learned from the experience. Then end the discussion by saying, "Thanks for letting me watch with you. I learned a lot."

While this technique may take longer than simply saying no, it accomplishes several important goals. First of all, you have diffused the possibility of rebellion by not creating a limiting situation. Second, by watching with your child and engaging him in discussion afterward, you have encouraged him to use his critical viewing skills and think about what he has watched. And finally, by agreeing to let your child watch and judge the program's merits for himself, you have helped your child learn a critical lesson about selective viewing and parental control. The next time the situation comes up, you will discover that your child is less likely to insist and more likely to think critically about what he is watching.

Q: Will my child be an outcast if she doesn't watch the TV shows and movies that her friends watch?

A: Although TV and movie watching is essentially a nongroup activity, most children like to compare notes about their favorite shows and movies. It is one way of identifying with each other and forming alliances. While this is not as difficult an issue for preschool and lower-elementary-aged children, it becomes more challenging as children enter upper-elementary and middle school.

If your child tells you that she feels left out of the TV conversation because her friends watch a program or movie that you don't approve of, offer to watch the show with her once, or go to the movie with her and discuss it afterward. She will then feel as though she can be part of the group and contribute to her peers' TV and movie conversations, and you will have had the opportunity to help her think critically about the show or movie.

Preteen group movie outings can be a bit trickier. By the time children reach the age of twelve or thirteen, they want to go to the movies together, without their parents, and telling your child that she may not go is setting yourself up for a rebellion. If your child asks to attend a group movie-date and the movie is one you aren't sure of, explain your apprehension and tell her that she may go, but she must agree to discuss the movie with you afterward. Then give your child a few questions to think about while she is watching the movie and plan to discuss it with her when she returns. This technique allows your preteen the independence and time with friends that she is desperately craving, but also helps you keep tabs on what she is seeing and how it is affecting her.

Q: How do I handle inappropriate TV viewing at friends' or relatives' houses?

A: This is always a difficult problem because no one wants to tell a friend or relative that they are doing something harmful to your child. The most effective way of dealing with this is to politely tell your child's friends' parents or your relatives that you are trying to improve your child's TV habits and need some help from them. Explain that you are allowing your child to watch TV only if there is a specific program he wants to see and not to use TV as a time filler. Explain that if your child asks to watch TV, he must say what he wants to watch and agree to turn the TV off when that program is finished. Delineate which TV programs are strictly off-limits for your child and why, and provide friends, neighbors, and relatives with a list of your child's viewing options. Most likely, your friend or relative will agree to support your work.

If, however, you discover that your child is still viewing TV inappropriately at someone else's house, you might talk to your child, explain the problem, and tell him that he will not be able to visit if he cannot control his own TV viewing while there. Although this is an extreme measure, it reinforces the idea that selective and critical TV watching is not something that your child does only at home but is a skill that must be practiced everywhere there is a temptation to watch TV.

If the problem is with a baby-sitter, explain the situation to the sitter and reiterate that you need her to abide by the rules as a condition of employment. If your child is not responding, remind him that if he can't abide by the rules, there will be no TV while you are out. Period. It is always difficult to guarantee that children are following your instructions when you or they aren't home, but with time and practice, your children will learn to view TV selectively and most likely will not be as interested in watching TV inappropriately at a friend's or relative's house or when a baby-sitter is caring for them.

Q: My preschool-age daughter watches only Disney movies and videotapes. Is there anything wrong with this?

A: Young children like to see things over and over again, and Disney movies are a staple of most young children's TV and movie diet. There is nothing inherently wrong with a child choosing to watch Disney movies frequently, if that is their selective choice. But as variety is the spice of life, parents should encourage their children to see other age-appropriate programs.

If your child appears to be hooked on one particular movie, which is common, you might consider offering her some alternatives. Rotate that movie with another appropriate movie or a previously taped program. But don't fret if she refuses to watch anything else. She'll tire of it soon enough and move on. Eventually, she will come to learn that there are other options out there and her TV and movie diet will expand.

Like any other program, however, Disney movies offer parents ample opportunities for TV Teaching, even with preschoolers. Pointing out animation techniques, talking about the characters and their actions, and even looking at stereotypes are perfect age-appropriate discussion activities for young children. Having children draw pictures or make up alternative endings are excellent follow-up activities. And remember, just because it's a "kid's movie" or your child has seen it several times doesn't mean it can't be a valuable lesson in critical and selective viewing.

Q: All my ten-year-old son ever watches on TV is sports programs. Is this bad for him?

A: If your son is spending all of his free time watching sports on television, then he is not balancing TV watching with other activities, and this can be harmful. If, as with any other TV show, he is watching sports shows selectively, there isn't really a problem.

Remember that sports programs have a tremendous appeal for young boys and many develop a near addiction to them. Look at your son's influences. Does his father or an older male in the household watch a lot of sports? Does your son play a sport? Look at your child's reactions to the sports programs. Is he overly excited or upset when a team wins or loses? Is he neglecting other activities or opportunities to watch sports on TV?

If you feel that your son is too involved in TV sports shows, you may want to help him become more selective and critical of the programs he watches. Ask him to choose one sport or one team to follow and allow him to watch only that sport or team for a month. Take the opportunity to watch with him a few times, pointing out production techniques, discussing sports ads, talking to him about why he likes that sport or team. Encourage him to talk about why he likes to watch sports.

If that doesn't work, limit his sports programs to one a day or one per week and try to watch with him and talk about what you see. Gradually, your son will become more critical of sports shows and more selective of the ones he watches.

Q: Do video games count as TV watching? How do I limit the time my children spend playing them?
A: Video games, such as Nintendo or Sega games, have reached national pastime status for many children. Although they aren't strictly TV, they have similar characteristics and are a specific use of TV. Consequently, they can be regulated in much the same way.

Rather than setting a time limit for video-game playing, as many approaches recommend, use your TV-Teaching skills to help children be more selective in their game playing. To begin, restrict game playing to only one area of the house and establish guidelines for when game playing is a choice, just as with TV. If your children want to play a game, ask them which one they would like to play, why they want to play, and inform them that they may play only two rounds of that game and then the game must be turned off. They may balk at first, but you must remain firm. If they refuse, tell them that if they cannot play by the rules, they may not play at all. If they agree, you may need to supervise their playing the first few times, to make sure that only two rounds are being played. If your children abide by the rules, you may allow additional rounds, if you feel it is appropriate.

It's a good idea anyway to watch them play the game a few times, as it will familiarize you with the game and give you the opportunity to talk to them while they play. Ask questions about the content of the game. Who are the good guys? Who are the bad guys? Why are they fighting? Is that a good reason for a fight? Encourage them to look at it critically. Ask them why they like certain games more than others or what they think makes a game good. Ask them if the game they are playing is good. If not, ask them to explain why they are playing it.

Don't purchase new video games unless a specific game is asked for, and do some research before renting or buying games. Ask your children to tell you why they want the game and rent or buy it only if you feel that it is appropriate for your children and only if they agree to abide by your rules of play. An even more effective measure is to have your children purchase the game with their own money, still agreeing to your rules. By following this method, you are encouraging your children to be selective and critical of their video games and, at the same time, giving them the tools with which to effectively regulate their own game playing.

Q: I'm still worried about the violence my children see on TV and in the movies. Is there any way to prevent them from being exposed to it?

A: There has always been violence in TV and movies and there always will be. It is next to impossible to prevent your children from ever seeing violence, unless, of course, you throw the TV out and lock your children in their rooms forever. The practical challenge is how to limit your children's exposure to screen violence, while making sure that if they do see it, they know how to think about it so it is less likely to influence or affect them negatively.

Helping your children understand the violence they see is the best prevention. Choose programs for young children carefully and be ready to talk about any violence that might be present. Explain to young children why the violence is there and what it is like in real life. Help them realize that TV and reality are very different. Discuss nonviolent conflict resolution as an alternative to physical violence. Teach young children that violence has consequences.

Older children who have already been exposed to a lot of screen violence need to discuss it too. You can help them be more selective about watching violence by talking to them about it. Tell them how you feel about violence and make a point of explaining the differences between screen violence and real life. You can even point out production techniques that make violence appear real on the screen! Most important, you should expose them to other TV programs and movies that don't contain violence, so they learn that violence isn't the only story to tell or see.

If you fear that your child is being adversely affected by the amount or type of screen violence he sees, you can help him be more selective about what he watches. If he is choosing to watch violent shows consistently, you might suggest that he alternate one violent program with one nonviolent program. Gradually introduce more nonviolent programs into his TV choices. Tell him that there are consequences for violent behavior in real life, and be prepared to follow through if you see him behaving violently. Be consistent, and you will see an improvement in his TV habits or behavior.

The Family TV Use Chart

Time of Day	Shows Watched	By Whom	Why?
6:00 A.M.			
7:00 A.M.			
8:00 A.M.			
9:00 A.M.			
10:00 A.M.			
11:00 A.M.			
12:00 P.M.			
1:00 P.M.			
2:00 P.M.			
3:00 P.M.			
4:00 P.M.			
5:00 P.M.			
6:00 P.M.			
7:00 P.M.			
8:00 P.M.			
9:00 P.M.			
10:00 P.M.			
11:00 P.M.			
12:00 A.M.			
1:00 A.M.–5: A.M.			

A Glossary of Basic TV Production Terms

Techniques: Different ways of making TV programs.

Video   the electronic recording of sound and image on a magnetic tape. Most TV is videotaped.

Film   the recording of sound and image on light sensitive material. Most movies are shot on film.

Live   when the action is shot and transmitted instantaneously without editing.

Taped   a prerecorded session which is often edited before it is shown.

Genres: Types of TV programs.

Animation   a technique in which inanimate objects or drawings are made to appear as though they are moving.

Documentary   a show in which real people are engaged in real events.

Fiction   a made-up story.

Drama   a serious fictional genre.

Sitcom   fictional situational comedy in which the same characters appear in a consistent setting.

Reality-based/Docudrama   a blend of documentary and fictional elements.

Production Personnel: People who make TV programs.

Producer   the person who is responsible for the concept and funding of the show.

Director   the person who makes the decisions about how a show is shot and edited.

Cinematographer/Camera operator   the person who shoots the program.

Scriptwriter   the person who writes the show.

Editor   the person who puts the show together after it has been shot.

Composition: The way in which objects and people are placed within the frame.

Close-up   a shot in which the subject seems close to the viewer, head and shoulders are visible.

Medium shot   a shot which shows the subject at a half distance, head, shoulders, waist.

Long shot   the subject appears very far away; full body.

Low Angle   the subject is shot from below. Makes subject appear larger.

High Angle   the subject is shot from above. Makes subject appear smaller.

Camera Movement: How the camera moves which affects the meaning of the shot.

Pan   the camera moves from side to side, horizontally.

Tilt   the camera moves from top to bottom, vertically.

Track   the camera follows a subject.

Dolly   the camera moves forwards or backwards.

Zoom   the camera lens moves to make objects appear near or far.

Sound: Music, voices and sound effects which add up to the picture's meaning.

Sync   synchronized sound with picture. Usually recorded at the same time as the picture.

Non-sync   when the sound and picture do not match. Sound effects and voice-overs often added in editing.

Voice-over   Dialogue or speech in which the speaker is not seen talking on the tape. Usually added in editing.

Editing: The process of putting shots and sounds together to create the final show.

Cut   a quick change from one shot to the next.

Dissolve   when one shot appears to melt into another.

Blue Screen   a technique in which two separate images are placed together, even if they are not shot at the same time, e.g. an actor in an alien landscape!

Recommended Resources for Parents and Kids

Advertising

Books

Marketing Madness: A Survival Guide for a Consumer Society. Michael F. Jacobson and Laurie Ann Mazur. Washington, D.C.: Westview Press, 1995. Ideas and activities to help children fight consumerism.

Selling Out America's Children. David Walsh, Ph.D. Minneapolis: Fairview Press, 1995. An easy-to-read analysis of the effects of advertising and consumerism on children. Includes wonderful suggestions for parents.

Sold Separately: Parents and Children in Consumer Culture. Ellen Seiter. New Brunswick, N.J.: Rutgers University Press, 1993. An insightful look at toys and television and their levels of meaning for parents and children.

The Sponsored Life. Leslie Savan. Philadelphia: Temple University Press, 1994. A very funny and well-researched look at contemporary advertising by the advertising critic for *The Village Voice.*

Magazines

Adbusters Quarterly. The Media Foundation, 1243 West 7th Avenue, Vancouver, B.C. V6H 1B7 Canada. Telephone: 604-736-9401. A Canadian magazine that produces some of the best cutting-edge and hilarious criticism of advertising. Good for older kids and teens, as well as adults.

Zillions: Consumer Reports for Kids. P.O. Box 51777, Boulder, Co. 80321. A packed-to-the-brim bimonthly magazine for kids ages nine to fourteen that analyzes advertising.

Videos

The Ad and the Ego. California Newsreel. Telephone: 415-621-6196. A comprehensive documentary on the impact of advertising in America with Sut Jhally, Jean Kilbourne, and other leading media critics. Good for teens.

Buy Me That, Buy Me That! Too!, and *Buy Me That! 3*. Ambrose Video, 1290 Avenue of the Americas, New York, N.Y. 10104. Telephone: 800-526-4663. Three kid-appropriate videos that expose the tricks in advertising. Coproduced by Consumer Reports and aired on HBO. Recommended for ages two and up!

Pack of Lies. Media Education Foundation. Telephone: 413-586-4170. An exposé of the tobacco industry's advertsing tricks and plans for selling cigarettes, with Jean Kilbourne. Good for teens and adults.

Production Notes. Produced and directed by Jason Simon. Video Data Bank. Telephone: 312-245-3550. A fascinating tape that exposes advertisers' objectives and manipulations using real commercials and their production notes. Great for teens.

Slim Hopes: Advertising and the Obsession with Thinness. Media Education Foundation. Telephone: 413-586-4170. A noted scholar's insightful and fact-filled look at how advertising images of women affect girls, with Jean Kilbourne. Good for teens.

Viewing Between the Lines. Produced by the Educational Video Center. Telephone: 212-254-2848. A nineteen-minute video, made by kids, that explains how to see through ads.

Stereotypes and Values

Books

The Beauty Myth: How Images of Beauty Are Used Against Women. Naomi Wolf. New York: William Morrow, 1991. A powerful examination of advertising's false ideal of beauty for women and its effects.

Hollywood vs. America: Popular Culture and the War on Traditional Values. Michael Medved. New York: HarperCollins, 1992. A vivid portrait of Hollywood's values and how they contrast with those of the American public. Written with humor and compassion by a noted film critic.

Where the Girls Are: Growing Up Female With the Mass Media. Susan J. Douglas. New York: Random House, 1993. A very funny and insightful look at the impact of media images on women and girls.

Videos

Color Adjustment. Directed by Marlon Riggs. California Newsreel. Telephone: 415-621-6196. The best video on racism in the media. Shocking and enlightening. Good for teens.

Warning: The Media May Be Hazardous to Your Health. Directed by Jenai Lane. Media Watch. Telephone: 408-423-6355. A highly recommended video for teens on sexism and violence in the media.

Violence in the Media

Books

Who's Calling the Shots?: How to Respond Effectively to Children's Fascination With War Play and War Toys. Nancy Carlsson-Paige and Diane E. Levin. Philadelphia: New Society Publishers, 1990. Developmentally appropriate suggestions, activities, and ideas for helping children play less violently.

Videos

The Killing Screens: Media and the Culture of Violence. With Dr. George Gerbner and Jean Kilbourne. Media Education Foundation. Telephone: 413-586-4170. A hard-hitting video that explains how media violence affects us all. Dr. Gerbner details his theories.

Does TV Kill? A Frontline documentary. Available through the Center For Media Literacy. Telephone: 800-226-9224. Probes TV's effect on children through sur-veillance cameras and interviews. With Bill Moyers and other media experts.

You Are What You Watch: Kids and TV Violence. Nick News, Nickelodeon Network. A great program for kids on violence in the media with Linda Ellerbee and a panel of kids. Ages nine through fifteen.

Teen TV

Books

Dancing in the Dark: Youth, Popular Culture and the Electronic Media. Quentin J. Schultze, Roy M. Anker, James D. Bratt, William D. Romanowski, John W. Worst, and Lambert Zuidevaart. Grand Rapids, Mich.: Eerdmans, 1991. Fascinat-ing essays on the impact of mass media on youth culture.

Media, Sex, and the Adolescent. Bradley S. Greenberg, et al. Cresskill, N.J.: Hampton 1993. A practical examination of how the media influences teen attitudes and beliefs. Good suggestions to help parents address issues surrounding Teen TV.

Videos

Dreamworlds II. Produced by Sut Jhally. Media Education Foundation. Telephone: 413-586-4170. An extremely hard-hitting, provocative, and disturbing look at mu-sic videos' portrayal of women. Banned by MTV. Recommended for mature audi-ences only.

Teen Sexuality in a Culture of Confusion, by Dan Habib. Media Education Foundation. Telephone: 413-586-4170. An award-winning video in which teens and scholars discuss media messages and their effect on teen sexuality and self-esteem. Good for older teens and parents.

News

Books

Censored: The News That Didn't Make the News—and Why: The 1995 Project Censored Yearbook. Carl Jensen and Project Censored. New York: Four Walls Eight Win-dows, 1995. An annual publication that reveals the big stories that "didn't make the news" and investigates the reasons and the effects. Always enlightening and sometimes shocking.

Deciding What's News: A Study of CBS Evening News, NBC Evening News, Newsweek and Time. Herbert J. Gans. New York: Vintage, 1980. The grandfather of news books. A very perceptive and thoughtful analysis of news judgment in the major news outlets and how it shapes our values.

How to Watch TV News. Neil Postman and Steve Powers. New York: Penguin, 1992. Absolutely the most readable and practical book on TV news analysis.

Out of Order. Thomas E. Patterson. New York: Knopf, 1993. A precise examination of how politics have been transformed by the electronic media and news.

Spin Control: The White House Office of Communications and the Management of Presidential News. John Anthony Maltese. Chapel Hill: University of North Carolina Press, 1991. A fascinating portrait of how the White House controls information that gets to the public through the media.

Unreliable Sources: A Guide to Detecting Bias in the News Media. Martin A. Lee and Norman Solomon. Secaucus, N.J.: Citadel Press, 1991. A great guide to media bias by the leaders of FAIR—Fairness and Accuracy in Reporting.

Magazines

Extra. Published by Fairness and Accuracy in Reporting. Telephone: 212-633-6700. A very well researched and essential guide to analyzing the biases and inaccuracies of the news. FAIR also has a special edition on newspapers for kids.

Videos

Fear and Favor in the Newsroom. California Newsreel. Telephone: 415-621-6196. An exposé on corporate ownership of the press and control of the flow of information. An indispensible guide to news judgment at its highest and most dangerous levels.

Video Games and Computers

Books

Being Digital. Nicholas Negroponte. New York: Vintage, 1996. An exciting and thought-provoking look at computers, the Internet, and the digital future by the head of the MIT New Media Lab.

Life on the Screen: Identity in the Age of the Internet. Sherry Turkle. New York: Simon and Schuster, 1995. A longtime computer and video game researcher takes on the Internet, exploring the ways in which electronic communication has changed our sense of identity and place.

Technopoly: The Surrender of Culture to Technology. Neil Postman. New York: Vintage, 1993. The darker side of technology and culture by one of the leading media critics and educators in the country.

Video Kids: Making Sense of Nintendo. Eugene F. Provenzo Jr. Cambridge, Mass.: Harvard University Press, 1991. A thorough examination of video and computer games and their effects on children. Important reading for parents of videogame junkies!

Internet

Brochures

Child Safety on the Information Highway. National Center for Missing and Exploited Children. Telephone: 800-843-5678. A useful brochure that informs parents of the risks and dangers of the Internet and provides guidelines and ideas for reducing the risks.

The Parents' Guide to the Information Superhighway. A publication of the Children's Partnership with the National PTA and the National Urban League. Parents' Guide, 1460 4th Street, Suite 306, Santa Monica, CA 90401. A helpful guide that gives a step-by-step introduction to parenting in an online world, with specific tools and rules for parents to use.

Videos and Movies

Books

Beyond TV: Activities for Using Video With Children, by Martha Dewing. Santa Barbara: ABC-Clio, 1992. The editor of Children's Video Report offers helpful tips and guidelines to maximize creative use of video with kids.

Stay Tuned! Raising Media Savvy Kids in the Age of the Channel-Surfing Couch Potato: The KIDVIDZ Family Video Guide. Jane Murphy and Karen Tucker. New York: Main Street/Doubleday, 1996. A guide to video by kid-video producers. Includes a first-rate listing of video producers and distributors and suggestions for choosing videos for kids.

The Screening of America: Movies and Values From Rocky to Rain Man. Tom O'Brien. New York: Continuum, 1990. An original examination of how movies have reflected and shaped the values of today's generation by a film critic and teacher.

Kid TV

Books and Guides

The Animation Book: A Complete Guide to Animated Filmmaking From Flipbooks to Sound Cartoons. Kit Laybourne. New York: Crown, 1988. An easy-to-understand explanation of how animated movies are made. Great diagrams, exercises, and projects. An excellent resource for the kid that's really into animation.

Make Your Own Video Movies! Lauryn Axelrod. East Arlington, VT: Green Mountain Media, 1994. P.O. Box 44, East Arlington, VT 05252. A video-making book designed for kids ages seven through fifteen. Explains everything they need to know to get started.

YO-TV Production Handbook. New York: Educational Video Center, 1994. Telephone: 212-254-2848. A videomaking guide produced by one of the top kid-produced video organizations in the country. For ages twelve and up.

Videos by Kids

Educational Video Center. Telephone: 212-254-2848. Wonderful videos on a variety of topics, all produced by kids.

Green Mountain Media. Telephone: 802-375-6849. Catalogue of award-winning videos produced by kids.

L.A. Freewaves. Telephone: 213-687-8583. Catalogue of fantastic youth-produced media in Southern California.

Rise and Shine Productions. Telephone: 212-265-5909. Lots of great videos by kids.

Video Data Bank. Telephone: 312-245-3550. Catalogue of kid-produced videos and media literacy videos by independent film and video makers.

VIDKIDCO. Telephone: 310-928-7403. Videos and CD-ROMS by kids.

Books on TV and Movies for Younger Kids

Arthur's TV Trouble. Marc Brown. Boston: Little/Brown, 1995. How does the popular character deal with TV advertising? Ages four through eight.

The Bionic Bunny Show. Marc Brown and Laurene Krasny Brown. Boston: Atlantic Monthly Press/Little Brown, 1990. An ordinary bunny is transformed through special effects on a TV show. Ages three through seven.

Lights! Camera! Action! How A Movie Is Made. Gail Gibbons. New York: Harper and Row, 1985. A behind-the-scenes look at the making of a movie from script to opening night. Perfect for ages six through nine.

Ramona: Behind the Scenes of a Television Show. Elaine Scott and Margaret Miller. New York: Morrow Junior Books, 1988. A photo essay that takes children behind the scenes on the set of a television series. Ages ten and up.

Television: What's Behind What You See. W. Carter Merbrier with Linda Capus Riley. New York: Farrar, Straus & Giroux, 1996. An ideal, beautifully illustrated book for seven- to twelve-year-olds which explains the behind-the-scenes workings of television, including ratings, news, and special effects.

Media Literacy Organizations

Citizens For Media Literacy, 34 Wall Street, Suite 407, Asheville, NC 28801. Telephone: 704-255-0182. Helps parents, teachers, and concerned citizens address issues surrounding children and TV, the First Amendment, and media in the schools. Produces a newsletter, *The New Citizen.*

Jesuit Communication Project, 300-47 Ranleigh Avenue, Toronto, Ontario M4N 1X2 Canada. Telephone: 416-488-7280. Father John Pungente is one of the most consistent and clearheaded voices in media literacy and produces a number of good resources for teachers including Scanning Television, a full curriculum with videos.

Media Literacy Website, http://interact.uoregon.edu/Medialit/Homepage. This one website will link you to hundreds of other media literacy organizations and websites around the world. One-stop shopping!

Media Watch, P.O. Box 618, Santa Cruz, CA 95061. Telephone: 408-423-6355. Media activism against sexist and violent stereotypes in advertising, magazines, TV, and movies. Produces *Action Agenda*, a very hard-hitting newsletter that usually contains ready-to-mail postcards requesting change.

National Telemedia Council, 20 East Wilson St., Madison, WI 53703. Telephone: 608-257-7712. The oldest media literacy organization in the country. Provides workshops and resource materials for teachers and parents and a newsletter, *Telemedium: the Journal of Media Literacy.*

The Association for Media Literacy, 40 McArthur Street, Weston, Ontario M9P 3M7, Canada. Telephone: 416-394-6190. The Canadian clearinghouse for curriculum materials.

The Center for Media Education, 1151 K St. NW, Suite 518, Washington, D.C.

20005. Telephone: 202-628-2620. Works with the industry, consumer groups, and community groups to improve children's television. Provides community action kits, videos, and booklets.

The Center for Media Literacy, 4727 Wilshire Blvd., Los Angeles, CA 90010. Telephone: 800-226-9494. The best source for media literacy curriculum and parenting resources. CML produces *Connect*, a great quarterly newsletter, as well as other useful magazines, videos, and workshop guides. Also has a wonderful resource guide from which you may purchase many of the books and videos listed here.

The Family and Community Critical Viewing Project. Telephone: 800-743-5355. A joint project of the National PTA, National Cable Television Association, and Cable in the Classroom which produces *Taking Charge of Your TV: A Guide to Critical Viewing for Parents and Children*.

The Media Education Foundation, 26 Center Street, Northampton, MA, 01060. Telephone: 413-586-4170. Produces a number of terrific videos on media with the leading experts.

The Media Foundation, 1243 W. 7th Avenue, Vancouver, BC, V6H 1B7 Canada. Telephone: 604-736-9401. Produces *AdBusters Quarterly* and is dedicated to creating a "new un-commercialized media culture."

The New Mexico Media Literacy Project, Albuquerque Academy, 6400 Wyoming NE, Albuquerque, NM 87109. Telephone: 505-828-3129. Teacher training and parent workshops in the only media-literate state in the U.S.! Produces a number of resources and a newsletter.

Strategies for Media Literacy, 1095 Market Street, Suite 617, San Francisco, CA 94103 Telephone: 415-621-2911. Provides media literacy workshops for parents, teachers, and community groups and has created a media literacy videodisk for kids, as well as *The Media and You*, a media literacy textbook for young children.

UNPLUG! 360 Grand Avenue, P.O. Box 385, Oakland, CA 94610. Telephone: 800-UNPLUG-1. A national youth organization which promotes commercial-free education and provides media literacy materials to parents, schools, kids, and community groups.

Guides for TV, Movies, Videos, Software, and the Internet

Great Videos for Kids: A Parents' Guide to Choosing the Best. Catherine Cella. Secaucus, N.J.: Citadel Press, 1992. The best video guide on the market. Rates and reviews over 450 videos for kids and looks for positive elements like nonviolence and nonstereotypical roles. Includes the names and addresses of major video distributors.

Inside KidVid: The Essential Parent's Guide to Video. Loretta McAlpine. New York: Viking Penguin, 1995. A first-class video reviewer's guide to kid's video with good listings and categories.

VideoHounds Family Videoguide, 2nd edition. Martin F. Kohn. ed. Detroit: Visible Ink Press, 1996. A terrific family movie guide that rates videos by category and age-appropriateness with warnings for language, violence, and other possible objectionable elements.

Child Safety on the Internet. Classroom Connect. Englewood Cliffs, N.J.: Prentice Hall, 1997. The CD-ROM included with this book provides free Internet access

and net-blocking software and the guide lists kid-safe net sites. Also available from Classroom Connect: *Family Internet Companion* and *Internet Homework Helper*.
The Multimedia Home Companion for Parents and Kids. Christine Olson, ed. New York: Warner, 1996. Provides ratings and detailed reviews of kids' software. Also discusses hardware. A great guide.

Video, Movies, TV, and Computers

Magazines

Better Viewing: Your Family Guide to Television Worth Watching. Telephone: 800-216-2225. A media-literate family TV guide with great articles and a listing that categorizes TV programs by age group and appropriateness.
Parent's Choice Magazine. Box 185, Waban, MA 02168. Telephone: 617-965-5913. Parent's Choice produces a terrific magazine with reviews of software, videos, and TV shows, awards those that are outstanding, and publishes a guide to video and software. Worth the subscription!

General Interest on Television and Kids

Books

Abandoned In the Wasteland: Children, Television and the First Amendment. Newton N. Minow and Craig L. Lamay. New York: Hill and Wang, 1995. Minow, the former FCC chairman, explains how things have changed since he first called TV "a vast wasteland," and makes a passionate plea for more responsible programming.
Amusing Ourselves to Death: Public Discourse in the Age of Show Business. Neil Postman. New York: Penguin, 1985. A thought-provoking look at how television shapes our lives and suggestions for surviving the media onslaught.
Children and Television: Images in a Changing Socio-Cultural World. Gordon L. Berry and Joy Keiko Asamen. Thousand Oaks, Calif.: Sage Publications, 1993. Thirty-five contributors identify the social and cultural impact of television on children.
Educating Students in a Media-Saturated Culture. John Davies. Technomic Publishing, date. Davies, a middle school teacher and administrator, puts forth a cogent and persuasive argument for teaching media literacy in American schools and gives the framework for a curriculum. Buy one and give it to your children's school!
No Sense of Place: The Impact of Electronic Media on Social Behavior. Joshua Meyrowitz. New York: Oxford University Press, 1995. One of the best books on the media's effects on social and emotional behaviors. A very well-written and thought-provoking exploration.
Prime Time: How TV Portrays American Culture. S. Robert Lichter, Linda S. Lichter, and Stanley Rothman. Washington, D.C.: Regenery, 1994. A scientific analysis of television's messages and meanings from the 1950s to the present, written by the directors of the Center for Media and Public Affairs. Fascinating and readable.
Smart Parents' Guide To Kids' TV. Milton Chen, Ph.D. San Francisco: KQED Books, 1994. Dr. Chen's public television expertise helps parents make the best of their young children's TV time.
Screen Smarts: a Family Guide to Media Literacy. Gloria De Gaetano and Kathleen

Bander. New York: Houghton Mifflin, 1996. Filled to the brim with media literacy activities for all media!

Teleliteracy: Taking Television Seriously. David Bianculli. New York: Touchstone, 1992. TV critic Bianculli defines, explores, and embraces what we know about and have learned from TV. Includes interviews with Peter Jennings, Linda Ellerbee, Bill Moyers, Fred Rogers, Bill Cosby, and others.

Television and the Lives of Children. Gloria DeGaetano. Redmond, Calif.: Train of Thought, 1993. A manual for teachers and parents that summarizes recent research and includes parent and teacher handouts.

The Age of Missing Information. Bill McKibben. New York: Plume., 1993. A well-known nature writer compares twenty-four hours of TV to one night spent on a mountain to point out how television appears to be providing us with important information, but really isn't. Readable, funny, and enlightening.

The Art and Artifice of Public Image Making. Kiku Adatto. New York: Basic Books, 1993. A fascinating exploration of how images on TV and in the movies manipulate our perceptions, ideals, and feelings.

The Media Monopoly. Ben Bagdikian. Boston: Beacon Press, 1992. An important book that details the growing concentration of media power and control. Big Brother is here!

The Parents' Guide: Use TV to Your Child's Advantage. Dorothy G. Singer, Ed., Jerome L. Singer, Ph.D., Diana M. Zuckerman, Ph.D. Reston, Va.: Acropolis, 1990. The early pioneers of children and television research provide good activities and excellent glossaries of production terms.

Watching Television: A Pantheon Guide to Popular Culture. Todd Gitlin, ed. New York: Pantheon, 1986. This superb collection of essays by noted media critics explains the how and why of TV ads, MTV, news, soaps, prime time, and children's TV.

Videos

On Television. California Newsreel. Telephone: 415-621-6196. A wonderful series in four parts which outlines the debates about television as a teacher, public interest, and purveyor of violence. Part four, "Media Literacy: The New Basic" is a great introduction to media literacy education.

Signal to Noise: Life With Television. Great Plains National. Telephone: 800-228-4630 In this three-part series, experts, producers, and consumers assemble to dissect and discuss television advertising, programming, news, and the future of interactive TV. Highly recommended!

Tuning In to Media: Literacy for the Information Age. Center For Media Literacy. Telephone: 800-226-9494. An excellent introduction to media literacy for parents, teachers, PTAs, and school administrators. The three ten-minute segments cover the basics of media literacy through analysis of the L.A. Riots and *Doogie Howser, MD.*

Select Bibliography

"Ads Called Most Persuasive in Enticing Kids to Smoke," the *Dallas Morning News,* 18 October 1996.

Barnow, Erik. *The Sponsor; Notes on a Modern Potentate.* New York: Oxford University Press, 1978, 4.

Bennett, Craig R., "Top Twenty Mega-Brands by First Quarter Earnings," *Advertising Age,* 16 August 1993.

Bennett, William J., ed. *The Book of Virtues: A Treasury of Great Moral Stories.* New York: Simon and Schuster, 1993.

Bernstein, Carl. "The Idiot Culture," *New Republic,* 8 June 1992.

Bettelheim, Bruno. *The Uses of Enchantment.* New York: Knopf, 1976.

Bowen, Wally, "Ads, Ads, Everywhere! Are There Limits?" the *New Citizen 2,* no. 2 (summer 1995).

Brinkley, David. *Everyone Is Entitled to My Opinion.* New York: Knopf, 1996.

Buckingham, David, ed. *Watching Media Learning: Making Sense of Media Education.* Basingstoke, UK: The Falmer Press, 1990.

Croft, Adrian, "Quayle Defends Murphy Brown Speech, Bemoans Lack of Values," Reuters, 8 September 1994. (Downloaded from AOL.)

DiMaggio, Madeline. *How to Write for Television.* New York: Fireside, 1990, 11–17.

"Distorted Viewing: TV's Reflection of Life," *USA Today,* 6 July 1993.

Douglas, Susan J. *Where the Girls Are: Growing Up Female With the Mass Media.* New York: Times Books, 1995.

Dover, Jay, "What Kinds of Stories Make the News?" *Connect* 12 (spring 1996).

Ellerbee, Linda, "Children Are the Victims in Television Battles," *Houston Chronicle,* 10 July 1994.

Faber, Adele, and Elaine Mazlish. *How to Talk So Kids Will Listen and Listen So Kids Will Talk.* New York: Avon, 1980.

Farhi, Paul, "Study: TV Violence Pervasive, Harmful," *Houston Chronicle,* 7 February 1996.

"Fatal Attraction: The Selling of Addiction," *Media and Values,* nos. 54–55 (spring/summer 1991).

Gerbner, George, and Jean Kilbourne. *The Killing Screens: Media and the Culture of Violence.* Amherst, Ma: Media Education Foundation, 1995.

Gray, Ellen, "TV Turn Off Week Begins Across Nation," *Houston Chronicle*, 24 April 1995.

Greenfield, Patricia Marks. *Mind and Media: The Effects of Television, Videogames and Computers.* Cambridge, Mass.: Harvard University Press, 1984.

Hansen, Barbara, and Carol Knopes, "Prime Time Tuning Out Varied Culture," *USA Today*, 6 July 1993.

Healy, Jane. *Endangered Minds: Why Children Don't Think and What We Can Do About It.* New York: Touchstone, 1990.

Hickey, Neil, "How Much Violence?" *TV Guide*, 22 August 1992.

"Hispanics Berate Racist Portrayals on U.S. Television," Reuters, 7 September 1994. (Downloaded from AOL.)

Hobbs, Renée. Lecture given at National Media Literacy Conference, Los Angeles, Calif., October 1996.

Jensen, Jeff, "Quaker, Big Mac, Yank Ads," *Advertising Age*, 16 August 1993.

Jhally, Sut. "Dreamworlds," "Dreamworlds II." Amherst, Ma: Media Education Foundation. 1991–1992.

Kaplan, James, "Why Kids Need Heroes," *TV Guide*, 10 March 1995.

"Kids Respond to the News—A Children Now Poll," *Connect*, no. 12 (spring 1996).

Kilbourne, Jean. Lecture given at National Media Literacy Conference, Los Angeles, Calif., October 1996.

Kunkel, Dale, "How the Media 'See' Kids," *Media Studies Journal* vol. 8, issue number 4 (fall 1994).

Lambert, Pam, et al., "What's Wrong With This Picture?" *People*, 18 March 1996.

Landler, Mark, "TV Turns to an Era of Self-control," *New York Times*, 17 March 1996.

Leeland, John, "Violence, Reel to Reel," *Newsweek*, 11 December 1995.

Lickona. Thomas. *Raising Good Children: From Birth Through the Teenage Years.* New York: Bantam, 1983.

McGrath, Tom. *MTV: The Making of a Revolution.* Philadelphia: Running Press, 1996.

McKibben, Bill. *The Age of Missing Information.* New York: Plume, 1993.

Mander, Jerry. *Four Arguments for the Elimination of Television.* New York: Quill, 1978.

Medved, Michael. *Hollywood vs. America.* New York: HarperCollins, 1992.

Meyrowitz, Joshua. *No Sense of Place: The Impact of Electronic Media on Social Behavior.* New York: Oxford University Press, 1985.

Negroponte, Nicholas. *Being Digital.* New York: Vintage, 1995.

Pipher, Mary. *Reviving Ophelia; Saving the Selves of Adolescent Girls.* New York: Ballantine, 1994.

Postman, Neil. *Amusing Ourselves to Death: Public Discourse in the Age of Show Business.* New York: Penguin, 1985.

———. *The Disappearance of Childhood.* New York: Vintage, 1994.

Postman, Neil, and Powers, Steve. *How to Watch TV News.* New York: Penguin, 1992.

"Prime Time," *TV Guide*, 14–20 September 1996.

Provenzo, Eugene F., Jr. *Video Kids: Making Sense of Nintendo.* Cambridge, Mass.: Harvard University Press, 1991.

"Readers to Execs," *USA Weekend*, 30 July–1 August 1993.

Ryan, James, "Hollywood Puts out a Welcome Mat in Cyberspace," *New York Times*, 10 November 1996.

Schrank, Jeffrey. *Understanding Mass Media*. 3d ed. Lincolnwood, Illinois: National Textbook Company, 1990.

Schultze, Quentin J., et al. *Dancing in the Dark: Youth, Popular Culture and the Electronic Media*. Grand Rapids, Michigan: Eerdmans, 1991.

Silver, Marc, "Sex and Violence on TV," *US News and World Report*, 11 September 1995.

"Talk Radio Meets Rock-TV," *The Economist*, 5 September 1992.

Tichi, Cecilia. *Electronic Hearth: Creating an American Television Culture*. New York: Oxford University Press, 1991.

Vadehra, Dave, "My, How TV Spots Have Changed," *Advertising Age*, 16 August 1993.

Walsh, David. *Selling Out America's Children: How America Puts Profits Before Values and What Parents Can Do*. Minneapolis: Fairview Press, 1994.

Westbrook, Bruce, "Toying With Kids' Buying Power," *Houston Chronicle*.

Wollenberg, Skip, "Liquor Industry Ends Voluntary Ban on Ads," *Bennington Banner*, 8 November 1996.

Index